# The Old Courts and Yards of Norwich

## A Story of People, Poverty and Pride

*Beckwith's Court, Quayside, c.1930*

*The 'Old Courts and Yards of Norwich' is published by Norwich Heritage Projects, an independent non-profit-making organisation which simply aims to encourage an appreciation of the heritage of a wonderful city.*

**The Old Courts and Yards of Norwich: A Story of People, Poverty and Pride**
Published by Norwich Heritage Projects
Norwich Heritage Projects
5, Cringleford Chase
Norwich
NR4 7RS
www.norwich-heritage.co.uk

Norwich Heritage Projects is an independent non-profit-making organisation which simply aims to encourage an appreciation of the heritage of a wonderful city.

Edited, designed and brought to production by Norwich Heritage Projects.
Printed and bound in the UK by
Barnwell Print Ltd, Dunkirk Industrial Estate, Aylsham, Norfolk, NR11 6SU

Every reasonable effort has been made to establish the copyright holders of all the photographs and information sources used in this book. Any errors or omissions are inadvertent. Anyone who has not been contacted is invited to write to the publisher so that a proper acknowledgement can be included in subsequent editions.

**Front cover:** A montage of four images: Jolly Butchers' Yard (page 197), Fox and Hounds' Yard (page 190), Self's Yard (page 147), Burrell's Court (page 102).

**Back cover**: Globe Yard (page 215).

**Image Credits**
We are very grateful to our interviewees and all of the following who have kindly allowed us to reproduce images. Where accreditation is not made in the text we have listed the page where the image is located with the exception of maps which have been used repeatedly. Subjects have only been specified where more than one person's work appears on the page. In cases where the photographer or artist is unknown the image is accredited to the donor.

**George Plunkett (permission from Jonathan Plunkett):** 16, 18, 22, 29, 39, 40 (Crescent), 45, 48, 49, 51, 53, 70 (GC), 72, 73, 74, 77, 81, 84, 85 (K&CY), 86 (BY), 87, 88 (AHY, BY), 89 (DY, GY, SY), 94, 98, 100, 101 (1956), 103 (CY, Hooks), 105, 110 (TT), 111 (KHY), 113, 114 (CY, LC), 115, 124 (AS), 128 (GY), 130 (FH), 138 (SBC), 141, 142, 145, 146, 147, 151, 153, 157 (MY), 159, 160 (HC, TC), 167, 170, 178, 179, 190 (building), 192 (ML), 193, 195 (LS), 196 (MY), 198, 199, 204, 206, 207, 208, 209, 211, 214, 223.

**Historic Towns Trust:** The representation of Anthony Hochstetter's plan of 1789, accurately redrawn in the light of Millard and Manning's Map of 1830 and the OS Map of 1883.

**Norfolk County Council Library and Information Service:** i, iv, v, 6, 21, 30, 33, 34, 40 (Fake), 55, 59 (rooftops), 61, 63, 68, 69 (dancing), 70 (JL), 71 (BoB), 75 (Globe), 83 (DY), 85 (GFY), 86 (OBY), 89 (RY, TY), 99, 102 (LCY), 103 (LY), 108, 110 (Mag. St), 111 (JoNY), 112, 119, 112, 123, 124 (pupils), 125, 135, 138 (CC), 139, 140, 143, 152, 156, 158, 160 (PHY), 163, 168 (CC), 169, 172, 175, 180, 181, 183, 187, 188, 190 (lady), 191 (GHY), 191 (people), 202, 203, 205, 215 (Globe).

**Norfolk Museums & Archaeology Service (Norwich Castle Museum & Art Gallery):** 1, 4, 127.

**Norfolk Record Office:** All plans of clearance areas.

**Nottinghamshire Libraries picturethepast.org:** 44

**Ordnance Survey Department:** All reproductions of the 1884/1885 OS Map.

**Paul Venn:** 23, 90 (K&CY), 101 (2009), 104, 117, 118.

**Philip Armes:** 3, 37, 38, 41 (TS), 43, 64, 66, 70 (oven), 83 (BHY), 88 (BY), 91, 102 (BY, BC), 103 (Hindes, NY),109, 114 (BY, CKY), 128 (GWY), 129, 130 (SY), 131, 132, 168 (BC), 194, 195 (MS), 196 (TC, WY).

# Contents

# Foreword

It was back in 2009 that together with a group of friends we first researched the old courts and yards of Norwich, often simply referred to as 'yards' or 'courts', the terms being interchangeable. At the time we concentrated on interviewing people who either lived in, or could remember, the yards in the interwar years. We then produced a selection of material, including a website, a short film that was shown on the Fusion Screen (in the Forum) and published a short pamphlet written by Brenda Reed.

Since then we have given many talks on the old yards which has made us very aware of the high level of interest in the subject. This is largely because so many people from Norwich discover that their families lived in the yards and so want to find out more about them. We therefore decided to revisit and expand our earlier project.

The story of the yards touches on many aspects of the City's history and heritage. Starting with their origins, when Norwich was England's second city, to the 1930s, when the City Council cleared the worst of the yards and there was a huge migration from the City centre to the new council estates in the suburbs. As in all of our projects, we bring that story alive by combining living memories with archive material. In particular we have integrated contemporaneous material from a variety of resources, including newspapers and books together with governmental reports and records. We have aimed to give a balanced view. This is very important, because clearly the yards divide opinion. In fact they are mired in controversy. At one extreme is the view that they were the worst hell-holes in Norwich and needed to be razed to the ground, at the other is the notion that they contained historic buildings and were the homes of bustling communities. We have aimed to address both sides of the argument.

In the bibliography we have included details of websites and sources of information which will help with further research. In particular, the Norfolk Record Office has extensive files on the interwar clearance schemes and our website, www.norwich-yards.co.uk contains a comprehensive yards' index. Additionally, we are all very lucky to have online access to the wonderful images on the George Plunkett and the Norfolk Library websites.

Finally, many thanks must be given to all those who shared their memories and recollections. Since we spoke to them, some of our interviewees have passed away. We dedicate this book to all who contributed.

Frances and Michael Holmes

*Ladies of Globe Yard, Heigham Street, c.1916*

# Introduction

Any visitor to Norwich's historic streets will soon become aware of the many narrow entrances accompanied by a sign proclaiming the existence of a court or yard. Some lead through to pretty squares containing restored or new properties, but often what lay beyond has long been demolished. Going through the same passageway in the 19th and early 20th centuries the visitor would have entered a world very different to the one we live in today; this was a time when the courts and yards were not only the homes of bustling communities but were also notorious for containing the City's worst housing.

In years gone by the alley generally led into a claustrophobic cul-de-sac containing dilapidated homes sharing inadequate water supplies and communal toilets. Although many houses in Norwich suffered from poor sanitation, most premises built in yards were also airless, dark and gloomy.

However, the story of Norwich's ancient yards is so much more than one of bricks and mortar. It is also the story of the people who lived there and who built vibrant, supportive communities, who despite living in conditions over which they had very little control, still had their dignity, friendships and standards to maintain. As explained by Joyce Wilson, who lived in Fairman's Yard, Barrack Street:

*'People living in the yards did struggle, but it was funny they had a certain pride. They were dark little houses with one door, but it was so strange often the door step outside was whitewashed and the door knobs were "Brassoed" [polished]. So, on the outside you had a shiny door knob and a gleaming white doorstep, which we were told to walk over and not to stand on, we had to stretch over it so we didn't leave a footstep. But, I think that the whitewashed step was a little bit of defiance, it was as if the women were saying: "Look it's not too bad after all."'*

*Pope's Head Yard , St Peter's Street, c.1935*

# The Rise and Fall of the Old Courts and Yards of Norwich

*Old Barge Yard, King Street, by Thomas Lound, c.1850*

## Origins: Before 1600

In 1066, when the Normans invaded England, Norwich was already a prosperous centre, and hence attractive to the invaders who built both a castle and cathedral as very visible signs of their authority.

By 1297 the City contained more than 50 churches and it was around the outermost of these and the magnificent cathedral that its defensive walls were built. Once completed (c.1334) the walls, together with the eastern boundary marked by the River Wensum, embraced an area some six miles in circumference. Located within the boundary were the large houses of the gentry and the merchant classes as well as those occupied by their less prosperous neighbours. There were also large open spaces and even farming took place on a limited scale.

There was a housing boom in Norwich between 1475 and 1525, partly fuelled by the need to rebuild some 700 houses which were destroyed by fire in 1507. Building continued through to the mid-16th century. In particular larger houses were built in the parishes of St Peter Mancroft and Mid-Wymer (including St Gregory's and St Andrew's) and north of the River Wensum. Despite this activity, Braun and Hogenberg's map (produced in 1581) shows that the City, which was mainly contained within the walls, still encompassed large, undeveloped tracts of land. Although the bulk of the population lived in the centre of Norwich, the still small suburbs of Pockthorpe and Heigham had already been established outside the walls to the north-east and west respectively.

For the remainder of the 16th century there is little evidence that larger houses were built, instead properties were increasingly provided for the working classes. In particular, demand was generated by an influx of Dutch and Walloon refugees who arrived in the late 1560s and early 1570s. Amazingly at a time when Norwich's total population was only 16,000 their numbers grew to around 6,000. This raised the tricky question of where the incomers would live. The obvious solution would have been to erect more buildings in the open spaces which existed throughout the City, but in general these were kept. Instead there are signs that large houses were adapted for multiple occupation. Excavations, for example in Oak Street, have shown that there was also a steady development of 'cottage housing' in the courtyards behind the large properties which fronted onto the street. The discovery of substantial amounts of imported pottery suggest that many were occupied by the refugees. Such developments became the main housing for the poorer working classes well into the 20th century. They already incorporated characteristics which would define the old courts and yards throughout their life time. In particular: these were speculative buildings, squeezed into a small space adjacent to, or behind, existing buildings; they were put up with little recourse to planning; they lacked light, ventilation and sanitation; they were owned by landlords who sought to maximise their return on a minimal investment.

*Braun and Hogenberg's map of Norwich, 1581*

# 1600 - 1800: The Prosperous Years

*An unnamed yard in Ber Street, by Henry Ninham, c.1850*

By the turn of the 18th century, Norwich's population had almost doubled to around 30,000, making it the second largest city in England. It had also grown rich. Its success arose 'from the City's capacity to combine its long-standing role as a centre of distribution and consumption, with a specialist industrial role as a centre of textile production' (Corfield). Put simply, Norwich owed its size and wealth to a combination of factors, including its strong trading links, its agricultural hinterland, the financial services it offered and its role of regional capital. Underpinning this was the production of high-quality textiles.

Although the City was generally viewed as prosperous, it was also a city of contrasts. Rich merchants owned the vast majority of wealth which was propped up by a broad base of poorly paid labourers, and of course the labourers needed somewhere to live. Such homes continued to be provided by the simple method of creating tenements out of large buildings or erecting small cottages in existing yards adjacent to these buildings. As a result, despite the increase in population between 1570 and 1700 Norwich's medieval street pattern remained largely unaltered.

In the 18th century the growth in population levelled out, and by the 1801 census it stood at 37,000. Although Norwich was still the tenth largest urban centre in England, somewhat ominously, ahead of it now were the expanding industrial centres of Manchester, Birmingham, Sheffield, Leeds and Liverpool.

## Definition of a Norwich Yard

In Norwich a typical old yard or court (the terms are interchangeable) was located behind an ancient building which fronted the street. It was entered through a narrow opening, often tunnel-like which led to a cul-de-sac. Around its perimeter were shoddy dwellings, often formed out of larger houses, which shared inadequate water supplies, toilets and waste-disposal facilities. Occupants living in yards suffered from both a lack of ventilation and dismal light.

# 1800 - 1914: The Growth of Norwich's Old Courts and Yards

*A yard in St Andrew's Parish, by Henry Ninham, c.1850*

Over the 19th century the population of Norwich escalated almost threefold to 112,000. In response, new houses for the working classes were increasingly built outside the medieval street plan. Beyond the City, new developments included Crook's Place which was located west of St Stephen's Road and comprised about 250 houses along three wide streets. Within the City, new terraces and cul-de-sacs were also built, for example in the area between King Street and Ber Street. However, this was insufficient to meet growing demand, and so buildings continued to be crammed into the yards behind old buildings, especially pubs, which fronted the streets.

There is some discrepancy in records as to how many old yards existed at the start of the 20th century. A special committee set up in 1897 to look at their conditions estimated there were around 650. The social historian, Charles Hawkins, writing in 1910, puts the number at 749. The variation is likely to be the result of the definition of a yard. The commission was set up to look at yards which had been squeezed into any nook and cranny available. As noted above, newer developments also incorporated properties built around a cul-de-sac and are assumed to have been included in Hawkins' calculations. Another reason for the inconsistency was identifying them. The courts and yards in question could also be called, squares, terraces, rows or even buildings. Some yards contained high-quality buildings, whilst others, such

as Thoroughfare Yard on Magdalen Street, had all the characteristics of an old yard, even though they were not cul-de-sacs but very narrow alleys.

In the circumstances it is impossible to definitively state how many people lived in the old yards at the turn of the 20th century. However, if we take the conservative figure of 650, and using a very rough estimate (based on government reports and other literature) the average number of dwellings per yard was seven and each household averaged three people. This would mean that around 11% of Norwich's population lived in such accommodation.

To explain the continuing dominance of yards as a source of housing we need to look beyond the growth in population. The dwellings built in the yards in Norwich's historic centre were amongst the worst in the City, and this raises a number questions, including: Why did people choose to live in such poor accommodation? Why did such accommodation form such a large part of the City's housing stock? Where were the yards located? To answer such questions we need to look at two aspects which are still important in today's housing market: demand and supply.

## Demand

Until the industrial revolution Norwich was one of the country's pre-eminent commercial centres. Its wealth was based on the production of high-quality textiles. However, from the end of the 18th century Norwich lacked the natural resources necessary to compete in the new industrial age. The centre of economic activity moved north and Norwich was left in decline. In 1750 worsted weaving was Norwich's major industry, but by 1901 there was not a single worsted weaver left in the City. This had both an impact on levels of employment and the general wealth of the City. The failure of the industry did not happen overnight, but In 1845 a Royal Commission examining living conditions in towns summed the position up: 'Norwich, it is feared, has seen its best days as a place of commerce and would appear to be in that painful state of transition from a once flourishing manufacturing prosperity to its entire decline, and must, ere long, revert to its original condition as a capital of an extensive agricultural district....Neglect and decay are now conspicuous in the streets and quarters occupied by the working classes, so as to render them places of the most dismal aspect.'

During the second half of the 19th century a diverse range of industries, led by shoemaking, emerged in Norwich. The growth of new trades was considerably aided by the low wages paid to Norwich workers, which in almost every sector were below the national average. Low wages themselves were a consequence of both the City's remoteness from the main industrial districts and the influx of agricultural labour from the surrounding countryside. Traditionally farming wages in East Anglia were amongst the lowest in the country. The depression in agriculture from the mid-1870s reduced rates further causing a migration into the City: between 1841 and 1911 the proportion of Norfolk's population living in Norwich increased from 14.9% to 24.3%. The social historian, Charles Hawkins, writing in 1910, had no doubt that low wages brought employment here: 'Norwich enjoys no special advantages in the actual processes of manufacturing blue starch and mustard and chocolate [which all flourished in Norwich]. The important factor is the cost of labour for packing the finished article ready for consumption. It is here that her advantage really lies and it is good cheap labour which enables Norwich to command a world market for these commodities.' Such work was better suited to women. In contrast, there was a shortage of regular work for men as many industries, including shoemaking and tailoring, mainly offered seasonal employment and relied on outworkers to maintain production. By 1901 43.2% of Norwich's workforce was female, well above the national figure of 31.6%.

Thus, four factors epitomised the local labour market over the 19th century: high levels of unemployment amongst textile workers; low wages; proportionately high female employment; and high levels of seasonal and casual labour. Which leads to the somewhat leading question: Where did people with both low and seasonal wages live? Obviously it needed to be somewhere cheap, and the vast majority of the cheapest and shoddiest accommodation in Norwich was located in the yards which were located within the parameters of the City walls or in the immediate suburbs of Pockthorpe and Heigham.

## Supply

The pattern set by speculative 16th-century builders, who either crammed poorly built cottages into existing plots or sub-divided large houses into meagre accommodation, gathered pace over the centuries that followed. Such developments would have been relatively cheap for landlords to acquire, which was important considering there was a high level of demand for low-cost housing. At the end of the century the average rent for a house in a City-centre yard, which would often be one-up-one-down was 2s. 6d. a week whilst rooms in a tenement cost around 1s. per week. Yards were found throughout the City but were particularly prevalent in Ber Street, St Benedict's, St Martin's, Botolph Street, Fishergate, Cowgate and Barrack Street. Probably the best document to show how and where they developed is the 1884 OS map. The map shows the west side of Ber Street stretching between two pubs, the Lock and Key (89) to the Bull's Head (135), from which we can derive:

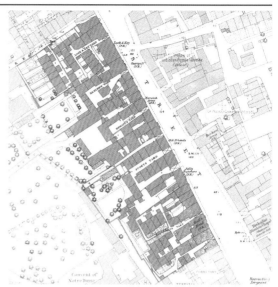

*Ber Street, OS Map, 1884*

- In this small area there are approximately seven yards (they are not all named on the map).
- In all cases buildings have been built around a space (yard) behind the line of properties fronting the street.
- Lock and Key Yard, Jolly Butchers' Yard (unnamed on the map) and Bull's Head Yard are all located adjacent to pubs, which give the yards their names.
- The yards are mainly entered through narrow passageways.
- Some of the yards are in two or more sections, e.g. Lock and Key Yard.

Although not shown on the map most yards were paved with cobbles. Water was supplied from a central pump, open drains ran across the middle whilst the toilets would either be midden or pan closets, shared by a number of households. This was an age when sanitation was universally poor, but what set the yards apart was their cramped, confined space and, as one end was enclosed, they generally had poor ventilation and light. We'll leave you to imagine what the smell was like! If you can't, it was summed up by a reporter from the *Norwich Mercury* who visited the yards around Oak Street in 1897: 'Each parish seems honeycombed with courts and alleys, and city life is at its lowest ebb here....In most instances the only entrance to these [courts and yards] is by a low and narrow archway abutting onto the main street....The stranger gropes his way up one of these passages, and his olfactory nerves soon let him know he has entered upon a new land – a land of stinking slops and refuse of all kinds. The comparatively fresh air of the outside world gives place to an ever-tainted atmosphere which at the first whiff, is well-nigh stifling.'

Sanitation, or lack of it, plays a big part in this book. At this point we thought that it would be useful to give a few definitions:

**Privy Pit**: A pit where sewage waste was dumped.

**Middens**: These consisted of large, pervious receptacles which held more than a week's sewage. Ash was used to cover the contents to create a more or less solid mass.

**Privy**: A toilet located in a small shed outside a house or other building.

**Ash Closets**: These were similar to middens but the receptacles were smaller and held less than a week's sewage.

**Pail Closets**: In some cases the receptacle used in an ash closet was reduced to the size of a pail (sometimes called a bin) which was located below the seat. These pails were either sealed for removal and cleansing at a central depot or emptied into a cart for immediate return. Although in theory they were cleaner and more efficient than large middens or privy pits, they often overflowed whilst wooden pails proved difficult to clean. The pails would be collected by a 'scavenger' in what was often, rather sarcastically, called the 'honey cart'. In Norwich the collectors, who were employed by the City Council, used to work at night because of the stench they generated.

**Water Closets**: A cheap and hygienic water closet for the working class was not developed until the last quarter of the 19th century but by 1890 the design of the 'modern' w.c. had been perfected. However, its widespread adoption depended upon the provision of water. In Norwich, in 1893 fewer than 5,000 houses had water closets but by 1914 around 96% of households had access to this form of toilet.

In the book 'The Seventeenth Child', Ethel George (b.1914) recalls growing up in Pockthorpe: 'Then there were the men what used to empty the toilet bins. They came with a big cart and two horses. They were different to the ordinary bin men. Someone told me that they had three eyes, but I never saw them, 'cause they came in the middle of the night. It probably took two men to carry a bin, 'cause it must have swirled around inside, mustn't it? Like when you carry a saucepan what's full of vegetables.'

*Wally Feeke's honey cart, Litcham, c.1950*

**The Norwich Cockeys were natural streams that flowed towards the river. They ran both along and across streets, and also underground. Between them they traversed large areas of the City and were used both as a water supply and to carry away effluent.**

# 1800 – 1914: The Road to Reform

During the 19th century Norwich's suburbs grew. Additionally, terraces for working-class tenants were built in the City centre. However, higher quality housing attracted higher rents which were beyond the lowest-paid workers, and so many had no choice but to live in City-centre slums. This was despite the fact that by 1911 there were over 1,500 empty houses in Norwich, mostly in the middle-class range. Poverty was rife, in fact in 1907 a Royal Commission calculated that around 11,000 of Norwich's population (exclusive of vagrants and pauper lunatics in the asylum) had been in receipt of poor relief for at least one day. The old courts and yards survived because they were all that a large portion of the population could afford. Charles Hawkins neatly summed up the position: 'There is in Norwich a very large under-employed, and therefore semi-employable, class who are always on the verge of destitution. Bad times, old age, widowhood, sickness, and any of the normal accidents of life leave them with absolutely no resources.'

## Legislation

In 1851 William Lee completed a report on living conditions in Norwich for the General Board of Health. He concluded that as a result of a diverse range of deficiencies, in particular an inadequate and bad water supply, improper and inadequate privies, defective dwellings and overcrowded burial grounds that '...there is a great amount of preventable disease and mortality in a city, that ought to be one of the most healthy in the kingdom'. Moreover he identified that 'by far the most numerous class of houses consists for the most part of old houses, very much varied in plan, that are built around irregularly-formed courts or yards'. He succinctly explained: 'A separate wash house is scarcely ever found attached to these houses, some have a wash house in common with three or more dwellings, and many are without any at all. The supply of water to these houses is almost solely by means of wells and pumps; they are most of them within reach of the water mains and in some cases the water pipes are made use of as well as the pumps. Sinks are most uncommon and the house-water is mostly poured on the surface, or into small surface drains and finds its way into the sewers or river. There are very few cesspools in these yards; the privy and bin are commonly found, and the latter is the receptacle of the worse portion of the house-sewage or water. In most instances there is no other open space attached to these buildings than the yard which gives means of access to the tenements around it. This space although often of a considerable length, is not often of a sufficient width to admit a proper quantity of light or air, and...is seldom found to be sufficiently cleansed or drained.'

Across the country, growing awareness of the links between public health and housing conditions led to the Government passing extensive legislation in the period 1850 – 1900 which was supplemented by a series of local government acts. Unfortunately, quantity did not necessarily equate to quality.

In 1858 new housing in Norwich was subject to by-laws which both regulated minimum dimensions and also stipulated that open space had to be left behind new dwellings. The latter should have effectively prevented the building of any more back-to-backs or squeezing properties into yards. However, the City authorities were somewhat lax in applying the legislation, and it was only after the adoption of the Public Health Act of 1872 that the City began to tackle the problems of poor housing. In 1873 Norwich appointed T. W. Crosse as its first Medical Officer of Health; sadly his reports made it clear that life for the very poor was as bleak as ever. However, increasingly the links between poor sanitation, abysmal housing and health were being recognised. For example, in 1880 epidemics of scarlet and typhus fevers in Norwich were directly related to the crowded and dirty conditions experienced in the City's densely populated areas, in particularly its yards.

The 1872 Act also marked the gradual involvement of Norwich Council in what is now known as 'slum clearance'. The first tentative steps occurred in the parish of St Paul's where 2.5 acres of land, containing 144 dwellings, occupied by 505 inhabitants was cleared, which led to the following entry in White's 1883 Directory: 'A rookery of disgraceful tenements in St Paul's has been demolished under the Artisans' Dwelling Act, and a colony of trim cottages erected in their place.' It was a costly exercise, as the Council had to pay some £11,000 for the buildings before it could even begin to demolish them, a sum which did not go down well with the rate payers.

Although other legislation was passed in the 19th century, it was the Local Government Act of 1888 that compelled Norwich City Council, which had been slow to accept its responsibilities, to take stock of its position. In August 1889, in a bid to clarify a mass of confused legislation, the Council passed the Norwich Corporation Act. This Act regulated every aspect of public administration, including sewerage, drainage and control of infectious diseases.

### Henry Mayhew

Between 19 October 1849 and 12 December 1850, this *Morning Chronicle* journalist (pictured), wrote over 80 bulletins (printed as letters) discussing the conditions of public health in England and Wales. In December 1849 he reported on Norwich.

Although the majority of the text concerned the weaving industry, he did refer to the living conditions of the poor. His article makes depressing reading: 'The houses inhabited by the working classes are generally in the most dilapidated condition. Within the boundaries of the City you must search for the working classes in narrow lanes, courts and yards, the entrance to which is from adjoining thoroughfares through low and narrow openings or archways. Here will be found rows of wretched cottages, built in most cases back to back, ventilation being almost entirely excluded. Where the cottages face each other, in many cases they are not more than three feet apart. Down the centre of these places an open kennel or drain – perhaps not even that – carries off the refuse water either into the adjoining streets, or into some receptacle, where it is allowed to soak away into the surrounding soil.'

### Health and Towns Commission

Between 1844 and 1845 this Commission reported that Norwich's working-class quarters '...were most likely to be found in narrow streets and lanes where courts and yards were linked by a single opening or doorway, some three feet wide, which led into the adjoining thoroughfares. They housed anything from a single family to as many as the 46 found in St John's Head Yard in Coslany....Toilet facilities were wholly inadequate and were consequently a prolific source of scarlet fever, a situation made worse where houses were built onto the City walls and the privies or bins placed close to their fronts.'

### William Lee

In 1851 Lee issued his report into the sanitary condition of Norwich. Although he made it clear that across the City both sanitary arrangements and the water supply were horrendous, he continually mentioned the appalling conditions in many of the yards. In particular he recognised that: 'By far the most numerous class of house in Norwich consisted of old houses built around courts or yards which gave access to the tenements around. This space although often of a considerable length, is not often of a sufficient width to admit a proper quantity of light or air, and...is seldom found to be sufficiently cleansed or drained.' For the historian Christopher Barringer, this was 'the first step in a movement which ultimately led to the clearances after WWI and the building of the new [council] estates.' However, the local press took affront at some of these finding, and in May 1850 (whilst Lee was investigating the City) they reported that they had also visited several courts and yards in the worst part of the City and found 'nothing whatsoever offensive'.

### A 'Norwich Mercury' reporter describes Reeves' Yard (the former Bett's Yard) on Oak Street, 1897

'The conditions of life in this yard must be hard indeed. An open channel runs in front of the houses containing sewage, slops and rainwater. The smell was neither imaginable nor describable. One battered pump, made in 1808, supplies water to the entire yard, or rather three yards in one. The water from this is said to stick around the cups and glasses like glue and sometimes more resembles soapsuds than water. Nearly all of the houses are uninhabited, and in those that are occupied the doors are almost off their hinges. Some of the garret windows have not a pane of glass and, as an inhabitant remarked, you might just as well lay down outside. There is no light, and inhabitants expressed the view that it wasn't safe after dark, adding the view that sometimes it was "as black as your hat". Five landlords provide just one pump for the tenants. One of the dwellers commented that the smell in summer was "enough to knock you back". Draughts and rats were two of the nuisances named.'

*The Sanitary Police, as seen by Punch*

# The Courts and Yards Committee: A Reforming Body

To sum up, despite there being a general consensus that living conditions in the yards were abysmal, by the last decade of the 19th century no real progress had been made to improve them. Then in 1897, Norwich Council formed a 'Courts and Yards Committee'. Following an early meeting, members made notes outlining the general scope of their work. Unsurprisingly, members adopted the principles that most of the courts and yards in the City were 'capable of substantial improvement', that their work would be guided by the dictates of public health and well-being and that they would have 'due regard to the outlay involved in any necessary improvements'. They summarised the principal defects of the yards as being: lack of ventilation, defective drainage, practically no proper paving, dilapidated housing and no lighting. It was these areas they particularly addressed. Note, that they did not concern themselves with the interior of the buildings.

Their reports contain very useful generalisations of what constituted a typical Norwich yard:

- Houses were built around a court, yard or square with an entrance from the street, generally through a narrow covered passageway.
- Generally, but not exclusively, they were of an 'ancient character'.
- They formed cul-de-sacs which were only used by persons residing or having business therein. However, some yards were included which were not blind alleys, but either led to the river or were very narrow thoroughfares. All were confined and 'badly situated' as regards ventilation.
- They had no lighting 'by gas or other means'.
- Often they were in two or more sections separated by a narrow opening.
- The outside communal areas were generally paved with cobbles that were in 'rough condition'.
- Residents had access to either midden or pan closets, which were normally near the houses, communal and were 'unsanitary and unsuitable'. Additionally drainage was deficient.
- Access to water was often, but not necessarily, supplied by means of a pump drawn from a well sunk in soil, which was either actually polluted or would 'of necessity be very liable to pollution'.

Although the Committee's remit extended across the City, they noted that yards were particularly prevalent in: Ber Street, St Benedict's, St Martin's, Botolph Street, Fishergate, Cowgate and Barrack Street.

The Committee did not make a general order applicable to every yard, but instead dealt with each on an individual basis. Payment for improvements was to be allotted as follows:

- Where the Committee decreed that a yard should be lighted this would be at the public expense, but only after the owners had paid for the cost of providing the means of lighting, e.g. pipes and lamp-posts.
- To require the owners, 'pursuant to the Norwich Corporation Act, 1889, to sewer, level and pave yards, as directed by the Committee'. In practice this meant that where the Committee deemed a yard to be a private street, they were within their powers to order owners to pay for such improvements.

Between its formation and 1911, when the Courts and Yards Committee was reconvened as the Private Streets Committee, it issued a series of reports, from which the following can be gleaned:

- In general, after works were ordered by the Committee, they were organised and completed by the Corporation, but paid for by the owners.
- By 1911, 280 yards had been, or were in the process of being, dealt with by the Committee. Improvements to private streets (mainly paving, drains and sewers) had cost around £17,000 (of which the Corporation had paid around £120) whilst improvements to sanitary conveniences had cost £3,251 (of which the corporation had paid less than £100).
- 266 lamps had been placed in various yards.

Only a handful of yards were demolished. One of these was an area which became known as the Priory Yard Estate. The case studies in the next section illustrates some of the major issues which emerged from this early attempt to clear the yards and replace them with better-quality housing.

Despite the work undertaken by the Courts and Yards Committee, by the time WWI started the vast majority of Norwich's lower working classes were still living in city-centre yards – those which Charles Hawkins had described as being 'as bad and insanitary as those to be found anywhere'. Although the Courts and Yards Committee had initiated improvements to the yards, it had done little more than address the peripheral issues faced by tenants living in them. It did not deal with major problems caused by their basic structure: they were airless and dark.

The Committee had no real mandate either to demolish the yards, or to provide replacement housing. New working-class accommodation was being built by private builders, but this was often beyond the means of those who lived in the yards.

## Local Authority Housing: An Alternative

As already noted, most of those on the lowest wages lived in the old yards. They lived there because they could not afford better-quality housing. To break the stalemate the government needed to intervene. During this period much legislation was passed which was eventually consolidated in 1890 into the Housing of the Working Classes Act. Although this gave local authorities the power to clear slum areas and obstructive buildings and also allowed them to make compulsory purchases, the Act did not address the real reason people lived in slums. In particular, it did not require authorities outside London to rehouse people displaced by slum clearance, nor did central government give any financial help to bridge the gap between the cost of municipal housing and the rents that working-class tenants could afford. Some areas, including London, Sheffield, Liverpool and Glasgow, did provide public housing, but by 1914 across Britain only 24,000 council dwellings had been constructed. In Norwich little was achieved. A tentative programme to rebuild following the clearance of housing around Priory Yard was dismissed because of cost. One of the few developments built in Norwich was on the Angel Road Estate where 12 tenements of two or three rooms were completed by February 1904. When one considers the scale of the problem, it is very clear that the Council had little appetite to act.

## The Floods: A Catalyst for Change

Would the lack of incentive to improve working-class housing be overcome by a major natural disaster? The plight of many yards' residents, especially those living in the Oak Street area was considerably worsened following floods in August 1912, as evocatively described in the *Eastern Daily Press*:

'Up to noon the north side of the river remained clear. Oak Street runs parallel with the river all the way from Drayton Road to St Miles' Bridge, and innumerable courts and yards run in gridiron fashion from Oak Street to the river bank. Up these yards the rising water crept steadily during the morning, and by noon the inhabitants of the houses nearest the river had to leave. It was at about one o'clock when the first trickle of water began to run into Oak Street through Queen Caroline Yard, a thin feeble stream which ran down the gutters. Within ten minutes the thin and feeble stream was transformed into a rapidly running cascade, which spread in a pool across the street, and spread up and down in either direction. Cyclists were still able to dash through it with much splashing and a crowd of people gathered around it to watch and wonder how far it would spread. Within an hour it was a foot deep. By this time it was evident that the whole district was in for it, and the forecast was very speedily realised. By five o'clock the whole area was under water.

'The scene in Oak Street as darkness fell beggars description. Darkness fell literally; for there were no street lights. The street was a turbulent torrent three feet deep in many places and down every court and yard the imprisoned people were eagerly awaiting the advent of rescue from their plight. Down yard after yard, often with the water up to the floorboards of the cart, the rescuers went, and the spectacle of women and children being removed from upper windows by the aid of a ladder propped upon so shaky a footing was one not readily to be forgotten. Load after load of children, many of whom had to be taken off in boats from houses where the water was too deep for carts to venture, were brought out, and speedily conveyed to St Augustine School where fires had been lighted, and arrangements were well ahead for the reception of the drenched and shivering crowd. As the evening wore on Oak Street was patrolled by police in boats, lights were out in the deserted houses, and the whole aspect of the scene was one of intolerable desolation' (18 August 1912).

Despite heightened awareness of the desperate conditions faced by tenants (as illustrated by the Rayner's Yard case study on page 28) there was no real appetite to instigate change. In fact public sympathy lay much more with the landlords of damaged properties than with the tenants whose already meagre homes had been ravaged by flood waters.

As WWI approached it was clear that without government intervention the yards would remain the principle working-class housing in Norwich. In turn intervention was only going to happen if there was a political incentive to change. It was going to be the war that would drive this change, and lead to the demise of the yards.

*St Margaret's Plain, Weswick Street, 1912*

## The Impact of WWI

Without the provision of an affordable alternative, the poorest members of society had no choice but to live in slum housing; in Norwich the majority of such housing was located in the old yards. To break the stalemate the government needed to intercede but, like other local authorities, Norwich City Council was reluctant to be involved in the supply of housing. However, WWI was to be the agent for change

The war helped undermine long-established class and gender barriers; it produced a situation where the state could no longer resist working-class demands for improved standards of housing. By 1918, after two decades of under provision, there was a severe housing shortage which for economic reasons private enterprise could not tackle effectively, and which for political reasons the state could not ignore. As early as 1919 the Housing and Town Planning Act required local authorities to provide council houses for families, many of whom were suffering from a combination of personal loss, mental anguish and physical injury. Soon, 'homes fit for heroes' were being built.

Norwich City Council was swift to react to new legislation. On 21 October 1919 the Medical Officer of Health for Norwich reported to the Town Clerk that 4,000 dwellings in the City were either back-to-back or had no through ventilation. In addition the properties lacked damp-proof courses, had deficient drainage and inadequate washing facilities, outside water facilities and shared outside toilets. (At the time 4,000 was considered to be a conservative estimate.) The majority of deficient properties were located in and around areas where the old courts and yards proliferated, including Oak Street, Fishergate, Cowgate, Barrack Street, Ber Street, Botolph Street and Magdalen Street. Interestingly, although the Courts and Yards Committee had found little evidence of overcrowding, it was now prevalent. This deterioration in living standards was probably caused by lack of building activity during the war years. In an attempt to address the issue, the Town Clerk indicated that the Council intended to construct 1200 houses on 420 acres of land that it had previously acquired. Building was scheduled on four major estates:

- The Angel Road Estate: 16 acres, proposed number of houses 147

- Mile Cross Estate: 102 acres, proposed number of houses 300

- Earlham Estate: 147 acres, proposed number of houses 453

- Harford Hall Estate: 151 acres, proposed number of houses 300

*English country-cottage-style council houses on the Mile Cross Estate, c.1935*

Ominously, such enthusiasm was tempered by the condition that completion of the estates was subject to access to funds and sufficient labour, and it was further estimated that based on current manpower only 600 of the planned houses would be completed. When one considers that a minimum of 4,000 houses in Norwich were 'seriously defective', it is very clear that the Council did not have the resources to address the housing problem.

In the event the Town Clerk's estimate proved optimistic, and by the end of 1923 only 293 of the planned houses had been built. These were mainly located on the Angel Road and Mile Cross Estates.

## Housing Acts in the 1920s

The 1919 Housing and Town Planning Act was repealed in 1921, to be replaced with the 1923 Housing Act, known as the Chamberlain Act (repealed 1929) and the 1924 Housing (Financial Provisions) Act, known as the Wheatley Act (expired 1933).

Both acts gave subsidies to local authorities to build houses. Particularly effective was the 1924 Act, which was introduced by Labour's first minister of health, John Wheatley, who hoped that municipal housing would replace private housing for the working class. To achieve this, councils were given higher subsidies and production targets. Across the country almost 600,000 council houses were built under the provision of the two acts, of these, 80% were attributed to Wheatley's Act.

This all sounds brilliant, but there was a major issue: housing policy was concentrated on reducing the housing shortage rather than slum clearance. Additionally the aim was to build high-quality houses at lower densities than had been the norm for private working-class dwellings before 1914. Unfortunately the combination of high costs, high quality and low density resulted in rents which were higher than those at the lower end of the private market. In Norwich, this meant early council houses were too expensive for yard dwellers.

Norwich City Council was now a landlord and, like private-sector landlords, officials sought desirable tenants who could afford rents, which in the case of the new council houses ranged from 4s. 6d. a week for a one-bedroom property to 8s. 6d. for three bedrooms. The allocation of houses in the new estates began early in 1921. In the early years relatively few of the successful applicants came from the slums. Although there were a few shoe operatives, many new tenants were clerks and teachers, with secure incomes. These were the preferred tenants.

Despite deficiencies in the legislation, the generous subsidies allocated to local authorities gave a tremendous boost to the growth of council housing

**Dorothy Dugdale recalls moving into a council house in 1930**

*Dorothy and her husband John, c.2005*

'One of my earliest memories was moving to Mile Cross from Spixworth when I was about five. It was a new house on Peterson Road [off Bignold Road], they were all new houses on the estate and none of our gardens had been made up. I moved in with my mum and dad and my younger sister.

'You walked into a porch and the toilet was on the left and then you went through a door into the kitchen. The bathroom was off the side of the kitchen. We also had three bedrooms and a living room. We thought it was lovely because everything was brand new. We didn't have hot water but had a copper [large metal container] in the corner of the bathroom, with a gas-fired flame underneath, where we heated water. You'd ladle the water out with a hand cup, which was a galvanised bowl with a wooden handle on, and put the hot water into the bath. My parents really liked the house. It was a friendly estate. We all knew each other. Those on our side of the road were real neighbourly.'

in Norwich, and between 1924 and 1930 around 2,600 such houses were built.

In 1925 new legislation gave local authorities the power to nominate improvement schemes where 'property was unfit for human habitation or in narrow, close or a bad or dangerous arrangement of the streets', but there was insufficient monetary incentive for local authorities to respond. Thus, despite Norwich having many properties which met the basic criteria, only 96 properties were built in Norwich following the clearance of areas around Baker's Yard (location unknown) and Robinson's Yard (Oak Street).

Although the early council estates did little to address the issues faced by those living in the City's worst slums, the Council's activity was impressive. By the end of the 1920s the following major estates had been established: Mile Cross, Earlham South (previously Earlham), Angel Road, Drayton, Lakenham (formerly Harford Hall) and the southern tip of Earlham North. These estates had a density of 10 to 12 dwellings per acre, residential roads were laid out in easy curves with wide, tree-planted grass verges. Additionally there was much concern about the aesthetics of the estates, in particular the aim was to create an interesting street picture by introducing different designs of houses. Interestingly, in the late 19th century, to prevent properties being built with restricted ventilation (a major problem for tenants in the yards) private builders had been banned from building cul-de-sacs. However, on the new estates cul-de-sacs were encouraged, as it was felt that houses grouped in this formation were more visually satisfying. Another notable feature in early council-house design was the importance given to air and space, simply because many people had been living without these two basic amenities. All of these factors were encompassed on the Mile Cross Estate, which was one of the first council estates in Britain with a design based on the principles of a garden suburb.

In the same way that the street layout on the new estates differed significantly from the City where yards were prevalent, the houses themselves contained facilities which were almost beyond the imagination of the tenants of the yards. All houses built in Norwich which were subject to the 1919 Act had a separate parlour and piped water. Cooking was done on a range in the living room. Both the range and the copper (which provided hot water and was located in the scullery or the bathroom) were heated by solid fuel. By 1924 a gas or electric stove, which was now located in a kitchen, replaced the range, whilst the copper in the bathroom was heated by gas. Initially most houses were built with a bath without running hot water which was located in a space off the scullery. Theoretically, 'fixed' baths were first made statutory in the Housing Act of 1923. Although practice lagged some way behind, by 1936 the law was being applied to all new houses.

In summary, the 1920s saw a significant change in national housing policy, resulting in over 900,000 properties being built. Conversely, little was being done to address the plight of the poorest, many of whom lived in appalling conditions but could not afford council-house rents. It is telling that across the country, despite the massive building programme, less than 11,000 slum dwellings were levelled. All this altered in 1930 when a change in building subsidies incentivised local authorities to commence massive slum-clearance schemes. In Norwich these were initially centred around the City's old courts and yards.

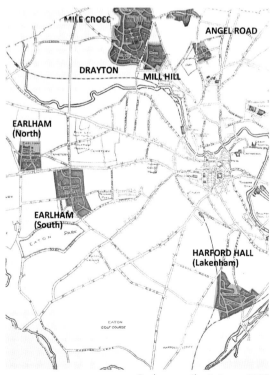

*Early council estates, c.1935*

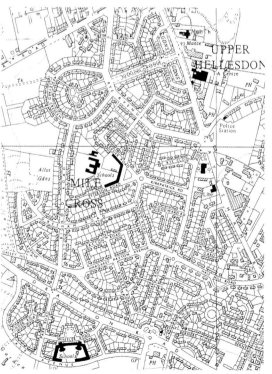

*Importance of street layout, Mile Cross, 1959*

*Don and Joyce Wilson, c1945*

'I now live at 72 Chamberlin Road, in a house that was originally occupied by my husband's [Don] family. They moved here in the late 1920s. They first moved into a council house at the bottom of the road, but it didn't have a parlour. The whole estate was more or less finished, then 72 – 78 Chamberlin Road were built on the land where all the supplies, such as bricks and sand, had been stored. The Wilsons were Freemen of the City of Norwich. Don's father worked at Greens, who were high-class gents' outfitters on the Walk, he was a porter or something like that. He wasn't anything important, but it was just a slightly elevated position. After the war, in 1946, when Don was sent back from Italy there was a housing shortage in Norwich because of the bombing, and my mother-in-law said we could have the rooms upstairs; I've been here ever since.

'In the early years, the tenant in the house across the road from here was a Mr Vines who had a thriving shoe-repair business in Pitt Street, on the other side of the road was the manager of Sainsbury's. A few doors down was the manager for the Trustees Savings Bank, even the mayor, a Mr Cutbush, lived a few doors down. Across the road was a man who had a flourishing tobacco business on Stump Cross, Policeman Dockra lived at the bottom of Blythe Road, he was an inspector at the finish. Don used to tell me that two teachers lived opposite at one time. Down the road was Mr Sabberton, who owned a jewellers' business. When you think that people with important jobs, bank managers and the like, were allocated these council houses. They were all middle-class people, not working class; you had to be somebody to live on Chamberlin Road.'

*Dorothy with son Terry and husband Bob, 1941*

Dorothy Holmes often told the story of her early life:

'My grandparents lived at 3 Finch's Yard. In 1915, my father Thomas Howell married my mother Alice. Of course he had to go to war, but he didn't return to a home fit for heroes, instead my parents moved into 5 Finch's Yard, where I was born in 1920.

'I was 15 when the houses in the yard were knocked down. I clearly remember moving to our new council house on Woodcock Road. We never dreamt of using Pickfords, and instead took everything on handcarts...but not quite everything. All our linen and soft furnishings, in fact anything that could contain fleas, was taken away to be fumigated, and so the first night in our new house we all slept on floorboards, but none of us minded. We couldn't believe it!

'Our new house had an inside bathroom and toilet, we could have hot water and even had a garden. I really think that mother thought she'd gone to heaven!'

## Government Policy Changes

'Local Authorities should concentrate their efforts on the provision of a type of house which can be built at a low cost and can be let at a rent within the means of the more poorly paid workers. The type of house which [we have] in mind is the three-bedroomed non-parlour house of about 760 square feet, which experience has shown gives adequate accommodation for the ordinary family with children.' Circular letter from Minister of Health to Local Authorities 12/1/1932.

197407 / P244 / 8582 / 032995

35523/190C68L5L00704

MRS VIOLET ARTHURTON
STONYCROFT HEATH ROAD
HOCKERING
DEREHAM
NR20 3JB

OFFER PRICE
£25.50

# Winter style for less

**25% OFF***
**EVERYTHING**
WITH CODE
**JAN25**

A71

1127

**25**%
OFF*
EVERYTHING
WITH CODE
JAN25

OFFER PRICE
£22.50

# Your new Winter favourites

Your new collection is here, with a fantastic
**25% off\*** everything in this catalogue! But hurry,
this offer **must end 31st January 2022!**

To receive your **25% off\*** discount, simply
quote **'JAN25'** when you place your next order.
If you're ordering online, please enter the specific 7-digit
catalogue code into the search bar, add your
items to your bag and apply the promotional discount
code **'JAN25'** at the online checkout.

## Stay in the know

**SIGN UP FOR OUR EMAILS VIA OUR WEBSITE**
See our new ranges first
Get personal product recommendations
Updates on your orders
Confirmation when you place an order
Updates on your deliveries

| FASHION SIZES | LINGERIE IN SIZES | FOOTWEAR IN SIZES |
|---|---|---|
| **10-32** | **32-54** | **4-9** |
| All sizes one price | and up to an L cup | and widths D-EEEEE |

OFFER PRICE
£19.⁵⁰

# 25%OFF*
## EVERYTHING
### WITH CODE
## JAN25

# AMBROSEWILSON.COM
## 0800 642 642

## DON'T FORGET YOU GET 25% OFF* EVERYTHING IN THIS CATALOGUE...

# 3 ways to order   ➤ ONLINE   📱 PHONE   ✉ POST

---

## Priority order form

MRS VIOLET ARTHURTON
STONYCROFT HEATH ROAD
HOCKERING
DEREHAM
NR20 3JB

LA71

**Choose the payment method that suits you best**

My personal account ☐    Cheque ☐
Existing personal credit account customers only

**Would you like to hear more from us about our great products discounts and special offers, and new ranges via email or telephone?**

Why not update your marketing preferences, visit **'My Account'** on our website or call us on **0871 231 2000.**

| CUSTOMER NO. | MKTG CODE | PROMO CODE | EXPIRY DATE |
|---|---|---|---|
| A1727002 | JAN25 | 8582 | 31.01.22 |

| Quantity | Item Number | Size | Colour | Description | £ Total P | Page No |
|---|---|---|---|---|---|---|
| ☐(✓) | J A N 2 5 | | | I would like to claim 25% off my order* | | |
| | | | | | | |
| | | | | | | |

Standard Delivery

TOTAL VAL'

# The 1930s: The Beginning of the End for the Old Courts and Yards.

In 1930 the Labour Government introduced the Greenwood Act which was specifically designed to tackle the problem of slum housing. It had two main thrusts. Firstly, the subsidies paid to local authorities were calculated on the number of people rehoused from slum-clearance areas. Secondly, and just as important for yard dwellers, local authorities could give rent rebates.

In October 1930 Norwich's Medical Officer of Health submitted a list of areas where slum clearance should be carried out 'if possible during the next five years'. It covered approximately 1,240 houses and more than 80 yards, encompassing areas of:

A.  Heigham Street, including Cooper's Yard, Baldry's Yard, Weston Square, Flower in Hand Yard and Crocodile Yard.

B.  Fishergate and Magdalen Street, including Blacksmith's Yard, Thoroughfare Yard, Rampant Horse Yard, Thompson's Yard, Long Yard, Red Lion Yard, Loose's Yard and Staff of Life Yard.

C.  Cowgate and Barrack Street, including Bennett's Yard, Ship Yard, Pestell's Yard, General Windham's Yard, Bradfield's Yard, Beckham's Yard, Stewardson's Yard, Nickall's Yard, Wrestler's Yard, Fairman's Yard, Palace Yard, Light Horseman Yard and Rock Yard.

D.  Golden Ball Street, including Woolpack Yard, and Chittock's Court.

E.  Coslany and Oak Street, including a section which had already been identified for improvement under the 1925 Act, comprising Sun Yard, Red Lion Yard, Havers' Yard, Dawson's Yard, Greenland Fishery Yard, Rudd's Yard, Chequers' Yard, Distillery Yard, Waggon and Horses Yard, Dial Yard, Tuns Yard and Saw Mill Yard.

Based on this information, in December 1930 the local authority put forward its first five-year plan, under which it proposed to build 250 houses per year and demolish the same number of slum properties. They also undertook to build 300 properties per year under the terms of the 1924 Act, although some of these houses would potentially be available to displaced persons they were also needed to meet existing demand and the needs of a growing population.

Such plans were laudable but over ambitious; especially when one considers the Council's poor track record in organising slum clearances.

Being fair, they recognised the difficulty of the task ahead and decided that they needed a 'trial run'. As a result they started small, and in February 1931 they elected to deal with part of the 'Sun Yard Area'. The scheme involved around 39 houses (three

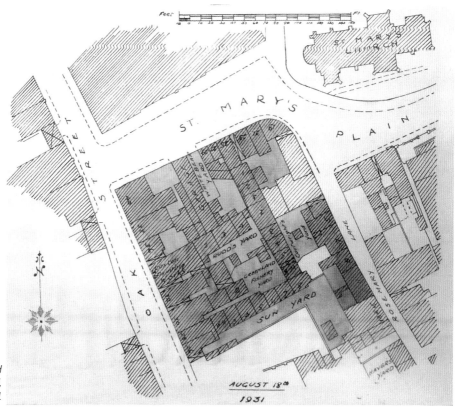

*Plan of 'Sun Yard clearance area', 1931*

were vacant) occupied by 35 families comprising 137 persons (in subsequent reports these numbers varied). The Council believed that the exercise would give them 'valuable experience in the working of the 1930 Housing Act'. By May 1932 it had been decided that residents from the Sun Yard area would be relocated to a combination of properties, including houses built on the Drayton Estate and flats at Temple Road. It was also decided to extend the clearance area to other properties in area E, including Distillery Yard, Chequers' Yard, Waggon and Horses Yard and, Saw Mill Yard.

Despite their good intentions progress was slow and by mid-1933 the Sun Yard Area, which eventually only covered 36 houses, was the only area fully cleared. However, other schemes to demolish 352 properties were underway, including plans to raze 173 houses around Barrack Street, 44 in and surrounding Cat & Fiddle Yard (Botolph Street) and 78 properties around Timber Hill.

It would seem that such sluggish progress was common, as in July 1933 Norwich's Health and Housing Committees received a circular from His Majesty's Government expressing the view that: 'The present rate at which the slums are being dealt with is too slow, and they look for a concerted effort between the central government and the local authorities immediately concerned to ensure a speedier end to the evil and an end within a limited time. The Government are further of the opinion that present conditions are favourable to the success of a vigorous campaign of slum clearance.'

In the same year national housing policy significantly changed. Initially it had been intended that the 1930 Act would run in tandem with the 1924 Act, but depression in trade coupled with the formation of a national government (1931), and the abysmal activity in clearing poor-quality housing led to the 1933 Housing (Financial Provisions) Act. This repealed the subsidy paid under the 1924 Act and decreed that in future 'the only subsidies provided for local authority housing would be to rehouse families from the slums'. This shift in policy was the incentive local authorities needed to tackle slum clearance, and as a result during the 1930s, some 273,000 homes were built across the country to rehouse people from clearance areas.

In Norwich, the first houses built under the new act were completed in 1934. By the end of the decade 3,290 properties had been erected specifically to rehouse tenants from slum-clearance areas. Many displaced residents were settled in new homes built on council estates on the City outskirts, including properties on the Larkman, Earlham, Catton Grove, Mousehold, Mill Hill and Marl Pit Estates. However, in response to high levels of demand from residents who wanted to stay in central Norwich, the Council also redeveloped City-centre sites. The two-or-three-storey flats built on cleared areas were quite distinctive in style and many, such as Bargate Court (pictured below) on Barrack Street, still survive.

Unlike the previous decade, it was now accepted that the function of public housing should be to rehouse the poor, leaving the private market to provide for the rest of the population. Although local councils were given discretion to apply rent rebates and subsidies, with so many people on low incomes being rehoused the easiest way to reduce the bill for such subsidies was to charge affordable rents. To achieve this houses needed to be cheaper both to build and maintain.

*Bargate Court, Barrack Street, 1938*

As a result council houses built across the country in the 1930s were, in general, inferior to the earlier estates, yet significantly superior to the properties they replaced. In Norwich, largely because more than 80% of the families rehoused consisted of less than four people, around 70% of the properties built by the Council under the 1930 Act were flats, rather than houses.

The clearance-scheme case studies, in the next section, show that after a jittery start Norwich Council developed a series of procedures which allowed it to move forward almost like a juggernaut, as they pushed through a comprehensive and far-reaching programme. By the end of 1937 the Council had issued in excess of 510 orders for either clearance, compulsory purchase, demolition or closing. These orders covered 3,294 houses and 9,886 people, by then around 1,420 houses had already been demolished or closed and 5,637 people been displaced. The vast majority of the areas cleared contained the City's worst, and oldest, courts and yards, including areas of Barrack Street, Ber Street, Oak Street, Heigham Street, Magdalen Street, Elm Hill, Pottergate, Cowgate, Little Bull Close, St George's Street and King Street. In fact, between 1932 and 1940 the Council's 'Registers of Slum Clearance' indicate that more than

230 yards, containing approximately 1,770 houses and 5,000 residents were subject to clearance orders, i.e. around 50% of the properties and people affected by slum clearances were located in yards. Such a shift could only be achieved by a corresponding growth in affordable housing.

Over the 1930s Norwich City Council acted decisively. Once inexpensive council housing had been built, the demolition of the courts and yards could begin. Critics of the programme did express misgivings, including:

- Along with slums, houses of great historical interest were demolished
- Property owners who were forced to demolish their assets were left with land of little or no value
- Some people did not want to move from the City centre to the suburbs
- Houses which were not slums were caught up in clearance areas and also demolished.

Notwithstanding these criticisms (which are considered in more detail in the 'Context, Controversy and Debate' section) there is no denying that as a result of the interwar slum-clearance programme, the living conditions of many Norwich citizens improved beyond recognition.

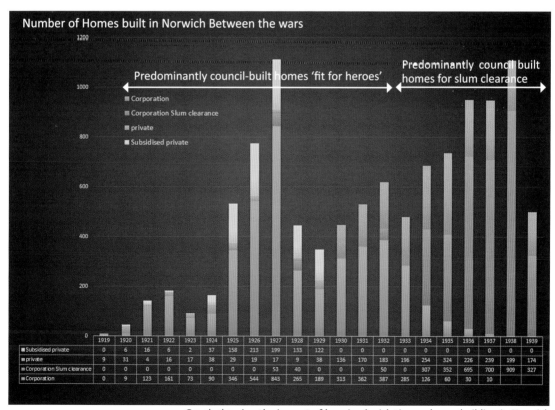

| | 1919 | 1920 | 1921 | 1922 | 1923 | 1924 | 1925 | 1926 | 1927 | 1928 | 1929 | 1930 | 1931 | 1932 | 1933 | 1934 | 1935 | 1936 | 1937 | 1938 | 1939 |
|---|---|---|---|---|---|---|---|---|---|---|---|---|---|---|---|---|---|---|---|---|---|
| ■ Subsidised private | 0 | 6 | 16 | 6 | 2 | 37 | 158 | 213 | 199 | 133 | 122 | 0 | 0 | 0 | 0 | 0 | 0 | 0 | 0 | 0 | 0 |
| ■ private | 9 | 31 | 4 | 16 | 17 | 38 | 29 | 19 | 17 | 9 | 38 | 136 | 170 | 183 | 196 | 254 | 324 | 226 | 239 | 199 | 174 |
| ■ Corporation Slum clearance | 0 | 0 | 0 | 0 | 0 | 0 | 0 | 0 | 53 | 40 | 0 | 0 | 0 | 50 | 0 | 307 | 352 | 695 | 700 | 909 | 327 |
| ■ Corporation | 0 | 9 | 123 | 161 | 73 | 90 | 346 | 544 | 843 | 265 | 189 | 313 | 362 | 387 | 285 | 126 | 60 | 30 | 10 | | |

*Graph showing the impact of housing legislation on house building in Norwich*

Joyce Wilson, who lived in Fairman's Yard, recalls:

'The big change when the yards started to come down was in the 1930s, I was still in the infant school. I clearly remember a man coming to the door with a book under his arm and saying: "Well Mrs Aspland I must condemn this house." He then turned and looked at us lot of rosy-cheeked kids and added, "…but I can't condemn these children". She thought that was a huge compliment.

'Many houses and yards were pulled down around Barrack Street. You have to remember, these were dreadfully put together hovels and so when they were demolished there were huge clouds of dust. Many of the houses were badly infested, and as the wood was pulled away they almost crumbled. I still remember the rats. Talk about the Pied Piper of Hamelin, there were rats everywhere…black rats, grey rats, white rats, even ginger rats. I remember people throwing sticks at them. Afterwards there was rubbish left about, water stood in green puddles and the stench was awful; it's a wonder there wasn't more disease. As houses were pulled down the people who remained would go and gather old gate posts and other bits of unwanted wood which they could put on their fires.

'It seems incredible now, but people who were moved to the council houses had to have their linen and any soft furnishings fumigated to destroy germs and pests. I remember there being a hoo-hah because people had a bathroom for the first time. They still had to heat a copper for hot water, but they did have cold running water in the house.

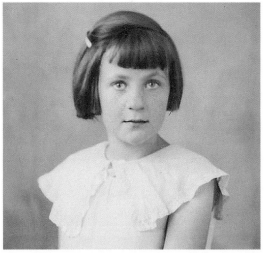

*Joyce Wilson, c.1930*

'People who lived there were moved to the new council houses. I think that some went to the Plumstead Estate, some to the Shorncliff Avenue area [off Aylsham Road], the Drayton Estate or Mile Cross. Often people were simply shifted out together, and of course that did mean that you didn't do away with the community spirit, because so many of the people who lived in the yards found themselves moved to areas where they were still with each other; your old neighbours still lived around the corner. As such although the yards were done away with, I think that spirit did go with them.'

*Lakenham Estate at the Barrett Road, Long John Hill junction, 1933*

# The War Years and Beyond: From Clearance to Recovery

By 1939 housing conditions in Britain were on the whole substantially better than they had been at the end of WWI. In Norwich the worst housing, which also meant the worst yards, had been demolished. Subsequent clearance schemes concentrated on other poor-quality housing.

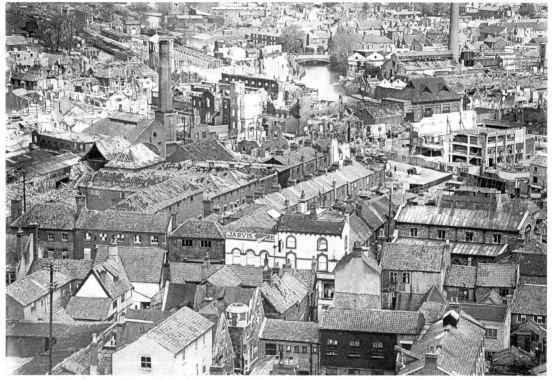

*War-damaged Norwich, looking across St Benedict's towards New Mills and City Station (top left), c.1942*

## The War Years

Across the country, apart from completing properties already under construction in September 1939, mobilisation for the war meant an immediate halt to slum clearance.

In Norwich, the Council's slum-clearance programme was basically abandoned for the duration of the hostilities, which left:

- 622 houses which had been the subject of a Compulsory Purchase Order (C.P.O.) or clearance order still occupied.

- An additional 374 houses that had been subject to a C.P.O. or clearance order which had not been confirmed by the Ministry.

- 908 houses that had been identified for inclusion in the programme where no action had been undertaken, and a further 286 houses that had been certified by sanitary inspectors and were in urgent need of 'slum-clearance treatment'.

Interestingly, although some of these properties were located in old yards, including Chapel Yard (Botolph Street) and Rayner's Yard (King Street) the vast

majority were not, simply because the worst of the old yards had been cleared. The programme had now moved on to encompass a vast area around Southwell Road and Trafalgar Street (part of the Peafield Estate, New Lakenham) and an extensive area around Shadwell Street (part of Crook's Place). The housing in both areas was built in the 19th century. Both areas contained cul-de-sacs, but unlike the traditional City-centre yards, these had been part of the original design, and not crammed as afterthoughts behind the original properties which fronted the street.

Enemy action significantly affected Norwich's housing stock. The City was particularly badly hit during the Baedeker raids of April 1942 when over two nights 297 high-explosive bombs were dropped. As a result of bombing Joan Banger (author of 'Norwich at War') reports that more than 2,000 houses were destroyed, a further 2,600 seriously damaged, whilst more than 25,000 suffered either slight or moderate damage. A number of old yards were destroyed during the raids, including many on St Stephen's and Oak Streets.

# The Post-War Years

## Housing Policy: The National Picture

Countrywide, during WWII some 450,000 dwellings were destroyed or made uninhabitable whilst an additional 3,000,000 were damaged. Over the same period labour and materials for housing repair and maintenance were in short supply, and so priority was given for work on war-damaged property. Simultaneously the population grew by around 1,000,000. At the end of hostilities the growth in popular demand for social reform culminated in Labour's massive election victory in July 1945. In the period after the war there was general agreement that there was a need for high levels of housing construction as a means of addressing shortages, removing slums and providing for a growing population. However, within this period there were three well-defined phases.

1. Immediately after the war, similar to WWI, the main objective was to increase the supply of dwellings and slum clearance was suspended. The vast majority of new properties were built by local authorities.

2. From around 1954, the Conservative government relaunched the slum-clearance programme, at the same time they removed the licensing system that had constrained private building since the outbreak of WWII. This clearly signalled that private builders were expected to meet general housing needs, whilst local authorities focussed on slum clearance and associated rehousing. During this period the government's attitude to poor-quality housing was the same as in the 1930s: deficient houses should be demolished and residents rehoused in new, modern properties.

3. In 1968 a White Paper, *Old Houses into New Homes*, marked a shift in policy from demolition to improvement. Legislation, including the 1969 Housing Act which introduced General Improvement Areas, and the 1974 Housing Act which added Housing Action Areas, followed. Unlike the clearance schemes of the interwar years, where an area was designated for betterment, rather than demolish and rebuild it in its entirety, plans were put in place to enhance the environment and grants made to owners which enabled them to upgrade and modernise their properties. There were a number of reasons for this change of policy, in particular it was a response to the growing public resentment of the loss of entire communities and the increasing emergence of unpopular new housing, particular high-rise developments. The very same points raised when Barrack Street, and numerous other areas were cleared during the 1930s.

## Norwich: Housing Policy and the Yards

After the war local housing policy reflected national trends.

A sketch of the type of redevelopment considered appropriate for the obsolescent residential areas outside the old City walls. Streets and Squares should be designed as a whole and not treated as a collection of semi-detached houses. Terraces of from eight to twelve houses should form units of the design ; the repetition of such large units will not lead to the monotony so evident in many pre-war suburban developments.

*Housing proposals, City of Norwich Plan, 1945*

In 1945 the City Corporation prepared the *City of Norwich Plan* for the Council. This was a comprehensive document which outlined their vision for the future which included plans to reform housing. The report clearly acknowledged one of the major criticisms of the 1930s' clearance programmes, decrying the fact that 'fine old buildings' had suffered from a 'deplorable lack of interest and negligence: actively and passively much harm [has been] done'. Although recognising that some buildings would need to be sacrificed in the name of progress, the document expressed a clear commitment, in theory at least, to 'the preservation, proper treatment, upkeep and use of valuable and interesting secular buildings'. Additionally the report stated that of the 36,000 houses in Norwich, around 25,000 had been built before WWI, and despite all of the work undertaken during the 1930s they estimated 80% needed to be rebuilt over the next 50 years. In line with the general attitudes of the day no mention was made of renovation, instead they considered inadequate properties 'ripe for demolition'.

In practice, repairing bomb damage also gave the Council the excuse to clear areas of substandard housing within the City and at the same time reorganise road systems. It also allowed the Council to put into practice a major principle they had learnt when the yards were cleared, namely that many residents wanted to stay in, or near, the City centre. Examples of new public housing in central areas included schemes in and around West Pottergate, Vauxhall Street and an expanse of land between Ber Street and King Street. However, as in the interwar years, the vast majority of new houses were located

*Sandy Lane, Tuckswood Estate, 1954*

*Heartsease Estate, 1954*

in new and expanding suburban estates, including Earlham, Tuckswood and Heartsease.

Despite the massive slum-clearance schemes of the interwar years and beyond, which resulted in the eradication of many yards, and the significant growth of council housing, in the mid-1960s around 30% of dwellings within the City boundary lacked one or more of the four basic amenities: a cold water tap, a hot water tap, a fixed bath and a water closet. The vast majority of such properties lay outside the medieval city walls and in the main had been built in the 19th century. How were these dealt with?

From the end of the 1960s, in line with national policy, strategy in Norwich began to change, and rather than demolish such inadequate properties the Council had a dual-pronged approach. Firstly they encouraged owners to apply for improvement grants. Secondly, because many of these houses were in the same location and collectively suffered from a range of environmental deficiencies, including lack of parking and children's play areas, they worked to improve entire areas. The 1969 Housing Act dealt with both these issues by legislating for environmental reforms to go hand-in-hand with house improvements. By 1976 Norwich had ten General Improvement Areas containing more than 4,100 dwellings of which 3,100 had already been dealt with. This switch from clearance to improvement covered many of the Victorian terraced properties now lying in the 'Golden Triangle' (a roughly wedge-shape area, spreading outwards from the City centre between

Newmarket and Earlham Roads to Colman Road/ Mile End Road). It is interesting that without this change in procedure, one of Norwich's most popular neighbourhoods might have been demolished. It also leads to the question of what would have happened if a similar policy had been adopted on Cowgate or Barrack Street in the 1930s?

Finally, although the old yards did not specifically feature in post-war slum-clearance programmes, many were demolished for a less-altruistic reason: the rise of the motor car. Their location in the City centre made them vulnerable to new road systems, in particular the building of the inner ring road and the Magdalen Street flyover.

### Council Housing in Norwich

Despite their early reluctance to be involved, by 1966 30% of the 61,100 dwellings within Norwich's urban area were owned by the local authority. It is particularly interesting to note that of the 42,700 homes within the City boundary 41% (17,500) were council properties. By 1977 the number of council properties in this area exceeded 22,500 (some 50% of the total).

*From 1970 to 1981 Bill worked for the City Council where he was a Committee Secretary for both the Public Health and Housing Committees.*

'By the late 1960s and early 1970s the City's clearance policy began to be questioned by some senior councillors, notably Patricia Hollis, the new Chair of the Housing Committee. The thinking was that clearance and rehousing destroyed and dispersed communities. One particular case involved a Miss Bullock, I can't remember where she lived, who was very distressed at the prospect of losing her home. She objected vociferously at every level and ultimately had to be evicted by bailiffs, throwing off her clothes in a final act of defiance and having to be carried out of her house wrapped in a blanket. Although Miss Bullock lost her home I believe her defiance and distress had a marked effect on councillors and gave added impetus to their determination to change policy.

'As I recall the main discussions whether to clear or improve centred around whether housing could be made fit at reasonable expense. One of the last of these battles was over Carlton Gardens in Surrey Street which the officers recommended for demolition on the grounds that they were both unfit and needed for road widening. By then, though, the councillors were sure of their ground and the recommendation was rejected. The Council subsequently entered into an agreement with Broadland Housing Association to renovate these houses. It's almost unimaginable now to think they were recommended for demolition.

'There were two elements to the renovation and improvement of substandard housing. Firstly there were individual Improvement Grants which could be given to owners to bring their properties up to standard (inside bath and toilet, damp proof course, etc.) which, very roughly speaking, covered around half the cost of improvement. Unimproved terraced houses were quite cheap and this allowed a lot of first-time buyers to become owners. Builders also bought unmodernised houses which they improved with a grant and then sold on. It resulted in the improvement of a lot of the City's housing stock in a fairly short period – a legacy we still benefit from today. Some tenants with low incomes were reluctant to allow their landlords to modernise since it would increase the rent. However, this could be got round by arranging financial help so they didn't have to pay the extra rent themselves. In this way the tenant got a properly modernised home, the landlord got a grant to improve the house and increased rent whilst the City got its housing stock secured for the future. It was win-win-win.

'Secondly, the Council could declare an area to be a General Improvement Area. This meant it made a plan for the environmental improvement of the area to go alongside the individual house improvements. This typically involved things like off-road car parks, play areas, traffic calming and planting. It might involve a limited amount of clearance to make space for these facilities but the emphasis was wholly on encouraging house improvement. The first of these was the Arlington Area [bordered by Newmarket Road, Unthank Road, Mount Pleasant, Essex Street and Brunswick Road]. At the same time the Council promoted and encouraged owners in the area to take up the grants available. This included owner-occupiers, who generally needed little encouragement, and private landlords of tenanted houses, some of whom were reluctant to pay for their half of the cost of the improvements.'

*Carlton Gardens, Surrey Street, 1987*

# The 21st Century

But what of the old courts and yards today? Despite the interwar slum-clearance programme and the many developments that have taken place in Norwich since, there are still numerous examples of old yards around the City. These mainly fall into one of two categories:

- Ancient yards that have been renovated and refurbished. Although they are now very pretty and contain desirable residences, their basic structure remains unchanged. Examples include Swan Yard (King Street) and Wright's Court (Elm Hill).
- A narrow entrance which bears the name of an old yard where the housing has been demolished often leading to an unused space or parking area. Examples include Stamp Office Yard (St Andrew's) and Loose's Yard (Magdalen Street).

Elsewhere new yards have been erected in the same area, sometimes on the same footprint, of an old yard, including Thoroughfare Yard (linking Fishergate to Magdalen Street) or Pye's Yard (St Martin-at-Palace Plain).

However, the story of the yards extends beyond buildings; it is also the story of the communities that lived there. What has happened to them? Although aspects of the interwar slum-clearance schemes can be criticised, one fact is not in doubt: they significantly improved the living standards of many of the City's poorest residents. Once coupled with the expansion of the Welfare State after WWII, which offered education, health care and social support, future generations were given opportunities that would have been inconceivable to their ancestors. Take Joyce Wilson, she may have been born in a yard and not allowed to go to grammar school, but she has four grandsons all with degrees, one went to Cambridge and two have PhDs. Similarly Dorothy Holmes was born in Finch's Yard, and had no opportunity to continue her education, but all three of her sons went to grammar school, whilst two went on to university. When Andy Anderson was a social worker in the 1970s and early 1980s he noticed a very definite trend: 'I always enjoyed talking to people about their earlier lives and I came across an interesting progression. For example, I'd visit a house somewhere off Drayton Road where people were becoming elderly and they'd tell me how they'd moved from an inner-city residence, maybe a yard, to a council house on the outskirts of Norwich when it was new, and their children were now buying a bungalow in the City suburbs – a gradual migration outwards.'

And so next time you walk the streets of Norwich and see the many signs of our old yards, please take a look, and imagine what living there was like. But more than that, look beyond the bricks and mortar, and spare a thought for the people who lived there and gave life to the old courts and yards of Norwich.

*A new development of an old yard, Key and Castle Yard, Oak Street, 2009*

*Mancroft Yard, St Peter's Street, 1938*

# Clearance and Demolition: Four Case Studies

During the 1930s more than 9,800 people and 3,200 properties in Norwich were subject to slum-clearance procedures. Around 50% of both the houses and tenants dealt with were located in the old yards. Demolition went hand-in-hand with the provision of alternative, affordable housing for those who were displaced. The vast majority of such housing was supplied by Norwich City Council, which built more than 3,000 homes, mainly on new estates located in the suburbs. This represented not only a massive migration of people but also a huge logistical exercise.

To put the achievement into perspective we review four clearance schemes which took place from the start of the 20th century through to 1938. Together they give a fascinating insight into how attitudes and procedures changed.

## Legal Procedures Used During Slum Clearance in the 1930s

*Clearance Order*: If a property was judged unfit for human habitation it was subject to a clearance order decreeing that it must be vacated. One order often covered a group of properties. Once properties were vacated they were described as 'cleared'.

*Clearance Area:* A specific set of properties covered by a clearance order.

*Compulsory Purchase Order (C.P.O.):* An order allowing specified bodies (e.g. local government) to purchase a property from its owner without their consent.

*Closing Order:* An order by a local authority prohibiting the use of premises for a specific purpose, such as accommodation.

*Demolition Order*: An order to an owner to demolish a property. In the 1930s if a property was subject to a clearance order, and not a compulsory purchase order, six weeks after the property was vacated it was the owner's responsibility to organise and pay for its demolition.

We also make reference to public houses that were **'closed under compensation'**, which happened as a result of the 1904 Compensation Act. The Act stated that when a licence came up for renewal, if the pub was considered superfluous its licence was rescinded, the pub closed down and the owner paid compensation – hence the expression.

# Case Study 1: The Priory Yard Estate Clearance Scheme

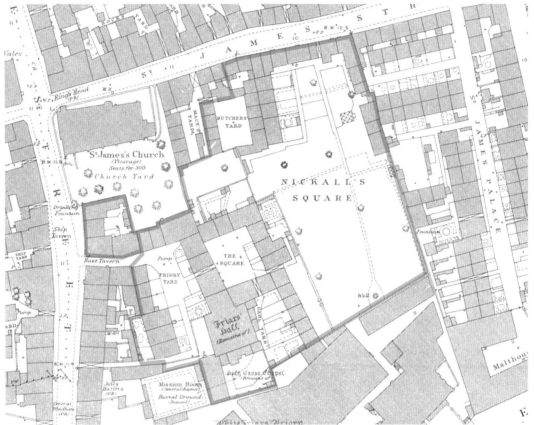

*The Priory Yard Estate Clearance Scheme' outlined in red on the 1884 OS map,*

In 1902 Priory Yard (Cowgate) was one of the earliest to be reviewed by the Courts and Yards Committee. A report printed in the *Norwich Mercury* in 1897 gives an idea why: 'Priory Yard has the reputation of being one of the worst yards in Norwich. It is really divided into three portions...the first yard is cobble-paved and contains 13 houses (more or less) for it is difficult to tell which are inhabited places and which are not. In the middle of the yard is a large pump, which one of the inhabitants stated supplied all the people of the neighbourhood with water. Nearby, entirely unprotected, was a midden, and all around the open drain there was stinking black mud....The second yard [The Square on the 1884 map] entered by a wide passage was in a terribly dilapidated state. Several of the houses were uninhabited and falling down, judging by the bricks and stones strewed over the yard. Eight or nine houses stand in the yard, but several are dismantled. In one these houses the juvenile population had accumulated wood, straw

and what refuse they could lay their hands on, and on the wooden floor they had lit a bonfire....The yard is partly cobblestoned but looks as if nothing short of a deluge could restore it to cleanliness....A narrow passage almost a tunnel takes one into the third of the yards [Gaol Yard] which collectively form Priory Yard. This contains five houses, and the machinery in the factory rattled and roared behind them. Two women were using language the reverse of parliamentary - very much the reverse. At the approach of a stranger they ceased, and in response to enquiries as to their water supply, harshly proclaimed that they have to fetch it from the pump in the outer yard: "A long way to go in cold weather or the fust [sic] of the morning." This pump supplies four or five yards, which have so many landlords and sometimes runs dry; then water has to be fetched from the street. Two dirty privies and a midden with the usual henhouse near the door, complete the equipment of the yard.'

The Courts and Yards Committee resolved that the owners of the properties should finance the cost of private street works, paving and sanitary conveniences amounting to some £688 18s. 11d. This was a colossal sum representing around 60% of the total value of the buildings.

At the time six landlords owned properties in the yard, some of whom made formal objection to the proposed works, and instead asked the Council to purchase the property from them. Eventually the Committee designated an area of one and a quarter acres between Cowgate and Barrack Street (St James Street on the 1884 map) as the Priory Yard Estate. It initially encompassed three yards: Priory Yard, which contained 33 houses and a Mission Room; Nickall's Buildings and Square with its 15 houses; and Butcher's Yard, which comprised eight buildings. It has the distinction of being one of the few areas where properties were demolished by the order of the Committee. At this point it is worth noting:

- At the commencement of the project there seemed to be no concrete scheme in place to redevelop the land, merely that it would be bought for 'improvement purposes', and more particularly that it offered the opportunity to be the site of 'a small scheme under the Housing of the Working Classes Act'.
- No reference is made to any plans to rehouse the tenants, who were probably left to make their own arrangements.
- The properties in the yards were generally owned by landlords who let them to tenants.
- It is unclear why this was one of the few areas subject to clearance by the committee. Yes, it was in exceptionally poor condition, but so were many other yards.

Over 1903 great progress was made with the project, and by the end of the year all of the premises in Priory Yard, Nickall's Building and Square, together with houses in Butcher's Yard (which allowed access to Barrack Street) had been purchased (at a cost of around £3,300), and at least some of the houses on Priory Yard had been demolished. Amazingly, little more occurs until 1906, when 25 houses still remained on the site of which 16 were occupied. In March the same year the Courts and Yards Committee put forward a number of options proposing road improvements and the construction of new housing for the working classes. Each scheme involved a capital cost and, controversially, an annual charge on the rates. It was therefore decided (six for, one against, one neutral): 'That in consideration of the financial aspects of each of the schemes put forward it is not advisable to utilise the Priory Yard Estate for the purpose of erecting thereon housing for the working classes.' The following year it was finally decided 'that the estate be utilised for recreative purposes (including swimming baths, a gymnasium and gardens), and street improvement.' Although this scheme never came to fruition, by the early 1930s the Priory Gym had opened on the site.

## In Conclusion

So what do we learn from the Priory Yard Scheme? Firstly, one is struck by the lack of planning. By the end of 1903 the properties had been purchased, but there were no plans in place to redevelop the land. Additionally, and in line with social and political attitudes of the time, although the landlords were reimbursed there was no concern for the plight of the tenants, and no procedures in place to rehouse them. Finally, although the initial intention was to build houses 'for the working classes', once the costs were taken into account there was no social or political incentive to carry the scheme through. None of which augured well for the wholesale clearance of the yards.

*Priory Gym display team, c.1935*

## Case Study 2: The Rayner's Yard Improvement Area

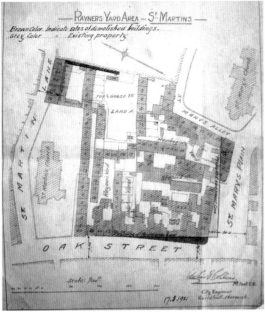

*Plan of the Rayner's Yard Improvement Area, 1921*

This area lay between St Martin's Lane, Oak Street and St Mary's Plain. It covered some 6,900 square yards and included Rayner's Yard, Fox and Goose Yard, Newbegin's Yard, Hen and Chicken's Yard, Gay's Yard, Benton's Yard and Dolphin Yard. In March 1914, according to the Town Clerk's Brief, the area consisted of: 'Main thoroughfares which are narrow and tortuous, and winding courts which are surrounded in many cases by old and tumble-down property, largely of the slum variety.'

In August 1912, when Norwich flooded, the area, which lay only 150 yards from the river, had been badly affected and lay under water for a week. Following the disaster commentators, including the *Eastern Daily Press*, began to raise awareness of the state of many houses in the flood areas: 'They stand low upon reeking saturated ground impregnated with impurities: and they are so congested and airless that even in their normal condition before the flood they could be only be considered habitable by a very restricted standard indeed of what is a humanly habitable place.'

Therefore, in this case, unlike Priory Yard, a single event raised public awareness of living conditions. However, there was little public sympathy for the plight of the tenants, instead this was reserved for the landlords. True, many observers reported on the terrible internal conditions of properties located in the yards, but they then took umbrage with tenants who 'took advantage' of the floods and refused to pay rent. Public opinion was in favour of the Council purchasing the flooded properties (which would benefit the property owners) and undertaking a programme of slum clearance, but little consideration was given to the views of the tenants. One exception was an article run in the *Eastern Daily Press* on 12 September 1912 which gave the opinion of a tenant that neatly summed up the position of many living in the yards: 'The great majority of people who live in these places do not do so from choice but from stern necessity... in the event of these slums being pulled down, what is to become of these poor people? Are they to be forced out of their little homes into workhouses, or are the Board of Guardians and others in authority prepared to make up the difference of rent etc. which will be charged for better-class dwellings.'

By the end of 1912 Norwich City Council had decided to clear the Rayner's Yard area; yet two years later no action had been taken mainly because of the Council's inability to decide what to do with the land. Meanwhile, the number of residents, which stood at 520 in 1911, had dropped to 270 and Harry Pattin, the Medical Officer of Health for the City, was of the opinion that 'the houses, courts and alleys are unfit for habitation'.

Eventually, it was decided that the land was an ideal location for a factory, and Arthur Eliston Collins, the City Engineer, supported a £4,000 plan to build 31 cottages on Starling Road on a site already owned by the Council for 115 displaced tenants. It is important to note that at this time there was no intention to rehouse all of the residents, a proportion of whom would not have met the criteria for council accommodation mainly because they could not afford the rent.

During WWI the scheme was put on ice, but by the end of 1919 the local shoe-manufacturing firm of Sexton, Son & Everard (Sextons), which already owned a number of properties in the area, had expressed an interest in purchasing the land for new factory premises. As it was owned by a variety of landlords, which would have made a private sale very complex, the Council agreed to purchase all individual properties located in what was now designated the Rayner's Yard Improvement Area which it would then sell on at a profit.

It was during this period immediately after WWI that there was a shift in attitude towards the plight of tenants as reflected in the eventual terms of sale. These stated that Henry Sexton could not demolish any housing until alternative accommodation had been provided on the new Angel Road Estate, or equivalent, for all tenants (not just the 115 originally stated) and that such housing should be available within three years.

In February 1921 (almost nine years after the flood) Sextons eventually completed the purchase of the site. By 1924 although 115 persons had been rehoused on the Angel Road Estate no other accommodation had been provided. In a letter from the firm to the Town Clerk dated 26 August 1924, it is made clear that housing provisions made by the Council had been woefully inadequate:

*'We purchased our factory site situated in St Mary's in February 1921, and if you will be good enough to refer to the terms on the contract you will see that the Corporation undertook to provide housing accommo-dation for those families residing on the estate within three years.*

*'We were compelled, owing to the necessity of erecting our factory, two years back, to accommodate the majority of these ourselves, but there still remains six houses covering 12 families for which further accommodation is necessary.*

*'We are now desirous of extending our present factory to cover the site concerned and shall therefore be glad if you will give instruction to have the terms carried out.'*

On 20 February 1925 Sextons were told that displaced tenants would be offered accommodation on the Mile Cross Estate. Three days later the firm wrote to Arnold H. Miller, the Town Clerk: 'We shall only be too pleased to demolish the houses on the Rayner's Yard area as soon as housing accommodation has been provided for the present occupiers.'

## In Conclusion

The scheme raises a number of issues:

- The vast majority of properties in the yards were let. Initially there was friction between landlords and tenant. Public opinion was generally in favour of the landlords.

- There was a lack of co-ordination between the various local authority departments.

- The attitude towards tenants improved after WWI, in a land which should have been 'fit for heroes'. Despite this, provision for tenants was woefully inadequate.

Even allowing for the understandable disruption caused by WWI, it took around 13 years from the time of the flood for this designated slum area to be cleared and (eventually) for *c.*150 tenants to be rehoused. How would the Council cope with the massive programme that was to follow?

*St Mary's Plain, 1936. The house on the far right is the sole survivor.*

# Case Study 3: Barrack Street Clearance Areas, Sections A and B

*Barrack Street, c.1900*

In the interwar years Barrack Street was altered beyond recognition. Not only were huge swathes of buildings demolished and new flats built, but also the road was widened. The clearance map opposite shows two of the earliest sections to be cleared which incorporated some of the most notorious yards in Norwich, including Palace Yard and River Lane. On 21 March 1933 a clearance order was made by the Council. Importantly, and controversially, at this stage properties were not subject to compulsory purchase (in both the earlier case studies the Council bought all properties). Instead, once the tenants had moved out of the buildings, it was the responsibility of the owners to demolish them, at their expense, within six weeks. In the vast majority of cases, this was to the detriment of the owner. Tenants were to be rehoused in 131 new dwellings, ranking from one-bedroomed flats to four-bedroomed houses, located on the newly built Mill Hill Council Estate. In line with recent legislation, and in contrast to earlier programmes, clearance and rehousing were treated from the outset as a combined exercise. Also they were designed to benefit the tenant not the property owner.

A journalist from the *Norwich Mercury* visiting the area in 1897 observed: 'There appears to be an abundance of contiguous open space. From one place especially a fine pastoral scene was observable, with the grand old cathedral in the background. Yet in spite of this open country in the rear, the houses are packed and jammed together as though every foot of ground on this planet were occupied.' Although by 1933 some improvements had been effected to the yards, living conditions were cramped and congested.

Make no mistake, clearing these two areas was a major undertaking. They encompassed 3.66 acres of land and a population of around 550 (400 adults and 150 children) living in properties owned by more than 35 landlords. Major corporate owners were the brewery firms of Youngs, Crawshays & Youngs and Steward & Patteson, together with Jarrolds. There were three public houses, 13 shops with dwelling accommodation, two lock-up shops, and 158 dwelling-houses, of which six were unoccupied. All the public houses and shops fronted Barrack Street which at the time was a narrow thoroughfare, with a distance of between 9 feet and 31 feet 6 inches dividing the buildings on either side of the road.

Describing the area in 1933 Mr B. D. Storey (Deputy Town Clerk) placed as much emphasis on the lack of light and ventilation in many of the properties as

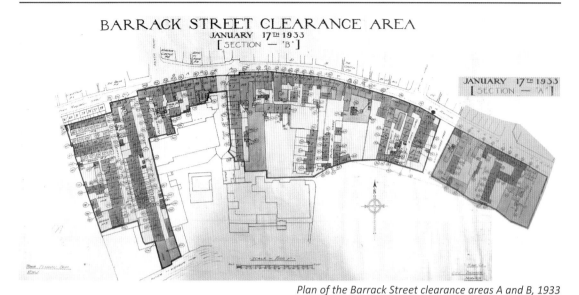

## BARRACK STREET CLEARANCE AREA
### JANUARY 17TH 1933
### [ SECTION — 'B' ]

### JANUARY 17TH 1933
### [ SECTION — 'A' ]

*Plan of the Barrack Street clearance areas A and B, 1933*

he does on the lack of facilities: 'The broad layout consists of a line of dwelling houses and shops fronting the south side of Barrack Street, with outbuildings, a line of small cottages and congested yards built at the rear. In many cases outbuildings are immediately behind houses fronting Barrack Street, which cut out sunlight and air from the backs of the houses and from neighbouring houses. 95 of the houses are below ground level. The structural condition of the vast majority of the buildings is appalling. They are dilapidated, with decayed or crumbling brickwork, low ceilings, rotten timber and plaster and inadequate ventilation.'

In summary: no property had a damp course; only 58 properties had an internal water supply whilst even fewer, 34, contained a sink; 142 properties showed evidence of dampness; 95 properties were below ground level; 91 water closets serviced the properties. Furthermore, based on the average of three years from 1 January 1930 to 31 December 1932, the death rate for Norwich was 11.71 per 1,000 of the population whilst infantile mortality was 51.75 per 1,000 live births. For these 'unhealthy' areas the corresponding figures were 14.63 and 75.47 respectively.

The schemes met much opposition. The majority of the arguments against them centred around five main areas:

- Properties were subject to clearance and demolition orders rather than a C.P.O.
- Notwithstanding the conditions some residents did not want to move.
- Were residents that unhealthy?
- Were living conditions that much worse than in other areas of the City?
- Should all properties be demolished?

## Clearance Order v. Compulsory Purchase

Because the Council had been concerned that central government would withhold their permission to build new housing on the cleared land (as had happened on the 'Sun Yard clearance area' in 1932), properties covered by the scheme were subject to clearance and demolition orders rather than a C.P.O.

In such cases, it was the responsibility of the landlords to demolish their properties, at their own expense, six weeks after tenants had moved out. As you can imagine, this was not a popular option for the majority of landlords who would potentially be left with small parcels of land of minimal value which they might not be able to sell. In particular, shop owners could lose both their homes and livelihoods. There were of course landowners who found the arrangements quite acceptable. At the time the Jarrold family owned a selection of cottages in Palace Yard. On 13 May 1933 on being informed of the scheme they wrote to the Town Clerk: 'The property adjoins our printing works and was purchased with a view to extensions in connection therewith. We have, however, never been able to get our tenants cleared from the cottages owing to the Rent Restriction Act. We shall be glad to have the houses closed so that we can utilise as proposed when the property was purchased.'

Luckily for some of the smaller landlords both Jarrolds and Steward and Patteson took the opportunity to purchase many of the cleared properties, which they subsequently flattened, enabling them to provide ancillary buildings for their respective printing and brewery businesses.

## Residents did not want to move

Despite the conditions, not all residents wanted to leave the area. A number of arguments were aired in the *Eastern Daily Press* during July 1933 after a letter was written by Hebert Pitts, Vicar of St James, under the heading 'Bedlam and Barrack Street'. Whilst acknowledging that many of the homes in the yard were not fit for human habitation the Revd Pitts was strongly of the opinion: 'Demolition without rebuilding would display a lamentable lack of statesmanship. There is no need to transfer any of these people to the new housing estates. They do not want to be removed from their old surroundings; they cannot afford the rents on the new estate, and it doesn't stop at the rent, because extra furniture is usually required and has to be procured on the hire purchase system. Many of those who have been removed would gladly come back.'

## Were residents unhealthy?

An area could only be designated as suitable for clearance if properties were assessed as being dangerous or injurious to health. Much debate centred around the relative high death and infantile mortality rates which pertained to a particular area, and whether they were truly reflective of housing conditions.

There was some argument that the high death rate in this section of the City could be linked to the proportionately high number of old people who lived there. Whilst it was suggested, with some justification, that the higher infantile mortality rate was also connected to relatively high levels of unemployment in the district and in consequence poor nutrition. Objectors to the scheme produced aged tenants who had lived for many years in the area as proof that local housing was not injurious to health. These included two female tenants, one aged 89 and the other 87, who had been born and lived in Dun Cow Yard all their lives. Whilst a gentleman aged 79 said he had lived in the area for 50 years and bought up 19 children, with 'no ill effects'!

Despite such anecdotal evidence, in some cases the statistics spoke for themselves. In particular, the rate of respiratory diseases, excluding phthisis (pulmonary tuberculosis), was 1.43 per thousand of the City's population but 5.06 in Barrack Street, whilst for phthisis the rate for the whole City was 0.67 and for Barrack Street 2.81. Such damning figures seemed to support the Council's claims that 'it was not a case of trifles in regard to the condition of the property, but an accumulation of defects'.

## Should all properties be demolished?

For a number of reasons this was one of the big questions which dogged the City's slum-clearance programme through to the 1970s, when policy moved away from 'clearance' towards 'improvement'. Firstly, Norwich is an historic city. Inevitably in its bid to carry out an extensive programme of slum clearance in a short period of time, the Council also demolished historical gems. Secondly, the programme resulted in the destruction of properties within an area, not necessarily within yards, that might not have been of particular interest, but were either in reasonable condition or with relatively little work could have been. Additionally the orders often encompassed commercial properties e.g. shops, where tenants were in danger of losing both their homes and livelihoods.

In Barrack Street, following an official hearing, a number of properties were spared demolition. These included the Dun Cow public house which was adjudged to be structurally sound leading to the conclusion that it had only been condemned because of its location.

## Conditions no worse than other areas?

Although few would disagree that many of the properties in the area were old and lacked basic facilities, the same could be said for many houses in Norwich. New properties on the council estates were being built with water supplies, indoor bathrooms and damp proof courses, but much of Norwich's housing stock lacked these facilities. For example, much was made of properties in the area having unventilated food cupboards, yet these were the same conditions that existed in 75% of houses in the City. Similarly, although none of the houses had damp-proof layers, as late as the 1970s many old terraces in the Golden Triangle were attracting grants to remedy such deficiencies. In fact, many opposers to clearance had the view that the City contained 'many ancient houses which may not have been satisfactory from a modern standpoint, but nevertheless housed the population perfectly well' .

However, what made many yard houses particularly bad was that on top of all of the other deficiencies, including lack of sanitation and an inaccessible water supply, they also suffered from an absence of air and light.

## The Outcome

Over 1934/35 approximately 13 yards, containing 130 buildings were cleared of 400 people, the vast majority of whom were rehoused in council-built properties. By the end of 1935 most cleared buildings had been demolished.

However, relief was short lived for the businesses and properties on Barrack Street that were exempt from the programme. On the 14 August 1936, as part of their plans to widen Barrack Street, the Barrack Street Compulsory Purchase Order was passed. Although, some traders just lost part of their land, others were forced to sell their businesses. On a more positive note, in this case owners were compensated.

## In Conclusion

This was an extensive scheme, which unlike the Rayner's Yard and Priory Yard clearances was pushed through at great speed, with almost military precision. Very clearly the shift in public opinion and legislation had fed through to practice, and the rights and needs of tenants living in slum properties had been moved to the fore.

From the rather amateur approach which was seen in the earlier schemes, in the 1930s the City Council perfected procedures which enabled them to move at great speed and effect extensive change to the living conditions of Norwich's poorest residents. Inevitably mistakes were made, but there were significantly more winners than losers.

One final, and very important point, was that subsequently, three-storey council flats were built on both Barrack Street and in other clearance areas. There were a number of reasons for this, including the cost, but also it would seem that the Revd Pitts had a point when he argued so eloquently that residents did not want to leave the area, as acknowledged by the City's Housing Committee in November 1935: 'Persons displaced by action under the slum-clearance programme frequently ask for accommodation within easy reach of the interior of the City... and there has been a considerable demand – greater than the supply available for the flats in Barrack Street.' Many of these flats, which enabled tenants to move out of the City's worst slums, have survived to this day, a testament to the work of the Council that did so much to improve the standard of living for so many citizens of Norwich.

*Barrack Street, c.1910*

# Case Study 4: Pye's Yard and St Martin-at-Palace Plain

By 1937, when this scheme was proposed, the City's slum-clearance programme was well advanced. There are boxes of documents at the Norfolk Record Office which show that though the Priory Yard Scheme may have been a shambles, by now process-driven, slick procedures were in place.

On 31 July 1937 Norwich Council ordered the clearance of properties in Pye's Yard and also the compulsory purchase of the adjoining land (all buildings numbered in red on the plan were included). The intention was for the site, together with that compulsorily purchased on Bedding Lane, to be redeveloped as 38 flats for the working classes. Of particular note is that of the 1.06 acres included in the scheme only 0.26 acres were 'unfit'. Although the scheme covered old yards, the emphasis was on building new flats rather than slum clearance; in this respect the scheme differed significantly from other projects. Most crucially the proposal encompassed one of the City's most attractive areas, comprising properties of both Tudor and Georgian origin. These included Cotman House, where the famous Norwich artist, John Sell Cotman, lived from 1824 to 1834, the very house where he had his school of painting and gave drawing lessons.

*Plan of Pye's Yard clearance area, 1937*

*Palace Plain, c.1920. Other than the White Lion, now the Wig & Pen (l) all the houses were included in the scheme*

## Background

The scheme was one of the 'Quayside etc.clearance areas' which were all located in a zone bordered by the River Wensum and Quayside to the north, Whitefriar's Street to the east, Palace Street and St Martin-at-Palace Plain (Palace Plain) to the south, and Wensum Street to the west.

At the time Cotman House was used as a 'house let in lodgings'. Even the Council admitted that it was in fairly good condition and an 'interesting specimen of Georgian architecture' although conditions at the rear were 'really rather bad'. Numbers 9 and 10 Palace Plain were also lodging houses, a Mrs Wright owned number 9 and was clearly upset when she wrote to the Council on 9 August 1937: 'I have been here for eight years and have to earn my living by letting and having boarders in my lovely old house. There are one or two little things wrong but it is a good house. The only way I earn my living is like this as I am not able to work. There is [sic] 11 rooms and all is conveniently placed. I do not want to be left on charity as I would have to if I could not earn my living after being in service all my life....I don't want you to give me anything only my home.'

## Saving Cotman House

By now the Council had systems in place which enabled them to bring schemes to fruition at a tremendous rate. Although hearings were held which allowed all parties to put forward their own opinions, City councillors made the final decision on what was recommended to central government. Once sent to the Ministry of Health, the vast majority of projects were 'rubber stamped'.

There was no doubt that Norwich's Labour run council were very focussed on improving living conditions in the City, but there can be a fine dividing line between being focussed and blinkered. In retrospect, in this case they seem to have overstepped that boundary.

Over the decade many ancient, historical properties in Norwich had been sacrificed in the name of improvement, and it was clearly recognised that without a well-organised campaign these wonderful buildings on Palace Plain would be lost. In response, local groups pooled resources, and on 5 October 1937 the Town Clerk received a letter from local solicitors Daynes, Keefe & Durrant informing him that: 'We have just been instructed by the Norfolk and Norwich Association of Architects, The Norfolk & Norwich Archaeological Society, The Norfolk & Norwich Art Circle and the Norwich Society to represent them at the public enquiry which is to be held tomorrow by an inspector of the Ministry of Health, with regard

to the C.P.O. made by your corporation in respect to Cotman House and the adjoining frontage on St Martin-at-Palace Plain.'

The scheme received national notoriety when *The Times* weighed in quoting Mr William Palmer, secretary of the Society for the Protection of Ancient Buildings: 'The houses now threatened with destruction form a very agreeable group of great value, and their disappearance would mean a loss not only to the historical attractiveness of Norwich but to the nation as a whole.'

Despite intervention by these august bodies and the housing committee indicating that the properties could be retained and 35 flats still be built, the Council stubbornly refused to reconsider the scheme. At the public hearing the Deputy Town Clerk (Mr B. D. Storey) said he did not press for the demolition of Cotman House and adjoining properties, but left the issue with the Ministry. It is unclear whether

COTMAN'S BIRTHPLACE.—Under a rebuilding scheme of the Norwich City Corporation the birthplace of the famous Norwich painter is threatened, with a number of adjoining houses. A public inquiry into the corporation's proposals is being held to-morrow.

*The Times, 5 October 1937*

he did so to distance himself from a controversial decision or, which we suspect is more likely, because he thought that the Ministry would accept their recommendation. As he said: 'It is a very good central site and could be used with greater advantage for modern requirements – housing the working classes near their work – if the Council could build as many flats as possible.'

This view was clearly not shared by the national government and on 21 February 1938 the *Eastern Daily Press* announced that the Minister of Health had decided to exclude both Cotman House and the adjoining Tudor and Georgian houses on Palace Plain from the clearance order. A letter from the Minister of Health is still held in the Council's files from which it is clear that Norwich's citizens were not alone in decrying the loss of their heritage and that in response to: '...a national groundswell of public opinion in slum-clearance operations in which buildings of historic, archaeological and artistic interest are concerned...[in future] careful consideration [should be] given to this aspect'.

## In Conclusion

Palace Plain was saved, but many important buildings and vistas across Norwich, which did not attract the same level of interest, were lost. Which leads to the question: In their quest to clear slum dwellings and replace them with higher quality housing did the City Council become over zealous?

It should never be forgotten that over the 1930s the living conditions of thousands of people in Norwich improved almost beyond recognition. However, such mass improvement inevitably led to individual losers.

*Palace Plain, October 2014*

# Context, Controversy and Debate

Writing in the *Eastern Evening News* in 1976 Jonathan Mardle aired a debate that has long raged about the demolition of Norwich's old yards. On the one hand are those who decry the loss of so many historic buildings and communities, on the other are those who rejoice in the razing of squalid houses which generated so much misery and disease. Were they so bad? After all in today's world of en-suite bathrooms, automatic washing machines and flush toilets, it could be very easy to overdramatise the conditions. Taking the discussion a step further we also need to consider whether the clearances were to everyone's advantage. Who lost out?

To place the yards and the interwar clearances into context we will:

1. Put the old yards into perspective at different times in their history. We will particularly evaluate living conditions in other types of housing.

2. Review whether the old yards were unique to Norwich.

3. Assess the issues raised when the yards were cleared, particularly the role of Norwich's Labour-run council. We will then consider who were the winners and the losers.

*Alefounders' Yard, Westwick Street, 1937*

Although there is a general consensus that the old yards contained some of the worst housing in Norwich, it is very clear that all yards were not slums and conversely that all slums were not yards.

## The Mid-19th Century

Let's start by considering William Lee's influential public-health report completed in 1851, in which he investigated the sewerage, drainage, water supply and sanitary conditions across Norwich. Although Lee reserved some of his most intense criticism for the yards, it is very clear that standards of hygiene were generally poor elsewhere too. In particular:

- **The Water Supply**: This was eloquently described as being 'bad in quality, deficient in quantity, and obtained with difficulty'. The report includes a vivid description of the River Wensum which once within the vicinity of the City became 'a receptacle for dye water, night soil, filth, garbage and every abomination...and in that condition the fluid is used by a multitude of the citizens in lieu of water and...actually taken with food.' In addition five of the City's ten public pumps were situated close to adjoining churchyards 'crowded with corpses', with all that implied. Even citizens who obtained their water via the Norwich Water Company were not safe, as the company in turn obtained their supplies from a polluted section of the river at New Mills.

- **Sewers and Drainage**: Not only were a large proportion of streets completely without sewers, where they did exist they were inefficient. In fact Lee concluded that house drainage did not exist in Norwich.

- **Pavements**: The yards weren't alone in being unpaved as a large number of streets in both the City and hamlets (suburbs) had either defective or non-existent pavements.

- **Burial Grounds**: The burial grounds within the City were crowded such that 'further interments of the dead in them would be incompatible with the health of the living'.

All of this led Lee to conclude: 'There is a great amount of preventable disease and mortality, in a city that ought to be one of the most healthy in the kingdom.' Although Lee highlights the deficiencies in the sanitary arrangements in the yards, houses designed for the better off were not necessarily significantly superior. For example, large houses in Bracondale rented out for between £20 to £100 p.a. had no drainage, whilst none of the 'respectable houses' located in Sussex Street had water supplied by the City's water company.

Along with the yards the report was also highly critical of new 19th-century developments, designed for the working classes which also contained poor-quality housing with abysmal sanitation and water supplies. One area which received particular criticism was

*Norwich Water Company, New Mills, 1897*

Peafield (New Lakenham). When Lee visited this suburb of modern cottages it had 500 houses and 2,000 inhabitants, no pavements, gas, water supply or drainage system. Refuse was generally retained on the surface, although some gathered in a stagnant ditch some 600 yards long and gave off 'noxious' gases. Another area of note was Crook's Place (west of St Stephen's Road) which comprised about 250 houses built along three wide streets with long front gardens. Located just beyond the City walls, Crook's Place was one of the first attempts in Norwich to design and build an ordered layout of small houses. Despite this, sanitary arrangements were poor, the area having neither paving nor drainage. Additionally, although some residents had access to pumps, the water was 'occasionally so bad the people will not use it for tea'. But these houses did have one major advantage compared with the majority of yard houses, residents had the benefit of large front gardens, and as a result they enjoyed better light and ventilation. However, Lee does point out that to the backs of the houses 'insufficient attention' had been given to these two points.

Another class of houses highlighted by Lee were the numerous cottages built 'upon the old walls of the City'. These included, houses on Duck Lane (later renamed Wellington Lane) about which the surgeon Henry Edgar, reported to Lee: 'The lanes are very narrow, the houses imperfectly ventilated and very badly supplied with privies...the locality is unhealthy.' Conditions here were comparable to dwellings

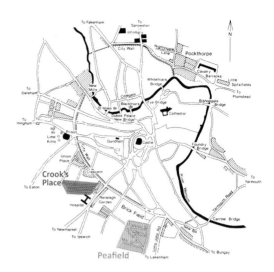

*Millard and Manning's Map, 1830*

located in a typical yard, and similarly tenants were 'compelled by their poverty to live there'.

Lee did make some positive comments about the old yards. Firstly, despite describing at length the horrific conditions in many yards and making particular reference to their woeful lack of hygiene, he notes that the interior of many of the houses were 'neat and clean'. Secondly, he points out that some courts were built around squares or open areas and even had areas of garden, which in the context of the period, would have made them relatively comfortable places to live.

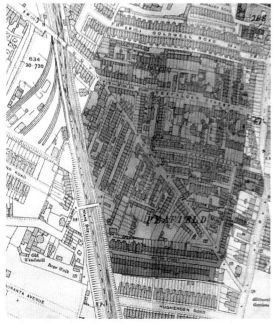

*Plan of Southwell Road, Trafalgar Street etc. Clearance Area, Peafield c.1938*

*Evidence of houses built 'upon the City wall', Wellington Lane, 1939*

## Pumping Water

*Pump in Old Barge Yard, by Thomas Lound, c.1850*

Poor water supplies were not unique to the yards as noted by William Lee in 1851: 'The private pumps in Norwich are of peculiar construction, being formed out of trunks, without casing, and standing from six feet to eight feet or upwards above the ground. They are exceedingly heavy to work, and it is common for two persons to unite in pumping especially women. The drawing of water from these pumps is too laborious an occupation for women. I did not meet with a cottage having a tap within-doors supplied by the company, and generally, where cottages are supplied, one tap is common to from 10 to 50 families.' An interesting postscript was provided by William Cooper, surgeon, who noted that '...[although] the labour of pumping water is injurious to people...hernia is not more common in Norwich than in other places'.

## Drainage and Disease

James Slapp Garthon, Surgeon, reported to William Lee in 1851: 'The Peafield is always diseased. There is no drainage there, and a very bad supply of water. That and Crook's Place are built on brick earth and the sewage water cannot permeate the soil.'

## Taste the Difference!

In 1850 it was reported in the *Norfolk Chronicle* that people taking their water from the River Wensum near the dye works knew what colours were being dyed as well as the dyers: 'They think the brown is best; they say that the black soils their tea, and so does the scarlet.'

## Upmarket Homes

*The Crescent, c.1960*

The Crescent, off Chapelfield, was made up of *c.*22 houses. In 1851, it would have cost around £40 p.a. to rent one of these upmarket properties. Despite the relatively high levels of rent (a 'basic' house in a yard would have cost around £4) residents had to put up with cesspools near the back doors, most had open-bin privies, although some did have water closets which emptied into the cesspools. Lee noted: 'These cesspools are intended to percolate into the gravel and the chalk below, but when the pores of the strata become closed the cesspool fills up and does no more good.'

## Digging for Water

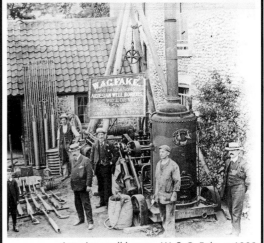

*Artesian well borers, W. & G. Fake, c.1900*

As late as 1893 25% of the City's population still depended on wells for water. By 1897, 84% enjoyed piped supplies and by 1906 the figure had increased to 98%. This did not necessarily mean that water was piped into a house, but meant that it could be obtained without working a cumbersome pump.

## Mid-19th Century to WWI

Between 1861 and 1910 Norwich's population grew from 75,000 to 122,000, and over the same period more than 10,000 new houses were built. Of these new dwellings, 7,000 were small houses designed for the working classes.

Houses built during this period included a section east of Unthank Road. Beginning with Essex and Trinity Streets in the 1850s, the area expanded, ending at Bury Street in the 1890s. Today these houses are much in demand as part of the City's 'Golden Triangle'. When built, they were designed for skilled workers and better-paid artisans, and their rents would have been around £10 p.a.

New houses had to meet certain criteria, which set them way above the standards experienced by casual and unskilled workers (10% of the population) who paid £3 – £5 p.a. to rent small dwellings in a yard, or for the 13% of the population who were charged £6 – £8 to live in one of the homes speculatively built around 1820 – 1840 (e.g. Crook's Place). Many will recognise the basic layout imposed in 1858, which of course can still be seen in many of Norwich's terraced properties. In particular:

- There was a major repositioning of the stairs which were now to be a straight flight between the two main downstairs rooms of the house, rather than the cramped stairs which had led up from the back room.

- To encourage the use of the parlour, front and back downstairs rooms had to be the same size.

- Houses had an outside coal shed, so that the coal did not have to be stored inside.

- Almost all new houses had a scullery added to the rear for cooking and washing. This freed the back room for use as an everyday living room.

- Every house was built with its own outside toilet, but this could have been a privy (earth closet) as in 1893 fewer than 5,000 houses in Norwich had access to a water closet.

Undoubtedly tenants in these houses enjoyed significantly better conditions than the majority of those living in yards. However, again there is evidence that some yards were reasonable places to live. Thus C.B. Hawkins, the social historian, wrote in 1910: 'In the courts and yards...are to be found housing conditions as bad and insanitary perhaps as those to be found anywhere.' However, he also makes the point that: 'Except in the smaller courts – unfortunately they are rather numerous – where the houses are apt to be sunless and probably damp, it is noticeable that even in the centre of the City the yards are often built around gardens. Many of these are quite charming in the summer when the flowers are out.' Of course, Lee had also noted that some yards did contain gardens, but how many really had them? Although, an examination of the 1884 OS map of the City, coupled with a review of documentation, e.g. reports made by the Courts and Yards Committee, makes it clear that 'often' is an exaggeration, a number of courts certainly did contain gardens, e.g. Turner's Square (Rose Lane).

In general, tenants lived in yards because accommodation was cheap and they could not afford anything better. However, tenants with higher incomes in stable employment, also chose to live in yards, leading to the conclusion that some accommodation was of a higher standard. One such family were the Sabbertons, pictured below outside their house, 5 Stamp Office Yard (St Andrew's Street) c 1904. At the time of the 1901 census, Frank, an engineer at Harmer's Clothing factory, lived here with his wife Emily and six children. Ten years later, the family were still there. Of the surviving children still at home four were working. This suggests that they chose to live in the yard, rather than doing so out of necessity. In addition the fact this lovely photograph was taken in front of their home, suggests that they were proud to live there.

*Turner's Square, Rose Lane, 1938*

*F. W. Sabberton and family, Stamp Office Yard, c.1904*

## The Interwar Years

Even in this period most yard dwellings had shared, communal facilities. In the early 20th century you felt really lucky if you didn't have to share your outside toilet with your neighbours. As neatly summed up by Joyce Wilson who lived in Fairman's Yard (Barrack Street): 'We were fortunate, because there was just one other house in our yard, and so we just had to share our loo, which was perhaps 10 yards from the house, with one other family. But in the main yards up the road, like Palace Yard, where we weren't allowed to visit, there was perhaps a dozen families sharing one loo, which sadly very often…well to say unclean was a euphemism, it was absolutely appalling.'

But it wasn't only yard dwellers who experienced such living arrangements. In the 1930s Daphne Way, lived on the Grove Place development, most of which was built in the early 19th century, when communal facilities were still the norm in smaller properties. She explains: 'I lived at the bottom of Howard Street and Lewis Street, on Cross Trory Street. Around the yard were five houses, we were in the corner of it. There were three toilets in the yard. We had one to ourselves, but the others were each used by two families. There was a shed, we had one half and someone else had the other half. My mother had a

great big mangle in her half but when it rained she used to get wet, because there wasn't enough room in the shed for her and the mangle! The linen lines ran across the yard and in the summer we used to sit out there and I used to have my tea sat on a stool. Mum used to do all of the washing in a copper in our kitchen, which had a water supply. The kitchen was very small but we had a big front room and bedroom. After mum had done the washing I'd arrive home from school and iron it all. The house was comfy we had nice furniture. My mother bought some lovely nick-nacks from her time in service. She had a lovely dinner set, I've still got it. We had a coal house in the sitting room at the back of mum's chair. When the coal man came, we had to move mum's chair and he'd put it all in. The house was infested with mice, I've never liked them since. One afternoon in the summer when we hadn't lit the fire, we had five mice in the fireplace, my father had to kill them when they came out.'

Betty King lived in a house on Portland Street, built as part of the Unthank development of the late 19th century. Unlike Daphne's house, it was self-contained, but would fall well below the minimum standards we expect today: 'It was really nice. We had our own

*Betty King, c.1937*

*Daphne Way, c.1937*

42

back garden, a communal pass through. We had three bedrooms and a reasonably good kitchen, with an iron cooking furnace at the end of the room. The cooking units were on the side of the fire, and the fire heated up hot water for the copper. We used to have our baths in a tin tub in the kitchen. We had our own outside toilet which, similar to many of our neighbours, my parents eventually converted into an integrated bathroom and toilet. It was really nice.'

John Curson lived with his parents at 82 Northumberland Street. Again much of the area had been developed in the late 19th century. He explains: 'It was a bit older than some in the area. I believe when the land was used for farming the group of houses we lived in were agricultural workers' cottages. Next to ours was a smallholding of several acres, and they used to keep pigs. Every time they used to clear the pigs out it was really smelly, and so we all had to close our windows and doors. The houses were nice six-roomed houses. We had a kitchen, we didn't have a bathroom of course, but luckily we did have our own flush toilet. They were outside and had been converted over the years. Originally they were just a container and the men used to come around once a week in the middle of the night and empty them, but once plumbing was fitted in to different houses we got made up with running water. There used to be a pump in our back yard, and I remember when I was about seven my dad was digging the garden and his spade disappeared. He'd found a well, he almost fell down. It must have been 20 to 30 feet deep.'

The facilities enjoyed by Betty and John were not that different to those experienced by Ruby Baker's family, who lived at 2 Stonemasons' Square (Yard) off St George Street: 'We had five bedrooms, a living room and a little scullery. In the scullery we had a cooker, a copper and a sink. On the other side of the house we had our own toilet alongside and my father built a little trellis around it, we had a dog's kennel there as well. You'd get to the toilet by going out of the front door.'

Finally, it must be remembered that although the demolition of yards was central to the City's interwar slum-clearance programme, which clearly indicates that they contained abysmal properties, it also encompassed many other dwellings. Some, such as those located on Cowgate, were in areas rife with yards, others, such as areas of New Lakenham, consisted of terraces built in the early 19th century, which were also unhygienic, unhealthy places to live.

## To Conclude

In summary, yes the yards did encompass some of the most insanitary and poor-quality housing in the City, but it must not be forgotten that not all yards were slums and not all slums were yards.

*Poor quality housing was not restricted to the yards. Norfolk Street cleared for demolition, c.1935*

# Were the Old Yards Unique to Norwich?

There are some who suggest that the old yards were unique to Norwich: but were they?

If you refer to the definition on page 3, the answer is a resounding no.

From the 18th century many urban centres experienced rapid growth, and the planning that accompanied such expansion was both patchy and lacked rigour. Across the country, in response to growing demand for accommodation from a working-class population, speculative builders constructed cheap housing at high densities. There were no national statutory requirements stipulating minimum standards for such developments, whilst local by-laws were inadequate to promote effective density, drainage, lighting or ventilation. As explained by the historian P. J. Corfield (writing in 1982), this resulted in 18th-century towns experiencing 'highly intensive settlement, in a maze of densely packed dwellings, around courts and off narrow streets and alleys, without systematic provision of public amenities and open spaces'.

If we take Leeds as an example, over the 18th century the population grew from approximately 6,000 to 30,000. To accomodate this increase, cottages for the 'lower orders' were built behind large houses on the main streets. In fact no entirely new street of houses was built in Leeds between 1634 and 1767. However, in the 19th century as Leeds evolved from a small town to a large manufacturing city (by 1851 the population had reached 101,000) this all changed with the construction of terraces of cheap back-to-back houses on undeveloped land.

In Nottingham in the early 18th century a population of around 10,000 lived in fairly spacious surroundings, generally within the boundaries of the medieval town, an area of some 800 acres. Then from 1750, as its knitwear and lace production became progressively industrialised, the population mushroomed and by 1831 over 50,000 people were living in the same area. Because the town was surrounded by open land subject to rights of common pasture, it could not be allocated for building. In such circumstances the most effective way to cram as many dwellings as possible into as small a space as possible was to build back-to-backs in cul-de-sac formations. Conditions were so bad that in 1845 the Health and Towns Commission reported: 'Nowhere else shall we find so large a mass of inhabitants crowded into courts, alleys and lanes as in Nottingham, and those too of the worst possible construction. Here they are so clustered upon each other, court within court, yard within yard....Some parts of Nottingham [are] so very bad as hardly to be surpassed in misery by anything to be found within

*Parr's Yard, Finkle Street, Nottingham, c.1931*

the entire range of our manufacturing cities.' The position was only alleviated when legislation was passed to enclose the land and abolish common rights, which in turn meant that blocks of land could be allocated for building. Thus, it is fairly conclusive that yards were not unique to Norwich. Although there were aspects of Norwich's old yards that give them distinct characteristics

Firstly, because of Norwich's early wealth, the origins of many yards can be traced back to Tudor and Stuart buildings, including Crown Court (Elm Hill), and Ragged School Yard along with many of its neighbours on Oak Street. A number could even trace their roots in the 15th century, including Mancroft Yard (St Peter's Street) and Old Barge Yard (King Street), which developed behind the magnificent Dragon Hall. This point is confirmed by the Courts and Yards Committee which in 1898 made the point that 'generally speaking the yards are of an ancient character'.

Secondly, as noted above, although during the 19th century many terraces, 'new' yards and back-to-backs were built in Norwich, builders continued to infill behind the old (often very old) properties that faced the street. The latter point is clearly illustrated by examining the development of the area behind 98 to 114 Oak Street. The main properties facing the street were all Tudor in origin. As can be seen on the

*106 to 114 Oak Street, 1936*

two maps below (on which Oak Street is called St Martin's at Oak Street) it was only between 1789 and 1884 that most of the cottages which made up the yards behind were built: namely Baldwin's Yard, Goat Yard, Dog Yard and Talbot's Yard.

Thirdly, many yards were located adjacent to public houses. By the 1880s, there were over 450 pubs within the City walls, often in historic buildings, and the pub yard was an ideal space to infill with small cottages. This leads to a final characteristic: the exotic names enjoyed by many of the yards. These included the Queen of Hungary Yard (St Benedict's), Flower in Hand Yard (Heigham Street) and Arabian Horse Yard (Oak Street)...sadly the names belied the conditions.

*Section of Oak Street based on Hochstetter's map (l), 1789. Yards behind 98 – 114 highlighted on OS map (r), 1884*

## Yards in Leeds

In 1845 James Smith reported: 'By far the most unhealthy localities of Leeds are close squares of houses, or yards, as they are called, which have been erected for the accommodation of working people. Some of these, though situated in comparatively high ground, are airless from the enclosed structure, and being wholly unprovided with any form of under-drainage or convenience, or arrangements for cleansing, are one mass of damp and filth....The ashes, garbage and filth of all kinds are thrown from the doors and windows of the houses upon the surface of the streets and courts....The privies are few in proportion to the inhabitants. They are open to view both in front and rear, are invariably in a filthy condition, and often remain without removal of the filth for six months.' It was noted during the cholera epidemic of 1832, that 75 cart loads of soil were removed from one of the privies in Boot and Shoe Yard.

## Overcrowding

By the 1930s the post-war issues of overcrowding had largely been solved in Norwich. Somewhat ironically in 1935 when a new housing act gave subsidies to specifically help with this problem a survey made under the act only discovered 763 cases of overcrowding made up of: 319 families in slum clearance areas, 168 families not in slum clearance areas, and 276 families (around one-third of the total) living in properties on council estates.

*Large families like Ruby Baker's were uncommon*

## Yards Across the Country

In 1897 the Courts and Yards Committee contacted other boroughs to ask whether: 'Ancient common passages through yards and squares having an unobstructed entrance from a main street but ending in a cul-de-sac were treated as public highways repairable by the inhabitants at large or as private streets.' The committee contacted 19 centres, including Birmingham, Manchester, Chester, Portsmouth and York. Their responses, which incidentally illustrated no common practice, give an interesting insight into how common yards were across the country.

- Only the railway town of Crewe, which was not planned until c.1840, had no ancient yards.
- In Birmingham, courts were 'so numerous' that the authorities required all paving, sewers and lighting to be done by the owners.
- In Cardiff, very few such places existed 'most having been obliterated by new buildings'.
- In Chester cases continually 'cropped up', suggesting a large number of yards.
- On the other hand, in Ipswich no case had arisen. In their response it was pointed out that their courts seldom contained more than 20 houses.
- Portsmouth had many yards with one 'entrance and exit'.

## Nottingham Comparison

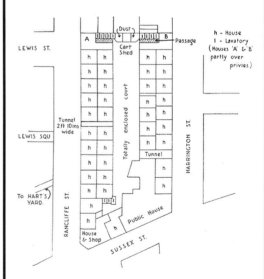

The plan is of a typical court In Nottingham (Source: The Report of the Royal Commission on the State of Large Towns, 1845). The properties lacked paving, lighting and adequate water supply and sewerage which meant that living conditions were very similar to those experienced in the Norwich yards.

# Clearance Schemes: The Issues, The Winners and The Losers

During the 1930s, national legislation paved the way for countrywide slum-clearance schemes and the building of council estates. However, what is particularly remarkable is that following the somewhat desultory nature of the early programmes undertaken in Norwich, during this decade more than 35 schemes of varying size were undertaken by the Norwich City Council. Without doubt the scale of change in Norwich was driven by the fact that from 1933 overall control of the City was in the hands of the Labour Party which had a clear commitment to provide improved services for the benefit of the working classes, especially in the field of housing. There was also another political element, as the rapid growth of council housing in suburban estates solidified 'safe' Labour wards.

There were two major reasons why it was in the Council's interest to adjudge a property a slum. Firstly, the Council had a mandate to improve the living conditions of the poorest members of society. To achieve this they needed funding to build more council estates. In the 1930s, subsidies to build new council houses were calculated on the number of people rehoused from slum properties. Secondly, if they needed to buy a property under a C.P.O. they paid less if it was designated as a slum.

But what was the definition of a slum? In the 1930s there was much discussion about this question. Decisions were generally made on the recommendation of the City's Medical Officer (a council employee), who justified his assessment in a report on general conditions. Typical statistics in this document included information on damp-proof courses, sanitation, relative death rates and the proliferation of specified diseases. However, many houses in Norwich outside the clearance areas lacked the same facilities, whilst poor health and high death rates could be credited to a multitude of causes of which poor housing was only one. As such, any assessment involved an element of value judgement. Schemes were of course subject to hearings, which allowed opposers to air their grievances. Although it is clear from council files that such hearings could be successful, it often took great effort, skill and finance to exempt a property from a scheme. As a result, as the decade progressed some argued that the Council had too much power to bring to fruition projects that supported their own political ideals.

On 13 April 1937 Percy Hatch, a solicitor, outlined a major deficiency in procedures:

'Dear Sir

'I have a case before me now, and it is undoubtedly typical of others. A man who spent his early life employed by others and served his time during the

**Clear Policy**

WORKERS!
Vote for Yourselves by
VOTING FOR WITARD.

The Landlord wants big Rents for Little Houses.

The Employer wants long hours for short Wages.

The Worker wants big Healthy Houses for low Rents and Higher Wages for Shorter Hours.

| 1. | HOTBLACK, LOMBE A. | |
| 2. | SMITH, JOSEPH DE CARLE. | |
| 3. | WITARD, H. E. | X |

Don't write anything on the paper, nor make any mark but a **X** opposite the name of **WITARD**.

[SEE OVER.]

Printed and Published by W. Moore, 16, Muspole Street, Norwich.

In 1903 Herbert Edward Witard became the Norwich Independent Labour Party's first City Councillor. He remained on the Council until he resigned in 1951. He became Lord Mayor of the City in October 1927 and in 1938 was given the honorary freedom of Norwich. In this early electioneering poster (exact date unknown) it is clear that working-class housing is high on his agenda for change.

Great War was, through hard work and thrift, able to save a few pounds and purchase a small shop and house in Norwich. A clearance order has now been made in that district.

'The clearance order directs that his property is to be pulled down and that site value only be paid for it. This will not even cover the mortgage he has on the property. The Housing Act provides that in certain cases compensation shall be paid for property in the clearance area, but if the property is unfit for human habitation then only site value is to be paid. This on the face of it seems fair enough. But who is to decide whether the property is unfit for habitation or not? In the first place a representative of the City Council inspects the property and gives his opinion, but however fair and scrupulous he may be, one has to remember that he is employed by the City Council. If the owner objects to his property being included as unfit he can send in an objection and the Government Inspector will hold an inquiry and decide on it. In the case in point, evidence was given by two well qualified and eminent Norwich men that the property was quite fit for habitation, but in spite of this it remained included in the Order as unfit.

'The vital point is that the unfortunate owner has no right of appeal: to any judge or jury or court of law. The decision of the Government is final.

'I believe I am right that both the Council who originate the scheme and the Government, whose inspector decides upon any objection, are financially interested in the scheme as they have to provide the money for paying the properties their site value. It therefore appears that they are interested parties and sole judges as well.

'Is not this contrary to all elementary principles of justice and equality? In spite of our claims to the best judicial system in the world, we might just as well be under the control of Mussolini or some other dictator.

'There is a growing feeling of resentment by people who are treated in this way, and one would like to see "the powers that be" help to put things right.'

The Council were driven to improve housing. Although their achievements were outstanding, they exhibited little sympathy for those who did not share their ideological views.

We did not discover any accusations that members of the Council, or their employees, were working for personal gain, but there is much evidence that once started on a particular track it was difficult, but not impossible, to divert their course. Their aim was to demolish slums and replace them with high-quality council dwellings, and they did not look kindly on those who stood in their way, a fact acknowledged in a council debate on procedures covered in the *Eastern Daily Press* on 23 November 1938. Here it was reported that one councillor (a Mr Finn) put forward the proposition that many houses had been cleared that were not hovels or slums although he did not believe that the Corporation had been using their powers unjustly, he thought that they had been going just 'a bit too far'.

One has to applaud the Council for achieving so much in so short a space of time. In effect they were correcting an inequitable situation that had existed for years, when both legislation and public opinion had favoured landlords and done little to help tenants. Not surprisingly both approaches generated a situation where there were many losers. As we move through the 1930s, in their understandable zeal to improve conditions for tenants, the Council saw property owners as collateral damage. Their properties were literally bulldozed over as one scheme after another came to fruition.

It would not be right to judge what happened using 21st–century ideals and standards. Luckily Council files, newspaper reports, correspondence and other documents give us a fascinating insight into public opinion at the time.

Archived material in the Norfolk Record Office illustrates how the Council's approach to slum-clearance programmes and the building of council housing resulted in many controversial situations. In particular:

- The treatment of landlords and property owners
- Lack of support for small businesses
- Properties of historical interest were demolished.

*17th-century houses, 10-14 Ten Bell Lane, demolished in 1938*

48

## Landlords and Property Owners

In general the Labour-run council had little sympathy for landlords, many of whom had little regard for the well-being of their tenants. For years legislation and public opinion had been weighted in favour of lessors, and the position needed to be redressed. However, there were good landlords and property owners, but the Council tended to assume that they were 'guilty' and it was up to them to prove their 'innocence'.

The main concern for property owners revolved around the question of compensation. Put simply, if a property was deemed unfit for human occupation and subject to a clearance order, once vacated it was the owner's responsibility to demolish the property and dispose of the land. If the property was subject to a clearance order and also a compulsory purchase order (C.P.O.) they received minimal compensation based on the fact that the property had been a slum. Alternatively, if a property was subject to a C.P.O., but not a clearance order, i.e. not assessed as a slum property, the Council would purchase the buildings at a market value. In the 1930s if an entire area was selected for clearance, it was then up to individuals to argue that their property should be excluded. Files at the Norfolk Record Office contain a multitude of letters from solicitors (who incidentally must have seen their incomes rocket during the decade, and really were winners) who rarely succeeded in protecting their client's position.

In theory, the principle is very sound, why should the owner of a slum property, which he may have exploited for years be paid compensation? Again it is useful to hear contemporaneous arguments. On 24 January 1924 this very subject was on the agenda at the Norwich Rotary Club, and was reported in the *Eastern Daily Press* the following day: 'It was agreed that a man might no more make money by letting bad houses than by selling bad meat or watered milk, and it was obvious that many landlords deserved to receive little or no compensation. In late years [it was observed] there had been speculation in slum property; houses had been bought at about £20 each which had brought their owner from 50% up to 300% return. But there were good landlords who depended for their livelihood on property which happened to be in a clearance area, property which was not slum property. It was felt that such landlords were entitled to proper compensation.'

Take the case of Mrs A. H. Prentice who owned four properties in Reeve's Yard (St Benedict's Street), which were included in the 'Queen of Hungary Yard Etc. clearance area', passed in 1937. In January 1938 she wrote a heart-wrenching letter to the Town Clerk:

*'Dear Sir,*

*I am an elderly widow whose sole means of support is the small properties left to me by my husband,*

*'Queen of Hungary Yard Etc. clearance area', 1937*

*and this loss of revenue to me is necessarily of great importance. I have no pension, or other means whatsoever, so you will readily see that compensation in my case is badly needed, and trust you will give me your experience in proceeding to this end.'*

Sadly Mrs Prentice's plight received little sympathy from the Town Clerk, who clearly received many such pleas. His terse reply read: 'With regard to the question of compensation, although I appreciate your difficulty, I regret I cannot assist you. The Council are not acquiring the property and therefore no question of compensation arises.'

To add insult to injury, as the yard was subject to clearance rather than compulsory purchase, Mrs Prentice was also responsible for demolishing her property at a cost of £45.

Unsurprisingly, in situations such as this landlords and owner-occupiers almost as a matter of course disputed clearance orders. The 'Queen of Hungary

*Reeve's Yard, St Benedict's Street, 1936*

Yard clearance scheme' was relatively small. It only encompassed 18 properties owned by five separate landlords. Although Mrs Prentice acted on her own behalf, Mr Burrage who owned eight properties employed the solicitors Cozens-Hardy & Jewson, who fared no better than 'the elderly widow'. As one of the later schemes, it is obvious from the files that the Council was not in the mood to take any hostages, as clearly illustrated in the case of 6 and 7 St Margaret's Street (incorporated in the same scheme) which were bought by Edward Hines, a mechanical-engineering firm owned by a rather ebullient Sidney Hines. He acquired these two residential properties for storage, after the clearance order had been passed, clearly thinking that he would be able to override the Council's edict. Little did he know. He used every method at his disposal, including solicitors and the intervention of Geoffrey Shakespeare MP. He then argued that he was involved in 'war work of national importance', a point backed up by Mr Shakespeare, but to no avail as explained by the Town Clerk: 'The committee have always set their face against permitting departure from the Act because they felt that one might be regarded as a precedent, and it would place them in a difficult position in the future. The present facts have been fully explained to the committee, and they are not prepared to depart from their usual practice.' They point out that if Mr Hines is urgently in need of a store for work of national importance he could readily and quickly erect a suitable building on the cleared site, and if he had 'done this at first instead of resisting the order of the minister he would have already had a store which would have aided him in the manufacture of his product'.

A note in the file dated 2 May 1939 indicated that finally Mr Hines had acceded to the order and demolition was underway.

However, the Council were not totally heartless, Mrs R. W. Hardingham, who lived on 12 Cherry Lane, received notification on 27 September 1935 that her property was caught up in the St George's Street (Section B) Clearance Order. In response, she explained:

'Dear Sir

1. The property is in a first-rate state of repair

2. The property was purchased with borrowed money, viz. £215 on 21st October 1925 and at the present time £150 is still owing, and if the property is included in the Clearance Area I should not be able to repay the amount still owing and pay rent for alternative accommodation, thereby bringing me undue hardship.'

Luckily for Mrs Hardingham, her plea was looked on with some sympathy and she was paid additional compensation in accordance with Section 64 of the Housing Act 1935. It remained unclear whether the compensation enabled her to clear her debts.

## Small Businesses

Many small businesses were located within the clearance areas. City traders faced a number of problems in the 1930s:

- The serious disturbance of trade which arose when large masses of the population were moved from one district to another.
- If they owned their premises and it was subject to a clearance order they were at best entitled to the site value.
- Any compensation for loss of business was at the total discretion of the Council.

In the same way they treated landowners, the Council often adopted a blanket approach in their handling of business owners, leaving them to fight their corner, which most did, with varying degrees of success.

Take the example of the grocer, William Pimm, who traded from 110 St Benedict's Street. In 1936 his property was included in the 'Neale's Square Etc. clearance area', where the Council planned to demolish slum properties and build a new road. Properties caught up within the scheme were subject to both clearance and/or a C.P.O. Mr Pimm was devastated to find that all of his property was subject to a clearance order. He wrote an impassioned letter to the Council:

'Dear Sir,

Further to my last communication to you I am making another appeal to you to save me from ruin and destitution even at the eleventh hour. I am informed you can do a lot for me, my building is sound, even the Sanitary Inspector stated so at enquiry. I am absolutely miserable.

Messrs. Southgate & Sons, Builders of Norwich, have inspected these premises and the report is enclosed. I ought to have full compensation or be left alone. This is my living and I am nearly 70 years of age. I want justice only.

Please do not reply to this as I am afraid if you do I shall do something desperate to myself immediately, but do your best for me.

W. Pimm

P.S. I am going mad with worry.'

The report from Southgates confirmed that: 'The premises are structurally sound and will last for years.' Eventually the 'front and middle units' of Mr Pimm's property were excluded from the clearance order, though still subject to the C.P.O.

Although Mr Pimm was successful, it is very clear that his property should never have been declared a slum. One of many examples where the Council pushed through a scheme, for the best of intentions, without having sufficient regard to the plight of individuals.

One of the problems faced by small businesses was that compensation was paid on a discretionary basis. Take for example the following who were all displaced by the 'Peacock Street – Cowgate redevelopment scheme' and claimed compensation with varying degrees of success.

### Frederick Cullum, 100 Cowgate

In Kelly's Directory, 1931, Frederick Cullum describes himself as a 'marine store dealer'. In a letter to the Council he lists his stock as including iron, rags, bones, boots, shoes and also some furniture, i.e. he was a rag and bone/ scrap metal merchant. On 16 August 1937 he wrote to the Council claiming £60 compensation, which today would be equivalent to around £3,000. He based his claim on the fact that his business had been established for 20 years, his average weekly profit amounted to around £2 10s. a week and the cost of moving his 12 tons of stock. On the 5 October he receive a letter from the Town Clerk informing him that he would receive an allowance of £40 when he vacated the premises; there was no explanation how the sum was calculated.

### Fred Wyatt, 118 Cowgate

In 1931 this 'fried-fish merchant' purchased the goodwill of his business for £200 (equivalent to around £9,500 today). After the purchase his business was badly affected by the migration of customers to the new council estates. Eventually his own property was listed for clearance. On 7 August 1937 he was offered £10 as compensation for loss of trade. Despite Fred contesting the decision, the Council refused to increase the allowance paid.

### R. Duffield, 98 Cowgate

This butcher did not fair well. On 22 October 1938 he was informed by the Council that as he had taken over his premises after the clearance order was made he was not entitled to any compensation. On 4 November 1938 Mr Duffield responded: 'I was informed that this area at that time [when I took it over] was not a clearance area, so I therefore sunk my money in it to get a living for myself, wife and six children. If no grant is made for loss of business and fixtures it simply means that I am cut off from getting another start in business.' Subsequently Mr Duffield was offered a payment of £10, which he pointed out would not even 'cover the cost for a side of beef much less anything else, so you see how useless such a small sum means in the butchering line'. His appeal for more money fell on deaf ears. In desperation Mr Duffield again wrote to the Council asking them to recommend him for work on the corporation, as he now had no means of supporting himself and family. In a brief note in the housing committee minutes of 12 July 1939, it was recorded: 'After hearing a further letter from Mr R. Duffield as to employment with the corporation that this committee is unable to take any special action is this case.'

### A. W. Cutmore, 31 Peacock Road

On 21 February 1938 Mr Cutmore wrote to the Council asking for 'some financial assistance' to cover loss of trade sustained over the previous five years as a result of slum clearance and to allow him to relocate his bakery as he was in 'the unhappy position of being turned out'. In April he was informed that on vacation of his property he would be the lucky recipient of £100. Happily, later the same month Mr Cutmore was able to inform the Council that as a result of their generosity he had purchased a new place on Harvey Lane.

*Cowgate to St James' Church, 1936*

Living next door to an area which was being demolished presented a few challenges!

Although Alice Groves saved her grocers' business from the Barrack Street clearance order it would seem that all was not plain sailing afterwards, as suggested by a letter dated the 25 January 1935 sent by her solicitors to the Town Clerk: '...as the result of the demolition of the property on each side of her shop, she has suffered and is suffering the greatest annoyance and inconvenience. Her shop and residence has been choked with dust and her goods injured.'

It is not clear whether Mrs Havers received any compensation from the Council following her complaint, but one suspects that she may have been relieved when the following year her property, along with those of many of her neighbours, became the subject of a C.P.O. to facilitate the widening of Barrack Street.

On 25 June 1937 Mrs E. Knights, who lived at 77 St George's Street, wrote a letter of complaint to the Council:

*'Dear Sir,*

*Would it be possible for the door of number 128 [part of the 'Stonemasons' Square Clearance Scheme'] to be made secure as nearly every day I go across and close it – sometimes twice a day.*

*Being directly opposite our house it is most unpleasant. The broken panes of glass are bad enough without getting a bad smell with a west wind.'*

The situation was more dire for the executors of Mr Alfred Hubbard deceased, who owned both 2 and 3a Pipe Burners' Yard. The yard was part of the 'Loyalty Court Etc., St Stephen's Street Clearance Scheme', but these two properties were excluded by order of the Minister of Health. Unfortunately when the Norwich Co-operative Society started to demolish numbers 4, 5 and 6 Pipe Burners' Yard, as they were legally obliged to do, they discovered that all five properties were originally one building. By then a previously internal wall was exposed to the elements and the roof had been partially removed.

The Council washed their hands of the position, and seemed reluctant to apply common sense, their stance being that under the terms of the order the Society were legally obliged to clear their site. Eventually the conundrum was put in the hands of solicitors, but the last letter in the Council's file came from the Society in which their Managing Secretary wrote: 'In passing may I say that if we proceed to demolish our property adjoining the house under review it will completely collapse.'

## The Destruction of Historic Properties

Many Norwich yards either contained, or were situated in close proximity to, ancient buildings. In general, as illustrated at Pye's Yard (Clearance Case Study Four, page 34), which was saved at the eleventh hour by central government, the Council took their brief to clear slums, provide new housing and improve road systems as being more important than retaining the City's heritage. Needless to say, this led to a number of disputes, particularly with the Norwich Amenities Preservation Society. In an article in the *Eastern Daily Press* (1 October 1936) the Town Clerk reportedly said that they did try without prejudicing their duties under the Acts, to work with the Society: '...but Norwich was "littered with old buildings" of archaeological interest and if they were never to interfere with any such, it would scarcely ever be possible to widen a street or make a new one.'

Under discussion were three Tudor houses located at 107 – 111 Pottergate. The properties were included in the 'Neale's Square and 107 – 113 Pottergate clearance area'. At the time the City Council were planning to construct a relief road for St Benedict's Street and its path was to cross the site of the ancient houses which were to be subject to a C.P.O. The Norwich Amenities Society claimed that 107 was one of the oldest houses in the City and indicated they were prepared to buy it. Meanwhile, solicitors for the owner (a Mrs Taylor, presented in the press as a widow) described the property as 'a Tudor house worthy of preservation'. One of the tenants sent a letter to the press singing the house's praises, saying that it was the best he had ever lived in and that its oak work was 'marvellous'. All to no avail. The houses were demolished, and then to add insult to injury because war intervened the new road was never built. The only consoling feature of this pointless destruction is that survival would have been short lived, as it is more than likely that in 1942, when St Benedict's was bombed, these ancient building would also have been destroyed.

Many buildings of archaeological interest were demolished in the 1930s. Properties lost included Sir John Falstolf's 15th-century house located at 104 – 108 Cowgate, which was condemned in 1936 as part of the 'Peacock Street and Cowgate development area'. Interestingly no effort was made to save this property owned by the famous English knight who is believed to have been the inspiration for Shakespeare's character, Sir John Falstaff. A similar fate was shared by an L-shaped block of Tudor houses located in White Lion Yard (Magdalen Street). In 1934 they were described as being well built and comfortable and having the appearance of a group of almshouses. Although it was suggested they could be quite pleasant if back-to-back houses in the adjacent

Gilling's Yard were pulled down to give through ventilation, they were not spared. Instead, the properties were compulsorily purchased as part of the 'Little Bull Close Etc. clearance area', all buildings were demolished and new council flats erected.

In defence of the Council it must be pointed out that a number of older properties were spared. For example, elsewhere on Magdalen Street the yards were cleared but many older houses fronting the street were excluded from schemes – this point is clearly illustrated in the compendium section. Also many individual houses were saved, including numbers 134, 135, and 136 St George's Street, which were caught up in the 'Stonemasons' Square clearance area'. These properties, which were admired for their 'architectural character', owed their survival to the Norwich Society.

In retrospect it is easy to criticise the Council's approach, but if we had lived in the abysmal conditions experienced in many yards, we would no doubt have demanded change and looked to a strong council to expedite improvements. Maybe one of the flaws in the Council's strategy is that they often adopted an 'all or nothing approach', in that they tended to raze an entire area rather than be selective. Needless to say this led to much criticism and heartache. A very balanced review of this approach was printed in the *Eastern Daily Press* on 14 August 1937, in a letter

from a Mr C. B. Jewson. Whilst acknowledging that progress was both inevitable and necessary, Mr Jewson suggested an approach, which if adopted could have led to many more buildings being spared: 'The unique interest of Norwich lies in its old streets, with varieties of styles of houses seen together and the resulting varied skyline. There seems to be a notion prevalent among many people that where new houses are to be built it is incongruous to leave old buildings, but this is an entire fallacy. Our old streets contain buildings of many styles, and where the new buildings are well designed they harmonise with the old.'

There are many examples across the City of old and modern buildings complementing each other. For example the modern Pye's Yard, which blends so well with older properties on Quayside and St- Martin-at-Palace Plain, clearly illustrating that Mr Jewson had a very valid point.

## In Conclusion

In the interwar years extraordinary improvements were made in the living conditions of many of Norwich's lowest paid families. Undoubtedly mistakes were made, but these have to be seen in the context of the incredible progress that was made, which is well summed up in an *Eastern Evening News* article printed on 25 August 1936, and reproduced overleaf.

*Tudor houses, 107 – 113 Pottergate, 1936*

# MOVING IN BEGINS IN NORWICH FLATS: FROM RAT-RIDDEN SLUM TO NEW HOME ON A TOP STOREY

The Lord Mayor will officially open the Norwich Corporation's new block of flats in Barrack Street on September 3rd, but the first dozen tenants moved in to-day.

The big building, set well back from the road, gives a new light and spaciousness to Barrack Street. There are 110 flats, of which 44 are now ready for occupation. Some are one-bedroom flats, intended for old couples, and the rest two-bedroom flats, for people with small families. They are light, airy little dwellings. Each has a hot water system, working from the stove in the living-room, a kitchen with a gas or electric cooking range, and a bathroom.

There is a big open space at the back, where the children will be able to play. On part of this space there are long rows of neatly built sheds, in which the tenants can keep their bicycles and perambulators.

## Contrast

The Corporation's housing manager, Mr A. Howard Burton, showed the "Eastern Evening News" reporter round the flats. He is rightly proud of them.

"Now", he said, after the inspection was over, "I will show you the sort of place our tenants are coming out of."

There was not far to go – a hundred yards or so down a side street – mean, but you would not say unfit for habitation, for the slums of Norwich are not apparent on the surface. We turned under an archway into a narrow little yard that was gloomy, although the sun was shining in the street outside. There were a dozen cottages there. Men were pulling two of them down. The cottages had all been vacated some weeks ago, but a smell of overcrowded humanity still hung about them.

We entered one. It was twilight in the downstairs room, for the window was only two feet square, and the wall of the opposite house was a bare three yards away. Scraps of rotting linoleum clung to the brick floor, which exhaled dampness. This room had served for living-room, kitchen and scullery. The only stove was an old-fashioned iron grate, and there was no sink. We opened a rickety door in the wall, and climbed a dark staircase that was more like a ladder. Here, with big holes in the floor, was the bedroom, low-ceilinged, cramped, and stiflingly hot, as the tiny window would not open. After that the air of the yard outside seemed purity itself.

## Water Supply

We examined the water supply – one tap in the middle of the yard, to serve the twelve cottages. Sanitary accommodation – a row of tumbledown outbuildings only a few feet from the doors of the houses. "Think," said Mr. Burton, "families of six and more have been brought up in houses like that one. I have not shown you the worst either. You can see that the brickwork of that place we have just been in is cracked, but there were one or two houses that almost literally fell to pieces a few days after the people had got out. It is a wonder that some of these Norwich slums have not collapsed with the people still in them."

We went to several yards like that. The house-breakers were reducing them to heaps of rubble, and on top of the rubble were bonfires in which the men were burning the woodwork. It all has to be burned, because most of it is impregnated with vermin and is not fit to be used even for domestic fire-wood.

## A Clear View

The reporter went back to the flats. For all their rawness and newness they were like Paradise after those yards. He went to see the first tenant. She and her family are on the top floor, and from her windows she can look right away to the top of Mousehold. These flats have opened up a great space in the cramped, despised Pockthorpe, through which sweeps the cleansing wind from the heath.

The first tenant had been in occupation of her new dwelling for less than 24 hours, but she had made it look like home already. She was hot and busy, and happy. She had polished the furniture till it shone, and there were bright new curtains at the windows, and a new, coloured cloth on the table. Everything was neat and spotless.

It was no sigh of regret that the tenant gave when she recalled the slum house she had just left. "It was swarming with rats and mice," she said. As for the new flat, it was just lovely, but she was too busy to talk long about it because she had not nearly had time to get everything straight yet, and she must have dinner ready in half an hour for her husband, and for the small son, who was happily running about among the builders' rubbish at the back, investigating his play-ground-to-be, no doubt getting finely grubby in the process and preparing a test for the new bath.

*Pump Yard, Lower Westwick Street by Holmes Edwin Winter, 1881*

# Memories of the Yards

There are many sources of information about Norwich's courts and yards. Some of the most evocative are photographs which, along with contemporaneous reports, give a fascinating insight into what it was really like to live in the City long before many of us were born.

In the pages that follow we recount the memories of people who lived in or visited the yards in the 1920s and 1930s. Their recollections of a bygone era bring the story of the yards to life.

*Philip Armes (centre), b.1923*

*Joyce Wilson, 1924 – 2015*

*Dorothy Dugdale, b.1925*

*Muriel Chilvers, b.1925*

*John Curson, b.1921*

*Daphne Way, b.1931*

*Dorothy Holmes, 1920 – 1995*

*Chris Baker, 1917 – 2013 and Ruby Baker, b.1921*

*Donald Read, b.1931*

*Betty King, b.1931*

*Irene Foster, b.1924*

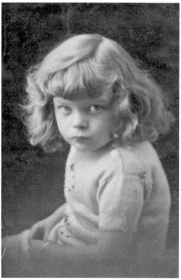

*Joan Banger, b.1927*

# General Conditions in the Yards

One characteristic of the yards is mentioned by everyone who knew them: the smell. When one considers the poor sanitation, this really isn't surprising. Neither is it strange that the subject of communal toilets and wash houses continually recurs, after all you really felt lucky if you had your own facilities. Also people did not have much in the way of possessions. However, they did not feel hard done by because, as pointed out by Chris Baker, 'we were all in the same boat'.

Speaking in 2011, Chris still had clear recollections of his youth: 'My father had a shop at 57 Rose Lane, where he made boots. My mother, father and us three children lived in Heald's Buildings, in a two-bedroomed house adjoining the shop. We had a living room, there weren't any lounges in those days, and a kitchen. Of course, we had an outside toilet that was right down the bottom of our yard. We were lucky enough to have a toilet of our own, but practically everyone else around there had to share. There'd perhaps be a row of three toilets, for about six houses or so. The houses in Heald's Buildings were very basic. Two bedrooms. No kitchen. No water in the houses. All the water was supplied from taps in the yard. The men of the house used to strip to the waist and go and wash under the tap in the middle of the yard and have a good sluice in cold water. There wasn't much in the way of furniture. You'd have a table and a few chairs. Maybe an easy chair, but that was about all. Cooking was done on little portable stoves. Maybe one or two had a little gas oven. Kettles would be boiled on the fire; there'd always be a kettle bubbling away. There were two wash houses in this particular yard and everyone shared them. In the wash house was a copper where clothes were laundered. We didn't have any washing machines or anything like that, just a copper and a mangle. Then we had washing lines in the little gardens, out the back of the cottages, each house had a bit of garden.'

Ruby, Chris' wife, can also recall her early family life: 'There were 12 children in my family, I'm the oldest. I lived off St George's Street, which we used to call Middle Street, at number two Stonemasons' Square. It was a big double-fronted house. We were all compact and it was in quite good condition compared with other houses in the yard. When we lived there my mother just had eight children. We had five bedrooms, a living room and a little scullery. In the scullery we had a cooker, a copper and a sink. On the other side of the house we had our own toilet alongside and my father built a little trellis around it, we had a dog's kennel there as well. You'd get to the toilet by going out of the front door. There was an alley leading to the Square. We lived in the main part near the road, and so we were away from the other houses. In the main part of the yard, there was a row of toilets shared by everyone, and they had a wash house too where they took turns rinsing their linen and things like that. They were little dwellings, I think they only had one bedroom.'

Although John Curson wasn't brought up in a yard, as a child he often visited his Uncle Bob and Uncle George who lived in Trowse Yard (Ten Bell Lane): 'We lived on Northumberland Street, where we had our own toilet, but on Trowse Yard they had a communal toilet stuck in the middle of the yard. I think there were two toilets and a wash house and it was up to the people who lived there to keep them clean. The yard where my wife was brought up, higher up on Ten Bell Lane, was similar. She used to tell tales of how some people never cleaned the loos....My mother-in-law was a stickler for cleanliness, a typical Victorian matriarch, and so I don't know how she coped with communal facilities.'

Muriel Chilvers and her parents moved to Ripley Close on the Earlham Estate when she was just three years old c.1928, but she often visited her grandmother, Harriet Lansdell, and neighbours on Three King Lane (St Benedict's): 'One of my grandmother's neighbours was a little old lady called Mrs Powell, for some reason we all called her Nanny Powley. The house where she lived with her husband [10 Three King Lane, which formed one side of Three Kings' Yard] was even more of a slum than my grandmother's, not because she was dirty, but because her house had nothing. She

## Chris and Ruby's first date in 1937

Chris met Ruby in Chapelfield Gardens at a Monday night dance when Ruby was just 16. From the first she thought, 'He's lovely', but when he walked her home she was nervous and talked too much and was concerned he'd never want to see her again. She needn't have worried: in 2010 Chris and Ruby celebrated 70 very happy years of marriage.

*Chapelfield Gardens, 2010*

*Muriel Chilvers' grandmother, Harriet Lansdell, c.1935*

didn't even have a gas light, the house was lit by an oil lamp which she kept in the middle of the table. I can't recall that she had anything to cook on.'

Betty King lived on Portland Street (off Unthank Road) but often visited the City centre: 'I remember using the yards as cut through. Yes, walking through the yards it was smelly and untidy, perhaps the buildings were a little on the ramshackle side, but it was a community. As a girl I felt intimidated walking through because it was different to the world I was growing up in.'

Like Betty, Joan Banger didn't live in a yard and was very shocked to discover their condition: 'When I was a small child in the early 1930s my grandmother lived in Orchard Street, and we children used to play in the street, skipping and what have you. A little girl often joined us; she didn't really speak to us, and when we finished she just left us and went home. One day I decided to follow her to see where she lived. We got to St Benedict's and I saw her pass down a narrow alley, and so I followed her to the sort of house that I'd never seen before. It was dirty. It had a toilet by its side and I could see water running from somewhere through a little gully. The toilet served all of the houses in the yard. I still remember the smell in the yard...it was indescribable. The house was just so dirty and ugly in my eyes. I knocked on the door and the child opened it, but she didn't hardly speak at all. Beyond her there was a table. I couldn't see any chairs. In the corner I could see a pile of what I thought were bedclothes. I think I just said hello to her, and she looked so embarrassed and I felt embarrassed, and so I just said goodbye and went...and we never saw this little girl again. I started to worry about people who lived in houses like this. What depressed me most was across Norwich were many little entrances and alleyways leading into yards, but once I knew what lay beyond I thought that it was absolutely terrible.'

## Betty King recalls that some yards were better than others

'The yards were generally tidy, residents obviously had a pride in looking after them. Of course some weren't. Along St Augustine's the yards were bad. Behind where the City Hall is now, there were a lot of yards, which seemed to be well looked after. They could be very noisy, especially when the children were playing.'

*City Hall site, c.1930*

## Joan Banger remembers the 1930s

'When I went up St Benedict's I can remember women standing in the narrow entrances that led to the yards. They had their arms folded and were chatting away. I suppose it was because the sun would never shine beyond where they stood. So they would come out for a little air. Sometimes people were inclined to laugh at them because they looked so dirty and they used to swear back.'

*Joan Banger, c.1950*

# High Standards and a Sense of Community

*Ruby Baker (circled) next to her mother and the rest of her family, c.1940*

Although general conditions in the yards were poor, there was one other fact which always came across, the importance of distinguishing between the fabric of the yard, over which residents had limited control, and the interior of a house which was in their personal care. People may not have had many possessions, but what they did have was looked after.

Ruby Baker recalls the high standards, set by many who lived in the yards: 'My mother worked hard, bless her. She'd be washing all day Monday. She'd already started when we went to school. She'd stop for dinner and fry us sausages and eggs and still be going when we came home in the evening. Our mothers were very hygienic and house proud. My mother used to scrub her table white. She'd always be polishing and cleaning. There were no table cloths and nothing fancy on the table, you had a plate and cup and a knife and fork. We all had our own. Cleanliness was very important.'

Joyce Wilson's mother was similarly industrious: 'Nobody had separate bedrooms, no indoor sanitation, no privacy. We had to go across the yard to pump the water out for the next day, but in spite of all this we did have high standards...The only day I can remember my mother not working was a Sunday

afternoon. She'd cook a big Sunday dinner, then she'd wash, put a clean blouse on and then sit and read the *News of the World*.'

It's easy to think that it was women doing all of the domestic work, but John Curson reminds us that was far from the case: 'Years ago if you lived in a six-roomed house, and maybe fell on hard times you'd let two of the rooms and give use of the kitchen, that's how my uncles came to live on Trowse Yard. They rented a little living room and bedroom and shared the kitchen. There were two communal toilets and a wash house outside in the yard. They didn't have their own furniture. In the bedroom they had a double bed, a wardrobe and a wash table with a jug. Everything was very basic, but they were always spotless. When they came to visit us on a Friday night, my uncles were always sparklingly clean. The facilities weren't there, but the effort was. My Uncle Bob used to have these big white starched collars, like the gentry used to wear in those days. When we used to go and see him on a Sunday morning he used to give us the job of taking them to Wensum Laundry, which was on Waterworks Road, who would clean and starch them. We'd take them back the next Sunday....I can still see my Uncle Bob and my Uncle George a couple of old codgers really.'

*Jubilee tea party, Rose Yard, 1935*

Although conditions were rough, and no-one wanted to see a return to them, when we asked if living in the yards was miserable, the general answer was a definite 'no'. Ruby summed up the situation when she said: 'We felt we had a duty to make the best of it.' People tended not to feel badly off, because everyone was in the same boat. Moreover, there were compensations, one of the most important being a very strong community spirit.

Ruby recalls that in Stonemasons' Square: 'All the kids got on and played together. We used to have a carnival every year when my mother used to dress us girls up. Once, when I was about seven or eight, she dressed me up as a powder box...and I got first prize.'

### Ruby Baker recalls her school days

Ruby was one of 12 children: 'I went to St Saviour's School. I remember being in the infants and sitting on a tiny chair and been shown how to knit. I left school at 14, by then I was ready to finish. That said, I didn't do much schooling because my mother kept having babies and she kept me at home to help her.'

Chris Baker had similar experiences: 'We all got on well, it was a very close community. Everyone was there to help one another. As a boy I used to run errands for people and help with gardens and things like that.'

Meanwhile on Three King Lane, Muriel recollects that her grandmother's neighbour, Nanny Powley, performed a weekly duty for her neighbours: 'Every Monday morning Nanny Powley made it her duty to visit her neighbours with a pram and collect anything that they wanted taking to the pawn shop. Then on a Friday she went back to the pawn shop to reclaim items. I think that she went to Boston's, on Orford Street. It always seemed a very peculiar thing to do to me.'

As Joyce explained: 'When you get this sort of situation when things are really bad and depressing, I do think that people try and stick together, and there was a terrific community spirit. The women didn't stand about a lot, there wasn't time, but especially in the yards where they had to share a copper to do their washing, and there'd be Mrs Jones waiting for Mrs Bernard to get her washing done, they had to get on....It was almost like the wartime spirit. When you're all in it together, you had to make the most of a bad job.'

# Recreation

*Dressing up in St Lawrence School Yard, c.1910*

All our interviewees had happy memories of playing in and around the yards. The contrast to today is enormous. There is no talk of expensive toys, instead girls skipped and boys competed with marbles and cigarette cards. There were no worries about playing on streets, instead there are tales of carefree days on Mousehold, kicking footballs and hitching the odd ride on the back of a horse and cart!

Although he lived in the City centre, Chris Baker and his mates found many opportunities to have fun: 'As a kid I used to play in the street with my friends. We had tops and marbles and in winter we collected chestnuts and played conkers. We played football in the street...that is until we were chased away by a local copper. We also used to play in wooded areas, mostly around the back of Wellesley Road. We never felt cramped in the City. We had plenty of parks. We went fishing at the Lakenham Cock and paddled in the river there and at Earlham Park. We went to Scotties' Meadow, in Trowse, where there was a lovely deep stream and waterfall.'

It was similar for children who lived just outside the City centre. John Curson recalls: 'I was pretty good playing with cigarette cards. I often won them from my mates: then lost them all. My favourites were the cards linked with sport, such as cricket. You'd most probably get 35 to 36 in a set. I remember often being just one short. We made our own enjoyment. We played marbles and football. There was no traffic and so you could play football in the street. The only thing you needed to look out for was neighbours, who came out and warned us if we broke a window our fathers would pay for them!'

Similarly Betty King and her friends found plenty of ways to amuse themselves on Portland Street: 'We all played in the street. We used to have big skipping ropes stretching across it. One girl's father was a bus driver and if he had a big trip the next day he used to park it in Portland Street overnight, and we used to play in it. We also had hoops and tops and all of that sort of thing. We didn't cause any bother, probably because everyone knew each other, and so you'd know they'd tell your mother if you'd been naughty. We used to wander up to Heigham Park as much as anything, we also used to cycle out and about.'

A time of great excitement was when the annual Easter and Christmas Fairs set up on the cattle market, where the Castle Mall now stands. Chris

*Norwich Fair on the old Cattle Market, 1950*

lived just down the road from the fair: 'It was a really special time for us. There were droves of people up and down Rose Lane. There were roundabouts, swings, waltzers, and of course side shows. You could see things like the "Fat Lady" or visit boxing booths. It was a big event.'

John also spoke fondly about going to the fair: 'I remember seeing it being built. There were the big swing boats and a waltzer and of course the side shows. The shows were really interesting, especially the boxing booths. As kids we enjoyed going into the booths and watching someone getting a hiding!'

Saturday was the day you went to the cinema – a very different experience to today. Now we go to multiplex, luxury venues to enjoy a 3D film; in the 1930s there was a very good reason why at least one City cinema was called the fleapit!

Betty has fond memories of her cinema visits: 'It was a perfect time to be a child. We had a happy upbringing. My brothers used to take me to the Haymarket Cinema [The Walk], which showed better films. Occasionally we went to the Theatre de Luxe [St Andrew's Street], where you mainly got cowboy films. Sometimes when children arrived in groups, one would pay and let all of the others in through

another door which was next door to the toilets. At the Theatre de Luxe you could "pay" with a jam jar or rabbit skin, but at the Haymarket it had to be money.'

Meanwhile on Saturday mornings Philip Armes enjoyed seeing films with his friends: 'Magdalen Street had "The Cinema Palace" – that was its actual name, although it was later renamed the Mayfair. On a Saturday morning we'd go there. It was a lovely place. One man who worked there seemed to be the general dogsbody and we used to see him cycling around the City putting up posters. As they had a change of programme twice a week he was constantly sticking up new adverts outside all the shops. He also looked after the cleaning inside, and on a Saturday he used to collect our tuppences. There were no tickets, there was just this horde of boys and girls waiting to go in, and he tried to grab as many of our coins before we pushed our way through. There was the usual yelling and screaming before the film started. We saw cowboy films, a cartoon and a serial which always ended in something dramatic. Then when you went the next week there was a real anti-climax: but we never minded.'

Chris and his wife Ruby also enjoyed watching the serials – though not in very salubrious surroundings:

*The Mayfair (previously the Cinema Palace), Magdalen Street, 1957*

'When we were youngsters the main entertainment was going to the pictures: the fleapits. They weren't pictures like you have today. They used to come around with a sort of antiseptic spray. The kids used to sit there and throw peel and things at each other... well they did at the Empire [Oak Street].'

John's favourite cinema was also the Empire and he chuckled when he recalled being involved in a riot: 'You used to be able get into the cinema for tuppence. A gang of us, about half a dozen, used to go to the Empire on Oak Street, it was best to travel in groups because one of the routes into the city from Northumberland Street was along Heigham Street, and that was a rough area. There was always someone wanting to thump you one, and so we went in groups hoping nothing would happen. On a Saturday afternoon it cost us tuppence and if you had a penny left after you'd paid, once the film ended you could get a pennyworth of chips from the chip stall on the corner, and so Saturday was a high day! You'd see maybe five short films in a two-hour programme. The Empire nearly always showed a cowboy film. We saw a lot of Charlie Chaplin, who was a great favourite with the kiddies. They made a film of King Kong in the 1930s, which was really popular, the rumour began that it was going to be on at the Empire. Well hundreds of us were crowding inside and a bloke came out to tell us it wasn't going to run 'cos we were all under 18. Well, there was a riot. There were seats being thrown about, it was mayhem because the Empire only told us they weren't going to show it after they got our money!'

*The Theatre De Luxe, St Andrew's Street, 1934*

## The yards made good playgrounds

Betty King recalls walking through the yards on her way to the market: 'You'd see children playing together in the yards. There'd be a good dozen and even more if the weather was fine. The parents would sit outside their front doors, to watch things.'

*Betty King with her four brothers, c.1938*

## Ruby and Chris Baker remember the long arm of the law

Chris and Ruby explained: 'There weren't many police about, but all kids were scared of the bobbies. If you saw one coming you'd scoot. Most doors had a couple of steps leading up to the door, and if they saw you sitting there they'd come over and say "off", as you weren't supposed to sit on them. In fact if they had a chance they'd clip you across the ear hole...but streets were safe.'

*Beckwith's Court, Quayside c.1930*

## From the yards to heathland

Donald Read lived in Mancroft Yard (St Peter's Street) until 1936 after which the family moved to a new council house on Gertrude Road (Mousehold): 'When we lived in Mancroft Yard I remember playing hopscotch and skipping, all sorts of things like that. We weren't allowed to play outside the yard, in fact I never realised how close the yard was to the church, I can't believe that it was only a road's width away. I loved living on Gertrude Road. We had the heath to play on. It was great when it snowed – because it was on a hill which was fantastic for sledging.'

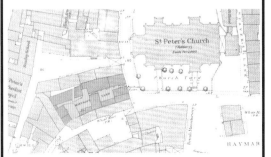

*Location of Mancroft Yard marked on OS Map, 1884*

## It wasn't only the boys who collected cigarette cards

Irene Foster recalls: 'As kids we used to stand outside the Ship Inn and ask people if they had any cigarette cards; the smokers were more interested in the fags and used to throw the cards down when they were all bright and clean. We all used to collect them and put them in little books, like albums, that we had to send away for. They ought to do cards like that now, It would learn the children a lot, you know. They had lots of different sets; there was every kind of flower, and animals and trains. I still have some tucked away.'

# Philip Ames Recalls his Childhood Haunts

*Cowgate looking towards St James' Church, Pockthorpe, 1937*

Philip has terrific memories of his childhood when he played in the yards and streets around Cowgate and Barrack Street or took adventurous trips up to Mousehold:

'We used to play on the street. It was quite safe because there was very little traffic. When a horse and cart came through some of the more adventurous boys would try and get a ride on the back axle. I particularly recall the water cart coming along on a hot summer's day. It was a waggon with sprays out of the back, a bit like an agricultural fertiliser, which was meant to lay the dust and stop it blowing around. It didn't do much good, but as kids we loved to run in and out of the cold spray.

'I remember playing with my friends in Brigg's Yard and Pestell's Yard, which were near us. The girls always wanted to get a concert together. One of them said I could be a cowboy, and so I went back home and told my mum who made me a felt hat. We always made our own entertainment. Another thing we always knocked up was a den. We used to go up to Mousehold a lot. In the summer, an older girl would come with us and we'd take a bottle of drink and sandwiches. We'd find a little flat area to be our base and then the boys would run off and play cowboys and Indians. The other thing we tried to find was a long straight piece of elderberry, we'd clean out the pith, and make it into a pop gun. We used acorns as

missiles. When it snowed we used to go tobogganing on St James' Hill using anything that could double up as a sleigh. In fact it wasn't even necessary to have snow, in summer we still tobogganed down the hill on a piece of cardboard. When I think back we used to go very close to the road but luckily there wasn't really any traffic.

*Philip playing cowboys, c.1934*

66

'It was quite safe to play on the pavement. We'd enjoy doing things like hopscotch and rolling hoops. If you had an old motor-car tyre you could run down the street pushing it along – then you really were somebody!

'Nowadays people hardly mention the comics we had. Our favourites in the 1930s were the Rover, Hotspur and Champion. They had proper stories in them, they weren't just picture stories. Champion was more of a sporty comic, it had football and that sort of stuff in it. On Barrack Street, towards the Silver Road End, there was a shop run by a man called Ketteringham. He used to have a pile of comics on his counter which were always on a "two-for-one" offer. You could either go in and buy them, or you could take in two comics and swap them for one in the shop. If you missed an issue you'd go through this pile hoping to find the one you missed.

'Of course we all had cigarette cards. All us boys had a wad of cards in our pockets, I still have some today. We used to swap them. I kept most of my cards in a shoebox. I had a big collection. You see my father and my uncles, who lived with us, all smoked and so I had four contributors. I used to learn quite a lot from them, because as I collected them I used to read what was on the back.

'I particularly enjoyed collecting cigarette cards about aviation. My lifetime interest in aircraft began when I was about six years old. I can still clearly remember playing on our front doorstep on Cowgate when I saw the R101, an airship made by Boulton & Paul, fly overhead. It was on its way to Sandringham, where the king was in residence. It hovered over us for some time and I can still recall it being a large silver object and the droning, humming sound that it made. Everyone came out and looked. It was referred to as a Pulham Pig.

'There was an airfield on Mousehold. On Empire Air Days the RAF would bring in stuff like Blenheims. I can even recall the prototype Spitfire coming over on one occasion. Norwich Flying Club were based there. At weekends, from when I was 11, I used to go and watch the flying and gliding. It was fascinating. They'd tow a glider across the field with an open car and when it was in the air they'd let it go. What started as a hobby eventually led to me joining the ATC [Air Training Corps] at the beginning of the war.'

# Education and Work

Education in the 1930s was very different from today. In particular: the minimum school leaving age was 14 (it was raised to 15 in 1947); at the age of 11 pupils took the 11-plus scholarship paper which determined whether or not they would go to grammar school; lessons were different, in particular the girls concentrated on 'home-making' skills. Additionally, because of home circumstances, many youngsters were not able to take advantage of the education on offer.

Daphne Way has happy memories of her school days: 'Until I was 11 I went to St Giles' School. After that I went to the Model School on Dereham Road, where we learnt cookery and how to wash, sew and many other home crafts. It was lovely.' Dorothy Dugdale learnt similar skills at the Dowson School on Valpy Avenue (Mile Cross): 'At the start of senior school we had needlework and had to make an apron and hat ready for cookery lessons. In another class we made a recipe book – we even had to bind the folder. In our housewifery lesson we had to learn to clean brushes, combs, silver and brass, and how to wash towels.'

Irene Foster enjoyed her time at Horn's Lane School, where she got on well with teachers, here she learnt 'reading and sums', and recalls that unlike the high-tech lessons of today, pupils had slates. However, when she moved on to Lakenham Council School, on the City Road, she found the classes and teachers very hierarchical: 'When I went to Lakenham School all the kids whose fathers had businesses sat on the front row in the classroom and when we went down to the games field they were the ones who got the tennis rackets and all that sort of thing, leaving us from poorer families with nothing. I often think that all we got of education was what was left over. I never got to play hockey or tennis, I just used to do running. One day at the end of games, a tennis racket had been left on one of the courts and I was asked to pick it up. I didn't see why I should, and so pretended that I hadn't heard. Well, that got me into a lot of trouble, I was called to the headmistress's study and I was told that I was in her black book and would never get a job. I left school at 13, because my birthday was in the summer holidays, and started work a fortnight before I was 14, at a shoe shop on Prince of Wales Road...so much for being told I'd never work.'

For those who passed the 11 plus, the opportunities were brighter, as recounted by Muriel Chilvers who was born in Three King Lane. Her family moved to a brand-new council house, 3 Ripley Close, on the Earlham Estate when she was three years old and she lived there until she married: 'I went to Colman Road infant and junior schools, and after passing the scholarship exam went on to the Blyth Girls' Grammar School in 1937, where five years later I

passed the school certificate. When the war started some of the girls left when their fathers were called up. Although you could legally leave school at 14, if you left the grammar school then your parents had to pay a fine. I didn't stay on for the sixth form, I think that by then my parents thought it was time I earned some money and I was ready to leave. I got a clerical job at the Norfolk Health Insurance Committee on Prince of Wales Road. I worked there until I married in 1950. Because my husband worked for the Norwich Building Society he was able to get a staff mortgage and we bought a house on Hotblack Road. We lived there for nine years before moving to Bluebell Road where I've lived ever since.'

However, it was no good passing the 11 plus if your parents couldn't afford to let you stay at school. Joyce Wilson and her sisters all had the ability to progress their education, but were not given the opportunity: 'We went to school at Bull Close, which is now St Augustine's. It was a good school. I remember the day I started, I was four. Mother wanted me to go because she had another baby on the way. Then when we were 11 we took the scholarship and the lucky ones were allowed to go to grammar school. The shame is that myself and my four sisters were all awarded scholarships. We brought the letters home saying that we were entitled to go, but my father just refused to

Irene Foster recalls: 'One year I was asked to present a bouquet to the Lady Mayoress on Empire Day [24th May]. My mother used to make all our dresses; me and my two sisters always looked very smart, we were always dressed alike. She used to make some with frills and others she used to knit. I was told to wear my lilac voile dress which had frills all around the bottom for Empire Day. To this day I remember that I was told to present the flowers and say: "Please will you accept these from the teachers."'

*Empire Day Celebrations, 1935*

have anything to do with it. He said that he left school at 12 and he didn't see why he should keep us; what was good enough for him should be good enough for us, and so we continued at Bull Close....I didn't want to leave and work in a factory because I loved school, especially when I became head girl which made me feel important. We all started in the shoe factories.'

In 1931 around 10,700 people, 17.5% of the City's workforce, were employed in the Norwich shoe industry. It is therefore not surprising that many of the people we talked to had links with the trade. Ruby Baker's father worked in the factories, whilst her mother, despite having 12 children, also managed to do some home working. Ruby recollects that her mum 'was always hammering away and solutioning [gluing shoes] and things like that'. At the age of 14 Ruby also started work in the shoe factories as did Dorothy Dugdale, whose mother also worked in the industry.

Our interviewees' fathers undertook a variety of jobs. Joyce's was a butcher, Irene's was a brewery worker at Youngs, Crawshay & Youngs, whilst Muriel's became a milk roundsman: all jobs that would be recognised today. Other jobs were a little more unusual. Until

she was eight years old Dorothy Dugdale's father was a well sinker: 'He worked away from home quite a lot with my grandfather. The business was called W. & G. Fake and based on Angel Road. When he had difficulty finding jobs, he started to look for work on the roads and eventually got building work on the council.' Daphne's father worked for the corporation in the sewer department: 'Part of father's job was to go down the sewers and crawl along the pipes with rats, and so it wasn't clean work'.

Households did not have the labour-saving devices we enjoy today, in fact they were lucky to have an indoor water supply. This meant that housework would have been backbreaking. Yet women often supplemented the family income by bringing home extra work. Philip Armes' mother worked hard in their house at 117 Cowgate bringing him up and also looking after her three-step brothers. Philip recalls that after the area was cleared and the family moved to Bull Close Road: 'She took in washing; when the weather was bad she used to hang it out across the living room to dry.' Similarly Joyce's mother took in sewing, whilst outwork from the shoe factories provided welcome extra money in many Norwich homes.

Muriel Chilvers admired the industry of the ladies who lived in Hipper's Yard: 'My grandmother, [Harriet Lansdell] lived at number 2 Three King Lane. Her house was located on one side of Hipper's Yard. She lived in four rooms. There was no water inside the house, to get water she used a communal tap and also shared a communal toilet in Hipper's Yard. The one thing I think was marvellous was despite such limited basic facilities, nearly everyone who lived in the main yard took in washing. Just think what you had to do just to earn a few pennies!'

*Pestell's Yard, Cowgate, 1938*

When she was five Dorothy Dugdale moved to a new council house on Peterson Road [off Bignold Road]: 'I never really went into the City as a teenager. Our main entertainment was going to dances at the Norman School on Bignold Road. They started when I was about 12, and were run by two teachers, a Mr Booth and a Mr Laithwaite who taught us how to ballroom dance. They were for the girls from the Dowson School [Valpy Avenue] and boys from the Norman School, and so just for the local, secondary modern school kids. There was live music! The group I remember was Charlie Hague with Ginger Edwards on the drums and Billy Duncan on the piano.'

*Samson and Hercules Ballroom, c.1940*

# Disease and Diet

*Jenny Lind Children's Hospital, 1927*

*Basic facilities, unknown date*

Childhood diseases were very different to today, when so many of us benefit from higher standards of living and of course treatment through the National Health Service.

Ruby Baker recollects: 'I think the worst illnesses were diphtheria and scarlet fever, which was why they had the fever hospital – it's the Julian Hospital now. There were two wards there. I was in there with diphtheria, and so was my sister. The hospital was very nice, but you weren't allowed any visitors. If my mother brought us anything to eat she had to throw it through the window. They were very strict because of the fever. They used to swab us every day. I was in there around three weeks. We recovered, but a lot died. Norwich had a clinic, where Churchman House is now, and all the mothers would take their kids there. In the clinic they had doctors and opticians, and so we were well looked after really. It didn't cost you anything. But it was half-a-crown if you called a doctor in at night, which was a lot when your father was only earning 30 bob a week and he had 12 kids to bring up.'

Chris Baker's father made surgical boots: 'There was also a lot of rickets about, kids with wobbly legs, also you'd see lame children wearing leg irons and built up boots, which was caused by polio.'

But what did people eat? John Curson sums up the situation in many households: 'We'd scratch around during the week and have whatever we could afford. But Sunday was always a roast.' This was despite the fact that many homes did not even have an oven. Chris explains how this was achieved: 'Many used to take their dinners to a baker's shop. You used to see the ladies walking down the road with a couple of dishes that they used to leave there to be cooked; they'd then go and pick them up later on.'

Although much of the food consumed in Ruby's household still sounds tasty, some of the cuts of meat may not go down so well today: 'We all came home for dinner when we had good old home cooking, things like meat dumplings and suet puddings, spotted dick and plenty of vegetables. We were fed well. Mother would make little individual puddings which were boiled in the same copper where she did her washing. Tea was perhaps plenty of bread and jam or banana sandwiches and a lump of cake. We were able to get extra meat because my grandfather worked in a slaughterhouse in Sprowston. He used to bring my father a sheep's head, which he loved. My father used to boil it and scrape off all the meat. He also brought father things like brains and chitterlings, which he cleaned, cooked and ate with bread and butter: he really enjoyed them.'

# Pubs

*Bess of Bedlam, Oak Street, 1907*

*The Golden Can, Alms Lane, 1937*

Since the Middle Ages Norwich has been well served with drinking establishments. It is often said that Norwich had a church for every week of the year and a pub for every day. This was not an exaggeration, as incredibly in the 1880s there were over 450 pubs within the City walls. Many would have been tiny ale houses occupying little more than the downstairs room of a house where a family would live at the expense of the brewery. Customers, many of whom lived in squalid conditions, resided within a few minutes' walk. After a hard day's work they returned to small overcrowded hovels. A visit to their local pub, to consume cheap gin and beer with friends, was their escape. After the passing of the 1904 Compensation Act, licensing judges had powers to close premises which were adjudged to be superfluous to requirements, and the number of city-centre pubs started to fall, the process being further hastened by the interwar slum-clearance schemes. One of the many examples of a yard and adjoining pub being demolished was the Wrestlers' Arms (58 Barrack Street) and Wrestlers' Yard, which formed part of the 'Cowgate and Barrack Street clearance area'.

Pubs were a place to escape, as described by Ruby Baker: 'Poverty was rife and there were no benefits, and so for some going to the pub was a way of letting their hair down. You'd be lying in bed and you'd hear a racket outside and someone singing, all on their own, and so they'd had a happy time. We always listened for one man in particular to come home, who had a club foot. He'd be singing psalms, and so his heart was in the right place.'

Ruby also recalls: 'After a full day at work my father spent all evening making and mending shoes, just to make the money go around. But at 10 o'clock he always went for his last pint in the Golden Can [Alms Lane]: sixpence it was. My mother was a Salvationist and she used to go to all of the meetings, but she was always home in time for my father to slip out. '

Pubs were very different to today, as described by Chris Baker: 'Most of the pubs on Rose Lane were little corner places, they were like the front room of a house. The only food would be crisps and nuts. They were a meeting place for locals, a bit like community centres today. You knew that your friends would be there on a Saturday night and that's where we'd all meet up. In most pubs you'd have bar games such as cribbage, shove ha'penny and darts. We mostly went out at weekends; I couldn't afford more than that. If I went out midweek, I'd have one drink and that would be that. Most pubs had a bar and a smoke room. Many had a snug. If you saw a chap skulking in there you thought they had gone there to get away from their wife. You could always get sweets in the snugs, they were like little shops. I used to like a weekend drink. I used to go to the Golden Can with Ruby's father. The landlord, like many of the others, used to organise fishing outings for the men. They often arranged a coach, but sometimes we cycled to places like Ludham and Wroxham.'

It wasn't only the men who went to the pubs, the ladies in Muriel Chilvers' family had links with the drinking establishments on St Benedict's Street: 'The number of pubs along St Benedict's always fascinated me; there was a pub every three or four shops. My mother worked in the Fountain which was at number 89 and my Aunt Mabel cleaned at the next-but-one pub up, the Stag. My father didn't earn a lot of money but on a Saturday night he'd have his *Pink 'Un* delivered, and so he was happy and quite prepared to stay home and look after me whilst my mother went to visit grandma in Three King Lane. He'd give mum a shilling which was enough to pay for her bus fare and two glasses of stout at the Three Kings [46 St Benedict's Street].'

John Curson's aunt, Mariah Land, was landlady of the Alma (later Micawber) Tavern on Pottergate from 1926 to 1952 and he remembers visiting the pub around 1930: 'When I was a little lad I recall sitting outside on the step with my bottle of pop and, if I was really lucky, a packet of crisps. It was very small then, I think they've extended it now by knocking out part of the living quarters. There was a bar and a snug that held two or three people, which was used by ladies who enjoyed a drink but didn't want people to notice.'

*The Fountain, St Benedict's Street, 1936*

*The Stag, St Benedict's Street, 1938*

# Moving to the Council Estates

*Woodcock Road from Aylsham Road, the Woodcock pub (centre left) prior to opening, 1934*

Unlike today, when the majority expect to own their own properties, in the 1920s and 1930s the norm was to rent. As the yards were cleared, tenants were given the opportunity to move to new council houses, often built on new estates in the suburbs. Frequently groups of neighbours were moved together, and so the community spirit prevalent in so many of the yards was not lost.

Dorothy Dugdale clearly remembers moving to one of the new houses on the Mile Cross Estate when she was five years old: 'It was a new house on Peterson Road [off Bignold Road], they were all new houses on the estate and none of our gardens had been made up. I moved in with my mum and dad and my younger sister. You walked in to a porch and the toilet was on the left and then you went through a door into the kitchen. The bathroom was off the side of the kitchen. We also had three bedrooms and a living room. We thought it was lovely because everything was brand new. We didn't have hot water but had a copper [large metal container] in the corner of the bathroom, with

a gas-fired flame underneath where we heated water. You'd ladle the water out with a hand cup, which was a galvanised bowl with a wooden handle on, and put the hot water into the bath.'

Until she was three years old Muriel Chilvers led a nomadic existence, until her family had a stroke of luck: 'I was born in Three King Lane, off St Benedict's, my grandmother lived opposite. When it became clear that my parents couldn't afford the rent, I've no idea what sort of money we are talking about, we all had to move. Over the next two years they just rented rooms in houses, the first was in Lady Lane and the second was in Rose Lane. Eventually, on my third birthday we were given a brand-new council house, 3 Ripley Close, on the Earlham Estate. It was one of the last houses built on the estate and located off Elizabeth Fry Road, which had been built at least two or three years previously. They really were good-quality houses. I was an only child, and so I don't know how my father managed to get the house, especially as he was unemployed at the time,

*Colman Road at the junction with George Borrow Road, Earlham Estate, 1933*

73

*Barrett Road with entrance to Martineau Lane on the left, New Lakenham Estate, 1933*

although he later became a milk roundsman for the Co-op. We had a decent-sized kitchen that had a gas oven. There was a little wicket [opening] in one of the walls that you could look through into the main room. We even had three bedrooms. The house was very modern at the time. We had a bathroom with a cold tap. We'd heat water in the copper, using a gas-fired flame, and then scoop the water out of the copper into the bath with a saucepan. It seems archaic today, but at the time I felt I was living in luxury compared to my grandmother's and aunt's houses [on Three King Lane, overlooking Hipper's Yard, and Neale's Yard respectively]. We even had a huge garden, which stretched to an eighth of an acre. My father was an ardent gardener, in fact he was very rude to one of the neighbours who didn't grow vegetables when they'd been provided with a plot which enabled them to do so. We never went short of vegetables or fruit. I recall that he even had six different types of apple tree. He also kept chickens and rabbits. Eventually in the late 1930s, when both my grandmother's and aunt's houses were demolished as part of the slum-clearance

### Fumigation

*On 5th December 1934 the Housing Committee reported to Norwich City Council:*

'In connection with the removal of tenants from clearance areas under the Housing Act 1930 to new Council houses the Housing Committee have found it desirable in the interests, both of the Council and of the tenants themselves, to arrange for the disinfection of the household goods and effects prior to the tenants moving into new houses. This is no reflection on the tenants, but arises from the condition of the houses being dealt with under the Council's programme…. The committee desire to add that while at first there was a disinclination on the part of the tenants to have their furniture and household effects disinfected, now that it is understood that every household moved from the clearance areas into Council houses will be dealt with in the same manner the Committee do not anticipate any objection on the part of the tenants.'

scheme, they both moved to the Catton Grove Estate. My aunt was thrilled to bits. I used to wonder what my cousins felt like when they moved from a two-roomed house to a four-bedroomed house on Palmer Road. I'd always been anxious for my cousins, who in my eyes lived in absolute poverty whilst I was lucky enough to live in a posh council house, though they never seemed to mind. I was really thrilled when they were able to move from Neale's Square.'

Although the vast majority were pleased to move to their new council house, this was not the case for Ruby's parents: 'When I was 15 we were moved to a council house on Stevenson Road on the Larkman Estate. My mother and father were pleased to move somewhere where there was a bathroom: it was lovely having a bath. We had five bedrooms. It was a lovely house, but we just didn't have the furniture to go in it. We lived in Stonemasons' Square for around 13 years, but my father never really settled at Stevenson Road and after that we moved house fairly frequently.'

However, the majority of families couldn't believe their luck when they moved from an old yard to a council house. Donald Read has very fond recollections of being moved with his family from Mancroft Yard: 'Two of our neighbours moved with us to Gertrude Road, one family lived next door to us and the other one, two houses up. I think that my mother thought that she was in paradise when we got there, 'cause there were four bedrooms, running water and a bathroom, she had everything that she wanted, which she'd never had before.' Finally Dorothy Holmes often told the story of her family's move from Finch's Yard on Cowgate to a brand new council house on Woodcock Road: 'We never dreamt of using Pickfords, and instead took everything on handcarts…but not quite everything. All our linen and soft furnishings, in fact anything that could contain fleas, was taken away to be fumigated, and so the first night in our new house we all slept on floorboards, but none of us minded. We couldn't believe it. We had an inside bathroom and toilet, we could have hot water and even had a garden. I really think that mother thought she'd gone to heaven!'

# Compendium of the Old Courts and Yards

## Compendium: Introduction

In this section we look in detail at the courts and yards located in 11 areas of the City using the 1884/85 OS map (referred to in the text as 1884).

Please note:

- The compendiums cover sections of Norwich which contained significant numbers of old courts and yards. They do not list every court and yard in each area nor do they cover all of the City.

- The names of the courts and yards constantly change. Where a name is given on the 1884 map, this is the one that has been used in the listing, unless we believe that an error has been made.

- Where a yard has not been named on the 1884 map we have taken the information from Kelly's 1908 Directory. Where a yard was not named on the 1884 map, nor in the 1908 directory, but it was named on the 1930s clearance maps, this name is used in the listing. Please note that some yards had different names in all three sources.

- Unless otherwise indicated, the address given for a yard is the **approximate** location of the entry as deduced from Kelly's 1908 Directory.

- Leading on from the above, the list of yards which is included for each section, gives the street number of the approximate location of the entry and the side of the street on which the yard lies i.e. N = north side of the street, S = south, E = east, W = west.

- The area highlighted yellow on the map is the area referred to in the text, apart from Heigham where the text refers to the entire map.

- Information on yard clearances and demolition has been extracted from clearance registers and maps held at the Norfolk Record Office.

- Major clearances from the 1930s are highlighted on the map. These give an indication of what happened, but they are not exact. The approximate area affected is coloured red. Please note that not all properties highlighted were eventually demolished, and not all clearance schemes are listed.

- The photo galleries give the name of the yard when the photograph was taken. Where this has changed the name of the yard given in the listing is shown in brackets

*Old Norwich yard, unnamed, c.1900*

# The Compendiums

We have divided Norwich into 11 sections which have been highlighted on the map below. Each compendium contains a selection of information, including a historical background, specific information on the main yards, the 1930s' clearances and what survives today. This is all supported with photos, reminiscences and contemporaneous reports.

We have excluded the City's main commercial centre and land around the Cathedral, which contain relatively few yards, and instead concentrated on areas where they predominated. Which, as can clearly be seen, was everywhere else!

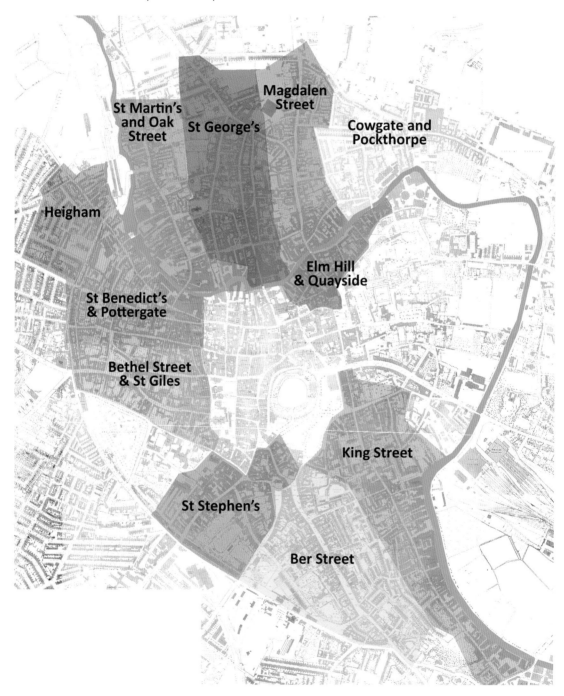

St Martin's and Oak Street

St George's

Magdalen Street

Cowgate and Pockthorpe

Heigham

Elm Hill & Quayside

St Benedict's & Pottergate

Bethel Street & St Giles

King Street

St Stephen's

Ber Street

# A Lost Tudor Heritage: Oak Street

Yards identified in this section of the City include:

## Coslany Street
- Red Lion Yard (26, E)
- Abb's Court (3, W)
- Chequers' Yard (13, W)
- Waggon and Horses Yard (19, W)

## Oak Street (St Martin's Street)
- Eight Ringers' Yard (12, E)
- Dawson's Yard (20, E)
- Sun Yard (24, E)
- Greenland Fishery Yard (30, E)
- Rudd's Yard (32, E)
- Gay's Yard (48, E)
- Dolphin Yard (54, E)
- Bream's Yard (60, E)
- Arabian Horse Yard (68, E)
- Little Arabian Horse Yard (72, E)
- Osborn(e)'s Yard (84, E)
- Fellmongers' Yard (90, E)
- Baldwin's Yard (94, E)
- Goat Yard (98, E)
- Dog Yard (104, E)
- Talbot's Yard (106, E)
- Little Brew Yard (120, E)

- Old Brew Yard (122, E)
- Royal Oak Yard (130, E)
- Angel Yard (148, E)
- Osborne's Yard (168, E)
- Swan Yard (178, E)
- Dial Yard (3, W)
- Tuns Yard (7, W)
- Saw Mill Yard (13, W)
- Distillery Yard (25, W)
- Betts' Yard (31, W)
- Buck's Yard (35, W)
- Unicorn Yard (39, W)
- New Mills' Yard (43, W)
- Barker's Yard (57, W)
- Queen Caroline's Yard (59, W)
- Little Queen Caroline's Yard (61, W)
- Bloom's Yard (71, W)
- Howman's Yard (75, W)
- Hawkes' Yard (79, W)
- Little Crown Yard (83, W)
- Bath House Yard (97, W)
- Ragged School Yard (103, W)
- Key and Castle Yard (105, W)

- Robinson's Yard (111, W)
- Horton's Yard (113, W)
- Saddler's Yard (115, W)
- Smith's Yard (119, W)
- Suffolk Arms' Yard (119, W)
- Flowerpot Yard (127, W)
- Hall's Yard (133, W)
- Buck Yard (139, W)
- Little Buck Yard (141, W)

## Rosemary Lane
- Cartwright's Yard (1, W)
- Haver's Yard (19, W)

## St Martin's Lane
- Butcher's Yard (3, N)
- Fox and Goose Yard (46, S)

## St Mary's Alley
- Bell Yard (3, N)
- Benton's Yard (5, N)

## St Mary's Plain
- Newbegin's Yard (20, N)
- Hen and Chicken's Yard (26, N)
- Marine Store Yard (31, S)

*Old Brew Yard, Oak Street, 1937*

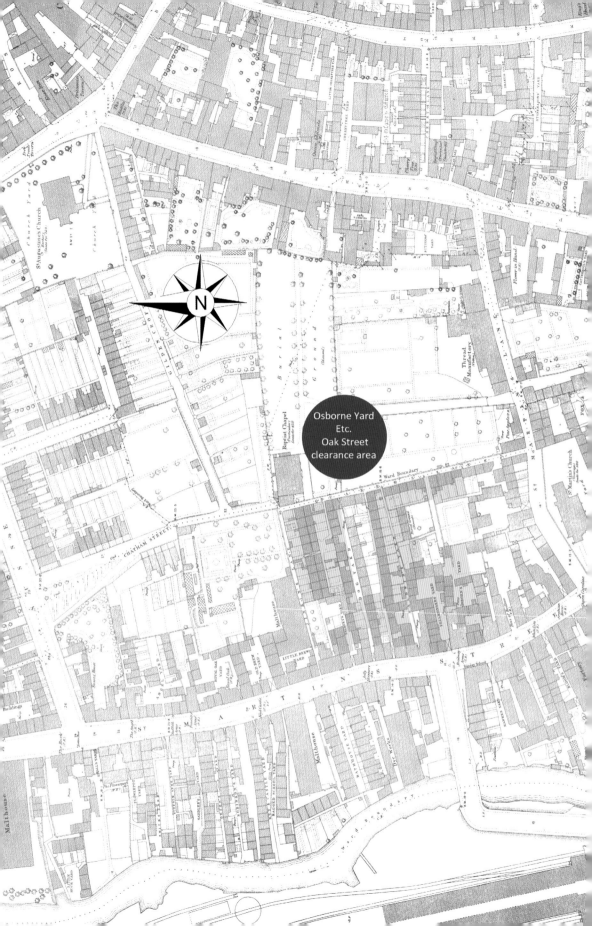

Osborne Yard
Etc.
Oak Street
clearance area

Sun Yard
St Mary's Plain
clearance area

12 – 14 Oak
Street Etc.
clearance area

60 – 78
Colegate
clearance area

Distillery, Saw
Mill and Dial Yard
Oak Street
clearance area

# Historical Background

For many years Oak Street was known as St Martin at Oak after the medieval church which lies on the corner with St Martin's Lane. The name was derived from a large oak tree that grew in the churchyard which was believed to bear the image of Our Lady, and as such was a big 'visitor attraction' in pre-Reformation days.

Excavations indicate that land in the vicinity of Oak Street was occupied from the 11th century. As in other parts of the City, one of the reasons for the early development of the thoroughfare was its proximity to the River Wensum. The river was an ideal conduit for transporting cargo, making Oak Street particularly popular with merchants and traders. In 1884, it was still the home of a range of commercial/industrial enterprises, including dye works, many malthouses, and a crape (a thin fabric with a crinkled surface) manufactory. New Mills' Yard ran from Oak Street to a mill, known as 'New Mills', which still stands at the highest point on the river. There has been a mill here since before the Conquest. It was originally used for both grinding corn and fulling cloth (the process of removing oil and grease from the woven cloth and pulling the fibres together ready for dyeing). Later it pumped river water to the Market Cross for drinking, and by the 19th century it was used as a sewage pumping station. The mill is one of only two pneumatic pumping stations in the country. Although it is now redundant the sluices remain in use as a means of controlling the river level.

Looking at Oak Street today it is hard to imagine that in the early 20th century it was lined with many Tudor houses. Of course in Norwich, ancient houses were where courts and yards filled with little brick cottages developed, and a brief look at the 1884 map clearly shows that this was the case here. In fact, when the map was drawn, in this one area there were more than 60 of them, which made for insalubrious conditions, as described in William Lee's 1851 report: 'St Martin at Oak Street contains many long, narrow courts. Filled with houses that drain along the surface into the adjacent river at the same places as the people take the water from. In Castle Court [exact location unknown] there is a pump supplied by filtration from

the river. The cesspool of about 16 houses is within five yards of it.'

Take for instance the properties behind 103 to 119 Oak Street. In this small stretch could be found seven yards: Smith's, Key and Castle, Suffolk Arm's, Saddler's, Horton's, Robinson's and Ragged School, all of which led down to the River Wensum. They were long, cramped spaces with narrow entrances, with all that implies for lack of air and unsavoury smells. Conditions were worsened by their proximity to the badly polluted river, which was a repository for sewage and waste, and the lack of clean water. William Cooper, a medical officer for St Martin's Parish, reported in 1851: 'The poor people use river water for [cooking] food....There are very few pumps in my district; they are in most instances difficult to work, and under certain circumstances, the labour of pumping water is injurious to people.' Luckily he was able to add: 'I should think, however, that hernia is not more common than in other places.' The other problem of being near to the river was the potential risk of flooding, which did happen in August 1912. Amongst the worst affected areas was an expanse of some 6,900 square yards lying between St Martin's Lane, Oak Street and St Mary's Plain. The area included Rayner's Yard (Bream's Yard in 1884), Fox & Goose Yard, Newbegin's Yard, Hen and Chicken's Yard, Gay's Yard, Benton's Yard and Dolphin Yard. The area consisted of: 'Main thoroughfares which are narrow and tortuous, winding courts which are surrounded in many cases by old and tumble-down property, largely of the slum variety' (Town Clerk's Brief, 24/3/1914). After much delay, all properties were demolished and the site become the home of the Sexton, Son & Everard boot and shoe factory (see Clearance Case Study Two on page 28 for full details).

A similar situation existed behind a row of Tudor houses that ran from 98 to 114 Oak Street. They lay just south of Jenkins Lane, which being barely a yard wide at its entrance, was popularly known locally as 'Chafe Lug Alley'! Behind the row lay four yards, namely Talbot's (erroneously called Talbert's on the map), Dog, Goat and Baldwin's. In February 1935 the row (with the exception of 114, the Anchor of Hope public house) was subject to an inquiry into the 'Osborne's Yard Etc. Oak Street clearance area'. It was subsequently agreed that the Tudor houses would be excluded from the scheme. The Norwich Preservation Trust were allowed to acquire the buildings subject to both renovating them and acquiring land at the rear to ensure residents in the renovated property had sufficient air space. Unfortunately numbers 110 – 114 were lost as a result of war damage, but numbers 98 – 108 have survived. These Grade II listed houses all

---

Before 1890, part of Oak Street (1 – 41 on the west side and 2 – 32 on the east) was part of Coslany Street. All references to the location of yards reflect the numbering system after 1890.

To confuse matters further, Oak Street used to be called St Martin at Oak Street whilst on the 1884 map it is called St Martin's Street. Other documents from the same period call the thoroughfare Oak Street – as we have done.

pre-date 1700. Numbers 100 – 106 (16th century) are timber-framed, plastered houses with jetties, whilst 108 (17th century) is a two-bayed house. The four yards behind contained 46 cottages mainly dating from the 19th century. In 1936 they were cleared of their 116 residents and subsequently demolished.

However, many other Tudor houses on Oak Street were lost in the early 20th century, including numbers 1 – 9 behind which lay Dial and Tuns Yards, and number 80 which for many years housed a pub named the Bess of Bedlam. Sadly, Coslany Street fared no better. Amongst the ancient buildings demolished here was number 23, parts of which dated from the 16th century and which for many years housed the Waggon and Horses public house, behind which lay a yard of the same name.

Today this area still consists of a mix of residential and commercial properties. Amongst recent developments are a series of newly built yards, blessed with both ancient and modern names, designed to standards not even dreamt of by the yard dwellers of yesteryear.

Although since 1930 many historic buildings have been demolished, a few tantalising clues to its past remain. Probably the most intriguing is a little medieval property located at 127 Oak Street. It would be very

*The Great Hall, Flowerpot Yard, Oak Street, 1955*

easy to miss, as it is now integrated into a commercial site, but the Great Hall is a flint and red-brick building dating from 1480. This 15th-century building was an integral part of Flowerpot Yard. All other buildings constituting the yard have since been demolished, but the Great Hall remains as 'a surviving northern outpost of medieval Norwich' (Norwich Preservation Trust).

*1 – 9 Oak Street, 1936*

Sun Yard Clearance

*Plan of the 'Sun Yard clearance scheme', 1931*

*Pilgrims' Hall, later the Rosemary Tavern, 2014*

Some of Norwich's earliest clearance schemes took place in this section of the City, which says something about the state the houses were in.

We completed a case study of the 'Rayner's Yard improvement area' (page 28). The next major project in this district was the 'Sun Yard clearance scheme'. The programme included the clearance of five yards, containing around 20 houses and 59 occupants. Subsequently the Council built flats on the site. The scheme excluded properties on Rosemary Lane, which though central to the site were of historic interest and still stand today. Of particular note is a 15th-century house once the home of Thomas Pyckerell, who held the office of mayor in 1525, 1533 and 1538. The pretty thatched property was known at one time as Pilgrims' Hall and also housed the Rosemary Tavern. In its early life the yard behind was called Pykerell's Yard, but by the time of clearance it was known as Cartwright's Yard (it is unnamed on the 1884 map) after the 19th-century licensees of the Rosemary Tavern. The house is now in the care of the Norfolk Archaeological Trust.

Other schemes followed, including the 'Osborne Yard Etc. clearance area' when concern for protecting ancient buildings was again in evidence. Thus, as already noted, a row of Tudor houses running from 98 to 114 Oak Street which fronted Talbot's Yard, Dog Yard, Goat Yard and Baldwin's Yard were excluded from the programme, but the main properties in the yards were demolished. Altogether, in 1936, as part of the scheme, six yards containing 71 properties were flattened and 197 people rehoused. It is worth noting that there was a burial ground in the centre of the clearance area – one wonders whether this had a

*Plaque reads: 'In this 15th-century house, Pilgrims' Hall & latterly "Old Rosemary Tavern" lived Thomas Pyckerell, thrice mayor of Norwich, 1525, 1533 & 1538'*

detrimental effect on the quality of pumped water! Once cleared the land was acquired by the Council and it was redeveloped to provide 24 flats and two three-bedroomed houses on the newly named Talbot Square.

Unfortunately, partly due to its close proximity to the City Railway Station, Oak Street was badly hit during the war. Yards that were damaged during the hostilities included: Angel Yard (which was completely gutted by fire), Bath House Yard, Royal Oak Yard and Swan Yard.

### The Baedeker Raids

During April 1942 approximately 140 Norwich pubs were either destroyed or damaged during the Baedeker air raids. Along Oak Street, the Anchor of Hope (114) and the Buck (139) were razed to the ground, but both the Key & Castle (150) and White Lion (73), though damaged, survived.

# Yards of Note

Oak Street not only had many ancient buildings but also many pubs, and hence many archetypal Norwich yards. The pubs gave the yards some wonderful names, such as Flowerpot and Arabian Horse. Sadly the conditions in the yards were not so wonderful, as discovered by a reporter from the *Norwich Mercury* who visited the area in 1897, and whose observations are included below. The following yards are of particular interest:

## Bath House Yard (97 Oak Street)

*Bath House Yard, Oak Street, 1957*

The yard took its name from the Bath House pub which traded at 97 Oak Street for around 30 years until its licence was rescinded in 1869. As can be seen on the 1884 map the yard had a relatively wide entrance leading to two rows of houses which faced each other. In 1897 the *Norwich Mercury reporter* explained: '[The row] on the left are called Oak Cottages. These are not very old and seem in good condition, having small gardens – very small – in front of each house. At the street end of this row is a disused pump with open drain and tap adjoining. In the rear there is one drain for every pair and one tap for each three....The ten houses on the right have one communal tap, with drains close to the doors, the open brickwork channel leading thereto running almost beneath the windows.' Very clearly the yard did not suffer from lack of air, but like most other houses in Norwich it suffered from poor sanitation. Although it was damaged during air raids in April 1942, the yard survived. As can be seen from the photograph above, by 1957 it was looking somewhat dilapidated and within ten years had been demolished.

## Betts' Yard (31 Oak Street)

Rather than take its name from the pub that stood at its entrance, Betts' Yard was named after its first landlord John Betts. The licence of the pub, variously known as the Bakers' Arms and the Staff of Life, was lost by 1890 and by 1897 the yard had been renamed Reeves' Yard, presumably after a resident.

The description of the yard in the *Norwich Mercury* highlights the lack of responsibility that the landlords had for their tenants. The journalist highlights the fact that an open channel which ran in front of the houses contained a mix of sewage, slops and rainwater, all contributing to the smell which

'was neither imaginable nor describable'. The five landlords provided just one pump which dated from 1808 and supplied water 'said to stick around the cups and glasses like glue, and sometimes more resembles soapsuds that water'. Obviously, you had to be really desperate to live there, and so unsurprisingly at the time of the visit nearly all of the houses were uninhabited and even those that were had front doors that were almost off their hinges, whilst some of the garret windows had no glass, causing tenants to comment that 'you may just as well lay down outside'. The yard was very dark, in fact it was sometimes 'as black as your hat'. By 1931 the yard was no longer listed in directories, and so had probably already been demolished.

## Dial Yard (3 Oak Street)

*Dial Yard, Oak Street, c.1930*

Until the 20th century a row of Tudor houses stretched from 1 – 9 Oak Street. The houses were of two storeys, timber-framed and faced with plaster, with upper floors that projected slightly over the street.

Dial Yard contained the remains of a mansion owned by the Clerk family. Gregory Clerk was sheriff in 1477. He was succeeded by his son, also called Gregory, a mercer who in 1497 also attained the rank of sheriff and was subsequently appointed as mayor in both 1505 and 1514. In its heyday the principal chamber of the Clerk's home was completely lined with richly carved panels of varied designs, including merchants' marks, monograms and the mercers' arms. Despite its grand ancestry by 1934 Dial Yard was declared a slum and demolished the following year.

## Dolphin Yard (54 Oak Street)

Named after the public house which stood at its entrance, at the time of the *Norwich Mercury* reporter's visit in 1897 this paved yard had a narrow entrance. Six houses were serviced by two taps, one privy and one midden whilst 'the brickwork channel was being flushed by a half-clad woman'.

## Flower Pot Yard (127 Oak Street)

In the early 1930s Flowerpot Yard was described as being 'the worst slum in Norwich'.

Interestingly, the Flower Pot public house, which gave the yard its name, was located at the rear of the yard, rather than on the main road. The pub was originally known as the Pot of Flowers and early in the 19th century it hosted flower shows at which tulips were the chief attraction. At the 1906 Licensing Sessions it was heard that the house was 'down a yard with the front door some way distant from the street', furthermore it was 'difficult for supervision by the tenant and the police'. The position was not helped by the fact that the tenant had a second job as a boat builder. As there were another 11 licensed houses within 200 yards, the premises was closed 'under compensation'. Subsequently the building was let to private tenants.

As can be seen on the 1884 map, the yard was in two divisions and contained a selection of buildings, including what is now known as the Great Hall. Built in 1480, the Great Hall was purchased and saved by Major (later Lieutenant-Colonel) S. E. Glendenning, after it had been condemned.

The Major wanted to demonstrate that old houses, as long as they had been well built, could be reconditioned and rescued. On 17 March 1942 the *Norwich Evening News* printed a letter from Major Glendenning in its Whiffler column in which he describes his property: 'The building on the right of the square at Flower Pot Yard was the Great Hall, in which everyone ate and most members of the house would sleep, warmed by a charcoal brazier. It was opened to a carved oak roof and the high table would be at the end toward Oak Street, next to the oriel window. The master's private room and the ladies' 'solar' or upstairs room, would adjoin at that end. At the other end of the hall is a beam which probably carried a curtain by way of a screen. One door led down to the kitchen, on the side toward the river, and a door each way to the outside gave access to the space behind the curtain.'

Over the years the building was further adapted. In particular, in the 16th century a floor was inserted half way up the building, and a fireplace and chimney added. As the area declined, the merchants moved out. Weavers' windows, designed to let in the maximum amount of light, were installed. These indicate that textile workers were amongst the tradesman who subsequently occupied the building.

Sadly in April 1942, much of the Major's work was undone when the yard was bombed. However, miraculously the Great Hall survived. Although all other buildings have since been demolished, in 1954 the Hall was restored to contain one massive ground-floor room with a great leaded window, and a large room and half gallery upstairs.

In 1961 the owner, Donald Pyle, established the Great Hall Theatre Company here and until 1964 the building was the setting for various productions.

All that now remains of the yard is the Great Hall itself, now commercial premises.

Although it now looks sadly out of place, at least this little piece of Norwich's heritage has survived, thus proving Major Glendenning's point.

*Flower Pot Yard from the rear, Oak St, 1937*

## Greenland Fishery Yard (30 Oak Street)

## Key and Castle Yard (105 Oak Street)

*Greenland Fishery Yard, Oak Street, c.1930*

*Key and Castle Yard, Oak Street, 1937*

This rather strange name, for both the pub and yard that stood behind, dates back to at least the 18th century when both Yarmouth and King's Lynn were involved with the Greenland, or whale, Fishery. Understandably, both these towns had hostelries with this name which, for reasons unknown, was copied by a Norwich publican.

This long, narrow yard stood behind the Key and Castle pub. It would be fair to say that when he visited in 1897 the *Norwich Mercury* reporter wasn't terribly impressed: 'On the right were 13 houses . In the wash houses were two taps for 13 dwellings, with six earth closets.' Looking on the bright side, it was noted that the public water supply was laid on. However, some 30 years earlier it was the pub's landlord who had been in the news. It was in 1869 that William Sheward, who had taken over the tenancy of the pub in the previous year, confessed to having murdered his wife back in 1851 when they had lived in Tabernacle Street. At the time the crime was committed portions of an adult female body had been discovered in various parts of Norwich, but it was decided that medical students were playing a practical joke designed to terrify local citizens. At his trial Sheward renounced his confession saying that he was drunk when he made the statement. Nevertheless, he was found guilty (at which point he again confessed) and subsequently hanged at the Old City Gaol at St Giles' Gate on 20 April 1869. It was the first execution to be held in private in Norwich, Until then the spectacle had been treated as public entertainment!

## Horton's Yard (113 Oak Street)

The yard (mistakenly called Orton on the 1884 map) was divided into two sections separated by a narrow archway. In 1897 the first half was made up of five houses. Compared to other yards it seems that the tenants were quite well provided for and shared between them two privies, one dustbin and one tap. In the lower part were nine houses which had small gardens 'two or three of these being gay with chrysanthemums'. This half of the yard was not as well serviced, only having one tap, two privies and a wash house. Although the drains were full of refuse, the *Norwich Mercury* journalist noted in 1897: 'The houses are in a fairly good condition, the yard being clean-looking on the whole.'

A Key and Castle Yard still stands in the same vicinity, but all it shares with its predecessor is the name. The tenants now enjoy high-quality accommodation designed to meet modern standards.

## Little Buck Yard (141 Oak Street)

*The entrance to Little Buck Yard, Oak Street, 1937*

The yard took its name from the pub located at 139 Oak Street which could trace its licence back to 1760. Over its lifetime the hostelry was known variously as the Buck, the Little Buck and also the Stag.

By the 1930s the yard was entered through a covered passageway which formed part of 141 Oak Street (pictured above). This 18th-century building was three storeys high and in the 1930s housed a small shop. It had a typical range of weavers' windows to light the top floor, indicating that at some time it housed a textile workshop. From the 1884 map it is clear that this is not your typical long, narrow airless yard, and in fact looks quite spacious.

Both the pub and yard were lost during the Baedeker Raids in April 1942.

## Little Crown Yard (83 Oak Street)

In 1897 there were ten houses in this yard, two of which were 'old-gabled dwellings'. Although the *Norwich Mercury* journalist did point out that the yard had smelly drains, there was only one tap serving all the tenants and that 'not five yards from the nearest window lay a heap of stable manure'. He did add: 'There were plants in the cottage windows: a respectable yard altogether.'

## Queen Caroline's Yard (59 Oak Street)

Visiting in 1897, the *Norwich Mercury* journalist commented that the yard contained ten houses and that it was 'cobble paved but not dirty, a remark scarcely applicable to the half-clad children thereabouts'.

## Old Brew Yard (122 Oak Street)

*Old Brew Yard, Oak Street, c.1930*

As can be seen on the 1884 map this was a spacious yard with a wide entrance; very clearly its inhabitants would not have suffered from the lack of air associated with so many Norwich yards. Together with the neighbouring Little Brew Yard it probably took its name from the St Martin's Brewery which in the latter years of the 18th century had a brewing office at 94 Coslany Street.

By the 1930s the houses on the south, which divided the two yards and were believed to date from the 17th century, had cement-rendered walls. The photograph (above) shows the west side of the yard formed by the houses facing Oak Street.

Along with its neighbours, properties in the yard were badly damaged during the Baedeker Raids.

### An unusual survivor!

On St Crispin's Road, next to New Mills, stands a small decagonal building. Although not particularly attractive, this pre-cast reinforced-concrete structure is Grade II listed. Designed in 1919, it is thought to be the oldest surviving concrete urinal in Britain! In the 1880s several of this type were made for the City of Norwich Corporation and set up in prominent City-centre sites. When built it would have been opposite the entrance to the City Station. It is no longer in use.

## Ragged School Yard (103 Oak Street)

*Ragged School Yard, Oak Street, 1937*

The yard was accessed by way of a wooden Tudor arch which spanned a covered passageway. The yard's name derived from the fact that during the 19th century a Sunday school primarily for the benefit of the poor was held in a room here.

## Saw Mill Yard (13 Oak Street)

In 1976 Jonathan Mardle wrote an article in the *Eastern Evening News* in which he reproduced a letter received some 20 years earlier from a man who was brought up in the 'slums of Coslany'. In his letter the man writes of the Hot Pressers' Arms (located at 15 Oak Street before it was closed under compensation in 1925) which stood at the entrance to Saw Mill Yard, which he calls Bagshaw's Yard (although the name was never officially changed), in reference to a business that traded there. The correspondent wrote:

'What a place this yard was! Cobbled and having a paved drain down the middle of it. It was common practice for the housewives to empty all and sundry of their pots and pans down this drain. Swarming with rats, and infested with fleas and bugs, Bagshaw's Yard was the playground of many kids, with their dirty feet, their sore eyes and runny noses. Bagshaw bought old rags, old bones, old bottles all culled from the dustbins of other parishes when people could afford to throw things away. As the piles of bones grew, so did the smell, but nobody seemed to mind.'

There is no indication as to the period referred to, but the Bagshaws were still trading there in the early 1930s when an entry in Kelly's describes, R. & R. G. Bagshaw as 'wholesale dealers in game & poultry; pheasant poultry & dog food manufacturers' and also 'rag, skin and paper merchants'.

Along with neighbouring Distillery and Dial Yards, Sawmill Yard was dealt with early in the slum-clearance programme when in 1933/4 it was cleared of its 47 residents.

## Sun Yard (24 Oak Street)

Along with its immediate neighbours, Sun Yard was one of the first yards to be demolished under the Housing Act of 1930. Although we do not have a photograph of the yard the *Norwich Mercury* reported that in 1897 it had a bricked entrance passage with a drain at the far end. Its 13 houses were served by three privies and a midden. Although a public water supply was laid on, of the two drains one was blocked and the yard had a bad smell. The journalist noted: 'Certain women suggested that their names were being entered in the notebook because they were not at school, a witticism which highly amused the inhabitants': but evidently not the reporter!

The yard was cleared of its 23 inhabitants in 1932. Along with other properties in the 'Sun Yard clearance area' the land was purchased by the Council for the erection of new flats.

## Unicorn Yard (39 Oak Street)

In 1897 the *Norwich Mercury* reporter had little more to say on this yard than: 'Seems alright'. This was high praise indeed, but maybe not surprising. From the 1884 map we can see that it was designed more like a modern cul-de-sac, with many of the houses having gardens. A modern Unicorn Yard has been built in the same vicinity.

*Entrance to Unicorn Yard, Oak Street, 1938*

# Photo Gallery of Yards in the Oak Street Area in the 1930s

*Arabian Horse Yard, 68 Oak Street, 1937*

*Baldwin's Yard, 94 Oak Street, 1936*

*Bell Yard, 3 St Mary's Alley, 1937*

*Georgian cottages, Dog Yard, 104 Oak Street, 1936*   *Goat Yard, 98 Oak Street, 1937*

*Robinson's Yard, 111 Oak Street, c.1930*   *Saddler's Yard, 115 Oak Street, 1937*

*Suffolk Arms' Yard, 119 Oak Street, 1937*   *Talbot's Yard, 106 Oak Street, c.1935*

# The Yards Today

Apart from the entrances to Talbot's Yard and Dog Yard, adjacent to numbers 108 and 106 Oak Street, there is very little evidence of the old yards that once lined the streets. However, what this section of the City does have is many modern courts and yards.

Some, such as Scholars' Court (a redevelopment based around the former St Miles' School) and Dyers' Yard have adopted new names. However, others, including Key and Castle Yard, New Mills' Yard, Unicorn Yard and Buck's Yard, have assumed the names of their predecessors. The standard of living in these new properties would be almost beyond the imagination of the tenants who resided in the Oak Street yards a few generations ago, but maybe they are a fitting tribute to the communities who once called them home.

*98-108 Oak Street, including entrances to Talbot's Yard and Dog Yard, 2014*

*Key and Castle Yard, 2009*

# Norwich Over the Water: St George's

Yards identified in this section of the City include:

## Botolph Street
- Sultzer's Yard (13, E)

## Calvert Street
- Baldwin's Yard (49, E)
- Hall's Court (12, W)
- Two Brewers' Yard (62, W)
- Crown and Anchor Yard (100, W)

## Colegate
- Guild Yard (49, N)
- Hook's Yard (55, N)
- Queen Anne Yard (57, N)
- Shore's Court (16, S)
- Nightingale Yard (24, S)
- Black Boys' Yard (32, S)
- Moon and Stars' Yard (56, S)
- Grapes' Yard (70, S)

## Cross Lane
- Betts' Court (14, E)

## St George's (Middle) Street
- Lowe's Yard (39, E)
- King's Head Yard (63, E)
- Appleton's Court (111, E)
- Crown and Anchor Yard (121, E)

- Barrack Yard (116, W)
- Cossey's Court (118, W)
- Stonemasons' Yard (122, W)
- Drake's Court (126, W)
- Little Cherry Tree Yard (160, W)
- Burrell's Yard (164, W)
- William IV Yard (166, W)
- Hill's Yard (184, W)

## Muspole Street
- Wright's Foundry Yard (29, E)
- Yeast Yard (16, W)
- Tubby's Yard (32, W)
- Archer's Yard (36, W)

## Pitt Street
- Whip and Nag Yard (3, E)
- Ely's Yard (25, E)
- Pelican Yard (33, E)
- Dark Entry (51, E)
- Adelaide's Yard (57, E)
- Mitchell's Yard (79, E)
- Blakeley's Yard (12, W)
- Cattermoul's Yard (16, W)
- Gilbert's Yard (50, W)
- Winter's Yard (84, W)

## St Augustine's Street
- Rose Yard (7, E)
- Hindes' Yard (13, E)
- Barnes' Yard (19, E)
- Bushel Yard (29, E)
- Nunn's Yard (33, E)
- Delph's Yard (35, E)
- Stonemasons' Court (39, E)
- Catherine Wheel Opening (61, E)
- Wine Coopers' Arms Yard (30, W)

## St Martin's Lane
- Butcher's Yard (3, N)

## St Mary's Alley
- Bell Yard (3, N)

Please note that there have been many changes in street names and numbering over the last century. In particular between 1884 and 1908 Middle Street was renamed St George's Street. The addresses give the approximate entrance to individual yards based on Kelly's 1908 Directory.

*Archer's Yard, Muspole Street, c.1935*

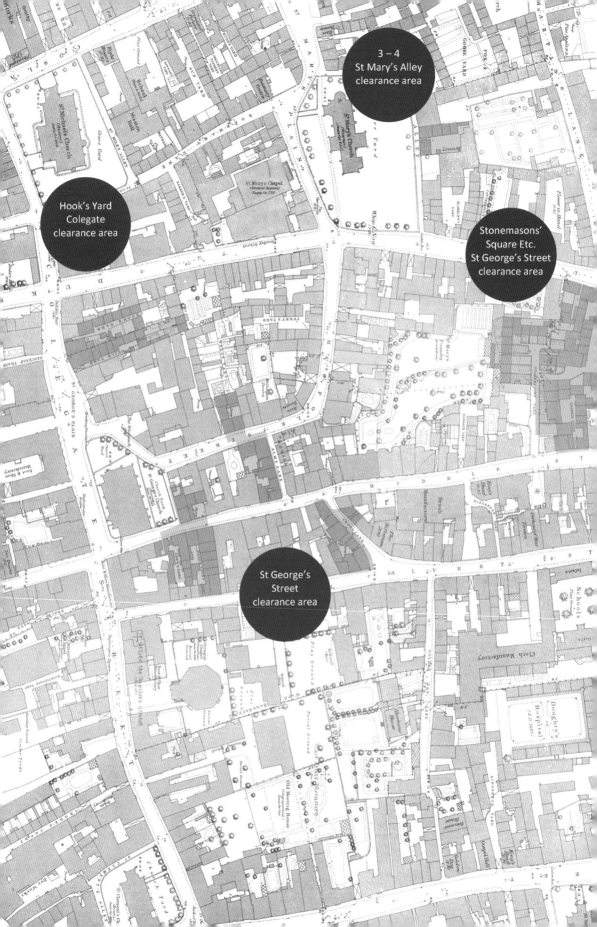

3 – 4
St Mary's Alley
clearance area

Hook's Yard
Colegate
clearance area

Stonemasons'
Square Etc.
St George's Street
clearance area

St George's
Street
clearance area

Cherry Tree
Yard Etc.
St George's
clearance area

*Corner of Muspole Street and Pitt Street, 1937*

There is much evidence that this part of Norwich was settled before the Norman Conquest. Some of the biggest clues are provided in the names of buildings and streets. Take for example the medieval church of St Clement Fybriggate. The dedication of this church suggests a Danish influence, St Clement being a popular saint in Scandinavian lands. It was in 870 that the Danes effectively conquered East Anglia, and although Brian Ayers (former Norfolk County Archaeologist) does not suggest that the original church and parish was of Danish origin he does believe it was established before 1066. St Clement was the patron saint of sailors, and characteristically churches dedicated to the saint are located, as here, near to river crossings. Further evidence of early occupation is provided by the alignment of St George's Street (historically called Gildengate) which appears to follow a line of a defensive bank and ditch constructed early in the 10th century. The alignment was paralleled by Calvert Street which lies immediately to the east.

The Danish influence is of course found throughout Norwich in the use of the word 'gate' meaning 'street': but why 'Colegate'? In her book 'Norwich: Street by Street', Pamela Brooks suggests it may take its name from the surname Cole, there being evidence for the name in the City from 1220. Writing in 1972, George Nobbs (local publisher) believed that

'per foot' Colegate was 'the architecturally richest street in the City'. Although this assessment is open to debate, few would argue that the street still contains some impressive buildings – both religious and secular. Ecclesiastical buildings include two medieval churches together with two of the 'most impressive Dissenter chapels in England' (Simon Jenkins, former Chairman of the National Trust). The first is the Old Meeting House which was built in 1693 as a gathering place for Congregationalists. Its exterior indicates the influence and association with kindred worshippers in Holland. The second is the Octagon Chapel, thus called because of its distinctive shape, which was built in 1756 for the Presbyterians, although it was handed to the Unitarians in 1820. Charles Wesley, the 18th-century English leader of the Methodist movement, described it as 'the most elegant meeting house in Europe...furnished in the highest taste and as clean as any gentleman's saloon.' Added to these, at number 31 lies a well-preserved Elizabethan residence called Bacon House, which was erected *c.*1540 by Henry Bacon (Mayor of Norwich in 1557 and 1566). He was just one of a number of mayors and rich traders who lived in the street, others included members of the Harvey family, one of whom was Robert Harvey of Catton (1696 – 1773). Robert ran the family's worsted business from his house located at 18 – 20 Colegate where he lived with his wife Lydia. He was renowned for his eccentric dress. He gloried in two pseudonyms the first being the somewhat dubious nickname of 'Snuffy Bob', earned for his habit of standing in front of his Colegate house taking snuff from his waistcoat pocket, and the second the somewhat grander 'Father of the City'. Unsurprisingly, it is the latter which is written on his wall tablet in St Clement's Church.

As in other parts of Norwich, early development meant later infilling of spare land, as is clearly evidenced on the 1884 map where we can locate around 50 yards. In William Lee's 1851 report, Thomas Crosse, medical officer for the parishes of St George Colegate and St Clement, where many of these yards were located, said of his patch: 'The people are supplied with water by pumps and by pipes. As far as I have observed I have not seen either a pump or a tap in the house. I should say that the average distance would not be more than 20 yards to fetch the water.' Although, in general Mr Crosse had: '...no reason to think that people would use more water if they had it in their houses...[there are] some exceptions, I think that the dirty people would perhaps to be induced to use more if they had less distance to carry it.'

A large number of yards in this section of the City were squeezed into the yards previously used by the pubs, which also gave them their name, including Crown and Anchor Yard (100 Calvert Street), Nightingale Yard (24 Colegate), William IV Yard (166 St George's Street) and Pelican Yard (33 Pitt Street).

Although not extensively cleared in the 1930s, a combination of WWII bombing, post-war road building together with new housing and commercial developments have led to many changes in this part of the City. But this really is a tale of two halves. Like Magdalen Street, the building of the inner ring road split the neighbourhood. North of the ring road a huge area was demolished in the 1960s to facilitate the building of the Anglia Square development and the now derelict Sovereign House, built as the home of Her Majesty's Stationery Office. But on the City side much has been retained. Here old buildings are juxtaposed with new, and maybe one of the main attractions is the way one comes across little gems. One such is the Whip and Nag Yard (located opposite St Mary Coslany Church), which looks like a renovated, old yard...but is it?

*The construction of the Magdalen Street flyover, Anglia Square and the Stationery Office (outlined above on the 1884 map) resulted in the demolition of most of the area highlighted in pink.*

St George's Plain is dominated by a Victorian red-brick building that in 1909 housed 'the largest boot and shoe factory under one roof in the Kingdom' (*Illustrated London News*). It was in 1856 that the firm which evolved into Howlett and White, and later the Norvic Shoe Company, first built a large factory on the site of a former coal yard between Claxton and Water Lanes, off St George's Plain. By 1936 the firm occupied a four-acre site which stretched from St George's Plain down to the river and along Colegate from Duke Street to St George's Street (Bridge Street in 1884). But it wasn't only the building that gave character to the area. During the lifetime of the factory the streets around St George's were a hive of activity and noise, and so when Norvic went into receivership in 1981 there was a very real fear that the whole area would become derelict. However, in 1985 the *Eastern Evening News* ran a story announcing a 'New Role for St George's' in which they explained that the building was being redeveloped for mixed usage, including offices, shops and a wine bar. The aim was to regenerate

this area of the City, now known as Norwich Over the Water. Although less attractive parts of the vast building were demolished, real efforts were made to retain attractive features, in particular the factory's imposing façade has been preserved and still dominates the street.

There were many other shoe-related businesses in this area of the City, in fact part of Muspole Street was once known as Soutergate, 'souter' being a medieval reference to shoemakers. Businesses came and went, but major players in the first half of the 20th century which were located here, included: S. L. Witton, later taken over by Norvic to produce its Kiltie brand; Phipps & Son Ltd, boot and shoe mercers; Norwich Wood Heels Ltd; and F. J. Andrews Ltd, general agents to the shoe trade. Similarly the boot and shoe trade was much in evidence on Pitt Street, which housed such organisations as the National Union of Boot & Shoe Operatives, the Norvic Social Club and the shoe manufacturing firm of John F. Kirby Ltd.

*The former Norvic (previously Howlett and White) shoe factory, St George's Plain, 2014*

# Major Clearance Schemes

Unlike other areas of Norwich, during the interwar years this section of the City was not subject to extensive clearance. In fact only around 10 yards were affected, resulting in the demolition of around 95 properties and the rehousing of 325 tenants. Stonemasons' Square (Yard in 1884) was by far the largest yard to be dealt with; here alone around 34 houses were demolished and 130 tenants rehoused. Other yards cleared during this period included:

- Pelican Yard, Ely's Yard, Drake's Court and Steward's Yard (the latter was unnamed in both 1884 and 1908). Overall, c.1937 45 tenants were rehoused from these yards and 17 properties

were demolished as part of the 'Stonemasons' Square Etc. clearance scheme'.

- As part of the 'Hook's Yard Etc. clearance scheme', 16 properties were cleared of 40 residents between 1938 and 1939 in Hook's Yard and Burrell's Yard (called Crook's Yard and Guild Yard respectively on the 1884 map).

- The 19 properties in Cherry Tree Yard and Burrell's Yard (Little Cherry Tree and Burrow's Yard on the 1884 map) were cleared of around 19 tenants in 1937 and demolished in the same year as part of the 'Cherry Tree Yard Etc. clearance scheme'.

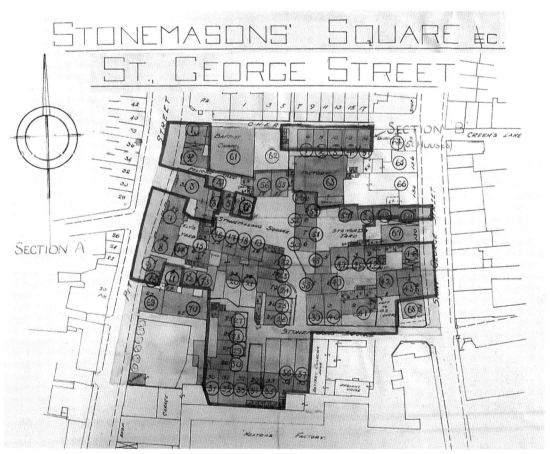

*Detailed plan of the 'Stonemasons' Square Etc. clearance scheme', c.1935*

# Yards of Note

In the late 19th century this area was full of nooks and crannies filled with ramshackle buildings. The following yards were of particular interest.

## Black Boys' Yard (32 Colegate)

The yard lay behind the Back Boys' pub, rechristened the Merchants of Colegate in 1980. The pub originally took its name from the Dominican Friary that started in Colegate before eventually moving to St Andrew's and Blackfriar's Hall. The monks wore a black cloak over their white habits hence the nickname 'Black Boys'.

During the first half of the 19th century in a building to the rear of the yard Miss Sarah Anne Glover ran a school. She was an excellent teacher, but her main claim to fame was her invention of the Norwich Sol-fa system of music notation on which John Curwen's Tonic Sol-fa was largely based.

For many years the way into the popular restaurant 'By Appointment' (25 – 29 St George's Street) was via the archway on Colegate which was the original entrance to the yard.

Both 32 and 34 Colegate were badly damaged during the war, but it is unclear when properties were cleared from the yard.

*Black Boys' Yard, Colegate, 1939*

## Muspole Street

The street's name is referred to as far back as 1250. It is possible that the curve of the street skirts a marshy area, whilst the name is thought to derive from 'Moss Pool', 'Mouse Pool' or 'Must Pool' – meaning muddy stream.

*Muspole Street, 1936*

## Pitt Street

The thoroughfare was originally known as Pit Street, in reference to an open pit at the end of St Olave's churchyard. The name proved quite fortuitous when the Pitt family rose to political prominence, and by simply adding an extra 't' homage could be paid to two of the country's prime ministers!

*Pitt Street, 1936*

## Rose Yard (7 St Augustine's Street)

*Rose Yard, 1939*

*Rose Yard, 1935*

This yard was located behind the Rose Tavern. An inn was first established on the site in the 14th century when it provided sustenance to knights and revellers after they had completed their jousting tournaments, and other exertions at the nearby Gildencroft. This large grassed area once filled the space between the City wall and St Martin at Oak, and between St Augustine's Street and Pitt Street on the east, and Oak Street on the west. In 1714 the Rose had yards, gardens, stables, an orchard and even pasture – a perfect place to build houses. From the 1884 map we can see that the yard was extensive and that many of the houses had gardens. But what were conditions really like? We have two interesting accounts which help us understand.

Firstly we have a vivid description of the yard in William Lee's 1851 report. At the time it contained around 70 houses. The only source of water for 50 of these, together with the Rose Inn, was St Augustine's churchyard [public] pump. The remaining 20 houses had access to three pumps. The inspector went on to say: 'The pumps are frequently locked up in the summer when water is scarce....The drainage and pavement is bad, some of the houses in the lower part of the yard are very dilapidated, and at the bottom is a large pool of nightsoil 15 feet by 25 feet from about 40 houses. There are privies, a stable and animals under dwellings, and the people complain much of stench. There has been fever in the yard...it was a bad locality of cholera in 1833.'

Then in 1976, the Canon Maurice Burrell (1930 – 2008) sent a letter to the *Eastern Evening News* in which he presents a somewhat different viewpoint:

'I was born in Rose Yard, and spent ten of the most informative years of my boyhood there. We had our Rose Inn, now the Old Crome, and two general shops, one of which my grandparents, and later my parents, were proprietors. We sold almost everything, not only to the 100 families living in the yard, but also to those living in the neighbouring Leonard Street and Esdelle Street and the constant stream of people taking a short cut between St Augustine's Street and Magpie Road.

'My memories are of a tightly knit community exhibiting a marvellous nurturing spirit to one another. This community spirit came into its own especially on great national occasions or when one of those living in the yard were married. Then an old piano would be trundled out into the middle of the yard. A yard which had been suitably decorated with bunting for the occasion, and not only the yard-dwellers themselves but even casual passers-by would be drawn into the joyful celebrations.

'Of course we had none of the essentials of modern city life. There was one outside tap, one wash house and one outside "privy" to every six or seven families. I am not suggesting that we should wish to return to such primitive conditions, though it is interesting to remember how many of those who moved out of the yard to the developing council estates gradually found their way back. On the whole, despite their hardships people were happy and they were not as careless about personal cleanliness and hygiene as [is often] suggested.'

The entrance to the yard, together with the building that latterly housed the Old Crome (delicensed 1981) and a few of the adjacent houses have survived. The rest were demolished during post-war slum clearance in the 1950s.

## Ruby Baker remembers life in Stonemasons' Yard/ Square (122 St George's Street)

*Stonemasons' Square, south side, 1937*

*Ruby Baker dressed up for her first dance, c.1937*

There is some debate about which stonemason gave his name to this yard. Amongst the contenders is Charles Milnes. In the 1851 census Charles, a master stonemason employing three men, lived in the yard with four children, including his son John (James) who was an apprentice in the same trade. Charles' younger brother Thomas, carved the statue of Nelson which is now in Cathedral Close.

The yard, which by the 1930s was referred to as a square, was subject to slum clearance and compulsory purchase in 1935/36. From the map produced at the time (see page 97), it is evident that although it is a yard within a series of yards, it is not particularly cramped. According to the Medical Officer of Health it was included in the programme, along with others in the area, 'on account of [its] sanitary defects and not on the grounds of [its] bad arrangement in relation to other buildings or the narrowness or bad arrangement of the street etc.'. Such insanitary arrangements do not appear to have impacted adversely on the residents' health. Figures collated for the 'Stonemasons' Square Etc. clearance scheme' in the five years to 31 December 1935 indicate that for the entire area the death rate per 1,000 of the population was 7.04, whilst for the City it was 11.89. The figures for respiratory disease were 1.73 and 2.15 respectively.

Over the period 1936/37 around 130 residents were moved from Stonemasons' Square. Most went to the new council estates. Once cleared it was demolished.

The original site of the square is now covered by St Crispin's House, which lies just south of the inner ring road.

Ruby Baker (born in 1921) and her family lived in Stonemasons' Square for 13 years, and so can give us an idea of what life there was really like:

'There were 12 children in my family, I'm the oldest. I lived off St George's Street, which we used to call Middle Street, at number 2 Stonemasons' Square. It was a big double-fronted house. We were all compact and it was in quite a good condition compared with other houses in the yard. When we lived there my mother just had eight children. We had five bedrooms, a living room and a little scullery. In the scullery we had a cooker, a copper and a sink. On the other side of the house we had our own toilet alongside and my father built a little trellis around it, we had a dog's kennel there as well. You'd get to the toilet by going out of the front door. On the left side there was a step down to another little room which had a door which opened up to a great big room with Elizabethan-type windows which looked over into Drake's Court [located behind Ruby's house]. My mother and father used to rent that out to a man that did woodwork.'

'There was an alley leading to the Square. We lived in the main part near the road, and so we were away from the other houses. In the main part of the yard, there was a row of toilets shared by everyone, and they had a wash house too where they took turns rinsing their linen and things like that. They were little dwellings, I think they only had one bedroom. They didn't have many children, maybe one or two at the most.

'In front of the house we had a little garden and running from the door to the gate was a little path made out of pink flagstones, the sort you sometimes got in a kitchen. On a Saturday, when I was a child, I used to scrub that path on my hands and knees, and my mother gave me tuppence and my father gave me a halfpenny. You could go to the pictures on a Saturday afternoon for a halfpenny, and so I was well pleased. Inside, we couldn't afford carpet and so we had lino on the stairs and I scrubbed that as well.

'Oh there was lovely community spirit in the square. All the kids got on and played together. We used to have a carnival every year when my mother used to dress us girls up. Once she dressed me up as a powder box...and I got first prize

'When I was 15 we were moved to a council house on Stephenson Road on the Larkman Estate. Some neighbours moved with us. others went to Mile Cross.

'My mother and father were pleased to move somewhere where there was a bathroom: it was great having a bath and five bedrooms. It was a lovely house: we just didn't have the furniture to go in it. We lived in Stonemasons' Square for around 13 years, but my father never really settled at Stephenson Road, and after that we moved house fairly frequently.'

## Whip and Nag Yard (3 Pitt Street)

Whip and Nag Yard has all the hallmarks of an old Norwich Yard. In particular it is a courtyard development of mainly timber-clad buildings set behind an ancient public house. We can even locate its position on the 1884 map. However, it was actually designed in the 1970s.

The Whip and Nag pub, which could trace its licence back to 1760, traded from 3 Pitt Street until 1960 (following changes in street layout it now stands at the corner of Muspole and Duke Streets). Parts of the building are believed to date from the early 16th century and there is some speculation that it may have been a hall-type dwelling which was later extended. Using a combination of the 1884 map, George Plunkett's 1956 photo and a current picture of the yard, it can be clearly seen that the entrance to the current yard goes through the centre of what was the public house. In the 1970s, plans were being made to demolish 3 Pitt Street to facilitate road widening. Instead, together with surrounding buildings, including rundown shops, derelict cottages and workshops it became part of a new 13-home development, built around a courtyard. Which maybe goes to show that with modern facilities and a bit of planning the old courts could have been pleasant places to live.

*Whip and Nag Yard, 2009*

*Entrance to Whip and Nag Yard, 2014*

*Entrance to Whip and Nag Pub, 1956*

# Photo Gallery of St George's Yards in the 1930s

*Blakeley's Yard, 12 Pitt Street, 1937*

*Bell Yard, 3 St Mary's Alley, 1937*

*Burrell's (Guild) Yard, 49 Colegate, 1937*  *(Little) Cherry Tree Yard, 160 St George's Street, c.1935*

*Cattermoul's Yard, 16 Pitt Street, 1937*

*Hindes' Yard, 13 St Augustine's Street, 1939*

*Lowe's Yard, 39 St George's Street, c.1935*

*Hook's (Crook's) Yard, Colegate, 1937*

*Nichol's (Barnes') Yard, 19 St Augustine's Street, 1939*

# The Yards Today

There remains much evidence of old yards in this section of the City. Examples include, Rose Yard (7 St Augustine's Street) where the entrance and a few buildings have survived. Similarly, Wright's Foundry Yard (29 Muspole Street) still contains buildings from the original yard although the northern end now lies beneath St Crispin's House. Elsewhere, signs indicate entrances to yards which are either blocked or lead to modern developments, examples include Hindes' Yard (13 St Augustine's Street) and Nichol's Yard (19 St Augustine's Street). Meantime, although Lowe's Yard (39 St George's Street) was demolished in 1937, a modern yard now stands on approximately the same spot. This spacious yard stands behind the 16th-century Bacon House. Finally the entrance to Queen Anne Yard (57 Colegate) lay adjacent to the pub of the same name which was closed in 1909. The main building, parts of which date from the 17th century, was renovated in the 1970s and the yard incorporated into the development. A sign over a crooked doorway still marks the former entrance to the yard.

There are also some interesting variations on the theme. We have already looked at Whip and Nag Yard. Another example of a modern yard which contains old buildings, is Balderston Court, which runs from Calvert Street to the Old Meeting House. In 1884 it was actually a lane which led to a school playground, which by 1931 was known as School Yard. By 1958 it was officially known as Balderston Court, after Timothy Balderstone (1682 – 1764) twice mayor of Norwich who lived in the parish of St George Colegate. Although the court contains predominantly modern buildings, at its entrance, at right angles to Calvert Street, is a listed 18th-century red-brick building of two storeys.

*Wright's Foundry Yard, 29 Muspole Street, 2009*

## Octagon Court - or is it?

A modern-day example of the difficulty identifying a typical yard by its name is provided by Octagon Court. Located at 1 Calvert Street this attractive development takes its name from the nearby Octagon Chapel. It is not a court, but one long building which was erected as a house in the 18th century and subsequently converted into a factory. In the 20th century this Grade II* listed building was renovated as individual dwellings which now constitute numbers 2 – 9 Octagon Court.

*Octagon Court, 2009*

# Beyond the Shops: Magdalen Street Area

Yards identified in this section of the City include:

## Botolph Street
- White Horse Yard (13, E)
- Cossey's Yard (25, E)
- Chapel Yard (31, E)
- Globe Yard (39, E)
- Fountain Yard (47, E)
- Sultzer's Court (61, E)
- Cat and Fiddle Yard (8, W)
- Howlett's Court (12, W)
- Grime's Yard (24, W)

## Fishergate
- Mint Yard (5, N)
- Barnard's Yard (15, N)
- Blacksmith's Yard (23, N)
- Thoroughfare Yard (27, N)
- Rampant Horse Yard (31, N)
- Thompson's Yard (37, N)
- Long Yard (43, N)
- Tiger Yard (45, N)
- Long Yard (14, S)
- Soman's Yard (20, S)
- Jolly Sawyer's Yard (24, S)

## Fye Bridge Street
- Jack of Newbury Yard (17, E)

## Magdalen Street
- Thoroughfare Yard (11, E)
- Red Lion Yard (19, E)
- Gurney's Court (31, E)
- Loose's Yard (41, E)
- Ling's Court (49, E)
- Bayfield's Yard (57, E)
- Fisher's Court (63, E)
- Abel's Court (65, E)
- Woolcombers Arms' Yard (77, E)
- Barnes' Yard (87, E)
- Zipfel's Yard (111, E)
- Addison's Yard (119, E)
- New Yard (125, E)
- Gilling's Yard (133, E)
- White Lion Yard (135, E)
- Paradise Place (139, E)
- Two Brewers' Yard (151, E)
- Red Lion Yard (159, E)
- Boswell's Yard (24, W)

- King's Head Yard (40, W)
- Cobb's Yard (54, W)
- Elephant Yard (58, W)
- Bishop's Yard/Court (60, W)
- Cremer's Yard (70, W)
- White Horse Yard (84, W)
- Hacon's Yard (92, W)
- Minn's Court (100, W)
- Cross Keys' Yard (104, W)
- Beckham's Yard (116, W)
- Royal's Yard (136, W)
- Foulger's Yard (140, W)
- Whiting's Court (150, W)

## St Saviour's Lane
- Harper's Buildings (21, N)
- Campling's Yard (18, S)

*Dolls' Hospital, Magdalen Street, 1935*

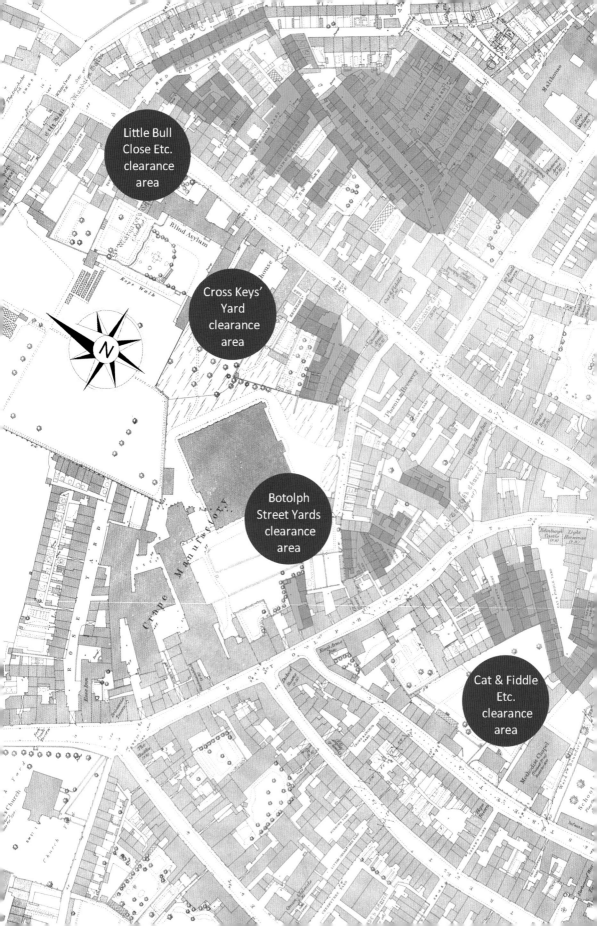

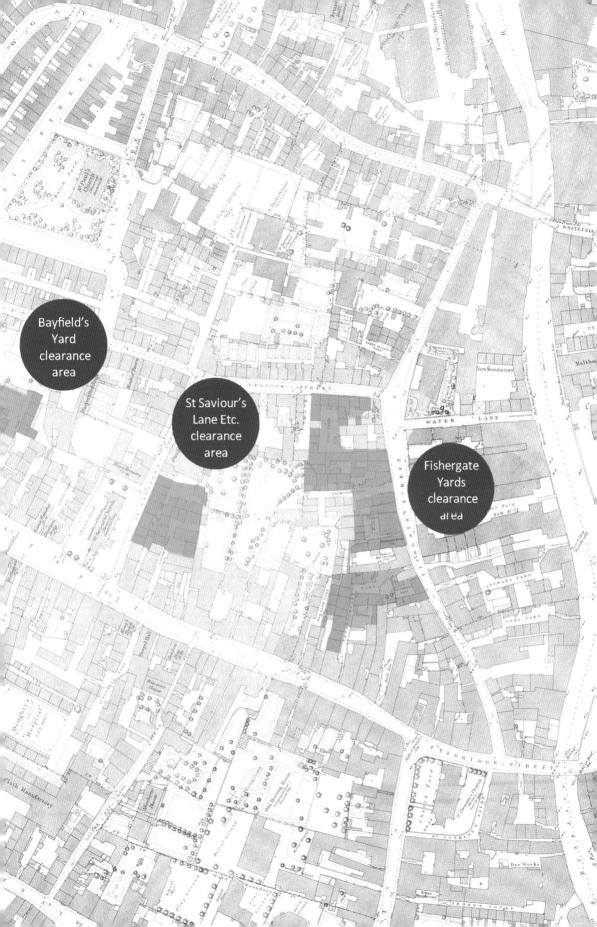

Bayfield's Yard clearance area

St Saviour's Lane Etc. clearance area

Fishergate Yards clearance area

*Magdalen Street, c.1920*

Magdalen Street has a long and illustrious past. It is believed to be the site of an important Middle-Saxon settlement, which formed part of the principal north-to-south route through the City. Until the late-19th century it was known as Fyebridge (or Fybrigge) Street after which the length stretching from St Clement's Church to the City gate was renamed 'Magdalen', in reference to a Leper's chapel that stood just outside the City walls. For many years Magdalen Street was one of Norwich's main shopping areas, in fact if you lived to the north of Norwich going 'down the City' meant coming here. However, a number of factors, including the migration of industry from the City centre, the construction of the controversial flyover, and the growing popularity of the shopping areas around of St Stephen's Street and Chapelfield, have all contributed to its decline.

Other major roadways in this area were Botolph Street and Fishergate. Until the building of the flyover, Botolph Street ran from St Augustine's to Magdalen Street, joining it at Stump Cross. Botolph Street derived its name from the former church of St Buttolph the Abbot (demolished in the early 16th century), which stood between Magdalen and Botolph Streets. Meanwhile Fishergate, also the site of a Saxon settlement, literally means the 'street of the fishers'. The name arose because of its location next to the river.

Because of their early settlement, many historic buildings lined these streets, which were also the home of many public houses – in fact in the 1880s there were more than 20 pubs in this relatively small area. Of course, in Norwich, the land around old buildings and pubs was a perfect place to build shoddy housing. Therefore it is not surprising, by the end of the 19th century to find more than 50 yards located in this section of the City. Those associated with pubs included: King's Head Yard (40 Magdalen Street), Rampant Horse Yard (31 Fishergate) and Two Brewers' Yard (151 Magdalen Street).

Although during the 1930s the area was subject to a number of clearance schemes, these did not seriously change its ambience. However, in the 1960s it was devastated by two controversial planning decisions.

In 1959 the outlook seemed positive. In this year Magdalen Street was the beneficiary of a 'Town Improvement Scheme'. With the help of the Civic Trust and the co-operation of the local council, shopkeepers and tenants, the street was given a face-lift. The local publisher George Nobbs recalled of the period: 'It is difficult to describe the atmosphere that existed at that time – everybody seemed excited about the scheme and proud of their City.'

Sadly, both the excitement and beneficial effect of the improvements were short lived, when in December 1961 Norwich City Council accepted a plan from the City Engineer to build a flyover across Magdalen Street as part of a new inner-link road. There were extensive objections to the proposal from many parties, including the Norwich Society and the Magdalen Street and District Traders' Association. The traders believed that the flyover would divide the shopping area, ruin the beauty of the street and lead to shops being closed. Despite an impassioned campaign by these two groups the new flyover was opened on 12 June 1972. Around the same time the massive Anglia Square complex was built, the first shops opening in 1970. The plan was that Anglia Square would extend to the west, over what became a car park, to join up with St Augustine's Street and Pitt Street, but Anglia Square struggled commercially and despite several revamps this never happened.

The building of these two structures has totally changed the character of the area. Amongst the casualties was Botolph Street, its southern half was totally buried under Anglia Square. Meanwhile, the Dolls' Hospital, which was housed in a 17th-century timber-framed building, was lost when the flyover was built. The White Horse Inn, parts of which dated from the 17th century, together with its adjacent yard were similarly demolished as were the Elephant public house and Elephant Yard.

The worries of the Traders' Association proved well founded. Today, the flyover still slices Magdalen Street in two. Yet despite all that has happened, it is still a busy shopping area with much to see. Somehow more than 20 listed buildings have survived together with a diverse selection of courts and yards.

## Stump Cross

The rather unusual name 'Stump Cross' perpetuates the memory of a stone cross which stood at the junction of Botolph Street and Magdalen Street. During Henry VII's reign (1485 – 1509) it was known by the more elegant 'Guylding Cross'. It is believed to have been rechristened after being badly damaged.

*Magdalen Street after the 'makeover', 1959*

*Magdalen Street: cranes loom as the bank (centre right) awaits destruction to make way for the flyover, c.1970*

Between 1934 and 1939 around 28 yards in the Magdalen Street area were affected by clearance schemes. These resulted in the demolition of more than 200 properties and the displacement of approximately 600 residents.

As can be seen on the map, unlike other parts of the City, the major interwar clearances along both Magdalen and Botolph Streets had little impact on the properties fronting the roads. However, many yards behind these buildings were either fully or partially demolished. The situation was very different on Fishergate, where buildings on the north side of the street between numbers 19 and 47 were subject to clearance. The Tiger Tavern (Inn), which stood at the corner of Fishergate and what was then Peacock Street, was a three-storey Tudor building. Although it was initially excluded, it was demolished when road works were carried out *c.*1938. The other survivor, in this run of buildings, was the Duke of Marlborough

pub, which stood at number 29 just to the right of the entrance to Thoroughfare Yard. It continued to trade until 1969. It has since been demolished.

As in Cowgate, alongside the demolition of the yards came the construction of new council-built flats, including the Thompson Yard development on Fishergate, where 16 flats were built, and the Magdalen Close Scheme, where 78 flats were constructed on the site of the 'Little Bull Close Etc. clearance area'.

To summarise, unlike other areas of the City, despite being subject to extensive slum-clearance projects in the 1930s, Magdalen Street retained much of its character. It was only in the 1960s, with the building of the flyover and Anglia Square, that the ambience of the street significantly changed.

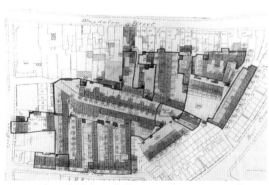

*Plan of 'Little Bull Close Etc. clearance area', 1935*

*The Tiger Tavern, Fishergate, 1934*

## Yards of Note

In the late 19th century more than 50 yards were located in this section of the City. Yards of particular note include the following.

### Gurney's Court (31 Magdalen Street)

*Gurney's Court, 2015*

The buildings making up Gurney's Court, a former home of the Gurney family, are amongst the many listed properties on Magdalen Street. Uncharacteristically, this court did not deteriorate into a slum.

The courtyard was formed by four building phases starting in the 16th century. Although, as is typical of an old yard, buildings were added over the years, very untypically the oldest sections do not front onto the street. Instead it is the buildings which lie parallel to, but away from, the street-line together with the north range which are the earliest.

Amongst the Court's most famous past residents are Elizabeth Fry (née Gurney, 1780 – 1845), renowned for her work with female prisoners, and Harriet Martineau (1802 – 1876), the English social theorist. In 1931, occupants included Ernest Bertram Hinde, London physician and surgeon, and Rev. Frederick Andrew Hannam, the rector of St Augustine's.

Today this pretty court contains high-quality apartments.

*Entrance to Jack of Newbury Yard, 1959*

### King's Head Yard (40 Magdalen Street)

*King's Head Yard, Magdalen Street, 1937*

The yard lies adjacent to the King's Head pub, where the licence can be traced back to 1760. The emblem of the Crown Brewery is still depicted above the entrance which dates back to the time the pub was tied to Youngs, Crawshay & Youngs, the brewery's owners.

Although the yard has been partially demolished, a three-storey, Regency, Grade-II listed building, believed to have been built in the early 19th century, has survived. The house was reputedly built for Barnabas Leman who was one of the first directors of the Norwich Union Fire Office. He became sheriff in 1804 and mayor in 1813 and 1818.

### Jack of Newbury Yard (17 Fye Bridge Street)

The yard was named after the adjacent pub, but who was Jack of Newbury? He was in fact a certain John Winchcombe who came from Newcombe (Berkshire) and was reputed to have been the greatest clothier in the world during the reign of Henry VIII (1509 – 1547).

## Mint Yard (5 Fishergate)

From the 1884 map it can be seen that Mint Yard contained a mishmash of properties, made up of at least two sections. In November 1897 it was visited by a journalist from the *Norwich Mercury* who noted: '[This yard] illustrates the way many tenements are packed together. Three low passages give exit to the street but the inhabitants are practically cut off from a supply of fresh air, whilst before their doors is the ever present drain.' It is unclear when the yard was demolished. It was still listed in Kelly's Directory in 1925, but had been removed by 1931. A new apartment block now stands on the approximate site of the old yard, bearing the name New Mint Court.

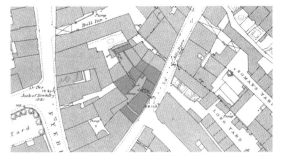

*Location of Mint Yard, Fishergate, 1884*

## Soman's Yard (20 Fishergate)

For many years Soman's Yard was the home of the Norwich Box Company, which in turn was owned by the shoe manufacturers P. Haldinstein & Sons Ltd (in 1946 the firm was taken over by Bally). Haldinstein's had been founded in 1799 by David Soman, a French émigré, and so the yard became known by the family name of its most prestigious occupier.

## Thoroughfare Yard (27 Fishergate and 11 Magdalen Street)

Unlike most Norwich yards, this one 'leads somewhere' – which accounts for its name. From the clearance map we can see the very narrow entrances, which are still there today, and it is a perfect example of how areas behind properties lining the street were filled in. In 1935 the yard was cleared of its 27 residents and in the following year its 12 properties were demolished. George Plunkett observed in 1987: 'It was formerly a quaint alley with numbers 4 – 9 on its north and east sides and number 11 in the corner opposite. Although they presented nice examples of architecture of about 1680, there were some indications that they may have been Tudor buildings which had been altered some generations after they were built.' As can be seen from the photograph, most of the properties were of three storeys and had a gabled roofline. Writing in the *Norfolk Annual* in 1936, Christopher Perks described the yard as being picturesque and mourned its loss, but acknowledged that it 'would have been well-nigh impossible to

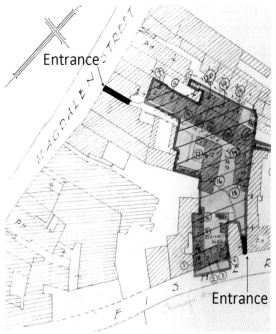

*Plan of the 'Thoroughfare Yard clearance area', 1934*

recondition on an economic basis'. By the 1980s the space was lined with commercial buildings. It has since been redeveloped and now contains residential properties, built using modern materials and in proportion to the space available.

*Thoroughfare Yard, Magdalen Street/Fishergate, c.1920*

## White Lion Yard and Gilling's Yard (133 and 135 Magdalen Street)

The White Lion Inn, which could trace its licence back to 1760, was housed in a small 17th-century building. At the rear of the yard stood an L-shaped block of Tudor houses. In 1934, when it was proposed that the yard should be cleared, the Tudor houses were described as being both well-built and comfortable and 'having the appearance of a group of alms houses'. The suggestion that the houses on the neighbouring Gilling's Yard should be pulled down to give the Tudor properties through ventilation was turned down in favour of a large area being cleared as part of the 'Little Bull Close Etc. clearance area'. Between 1936/7 ten properties were demolished in each yard and around 50 residents were rehoused. In both cases the buildings facing Magdalen Street, together with adjacent properties were retained and have since been renovated. Both yards (White Lion is now called Hartley's Court) can still be visited today.

Despite the clearance of the properties behind the White Lion it continued to trade as a pub until c.1962. However, for many it will be best remembered as the second home of the Jacquard Club (a jazz music venue). The club was set up by Albert and Tony Cooper in 1971. Over the next seven years it played host to an impressive list of musicians, including George Melly, Ronnie Scott and Stephan Grappelli.

## Woolcombers Arms' Yard (77 Magdalen Street)

Numbers 77 – 85 Magdalen Street used to be a block of three-storey timber-framed Tudor buildings. For many years the small yard lay between two pubs. The Woolcombers' Arms, which lay at number 79 and obviously gave the yard its name, was first licensed c.1840 and traded until 1908 when it was closed 'under compensation'. On the other side was the Rose (also called the White Rose and St Paul's Rose), which similarly started trading in the 1840s, but survived until July 1972 when a fire swept through the upper floors. Unfortunately, so much damage was caused that it was deemed unsafe, and a few weeks later the entire site was cleared.

*White Lion Yard, Magdalen Street, 1936*

*Hartley's Court (White Lion Yard), Magdalen Street, 2014*

*Bayfield's Yard, 57 Magdalen Street, c.1930*

*The entrance to Bayfield's Yard was marked by a Tudor doorway complete with carved spandrels, c.1930*

*Chapel Yard, 31 Botolph Street, 1936*

*Cross Keys' Yard, 104 Magdalen Street, 1938*

*Ling's Court, 49 Magdalen Street, 1937*

*Loose's Yard, 41 Magdalen Street, 1936*

*New Yard, 125 Magdalen Street, 1937*

*White Horse Yard, a thoroughfare leading between 84 Magdalen Street and 13 Botolph Street, 1936*

Despite the difficulties wrought by the building of both the flyover and Anglia Square, Magdalen Street still contains a collection of historic buildings and yards. Add to this some 1930s flats, and the street gives an interesting insight as to how housing has developed and evolved in the City.

Take, for example, Thoroughfare Yard. Originally the yard, as already noted, consisted of a narrow alley which contained very large three-storey houses with basic sanitation. Today, it contains attractive smaller properties, built using modern materials. The modern houses even have access to a communal garden. What does remain is the narrow, almost tunnelled entrance from Magdalen Street: an interesting link with the past.

*Zipfel's Court, 2014*

*Thoroughfare Yard, 2009*

By 1908, Foulger's Yard (144 Magdalen Street) had been renamed Webb's Yard, a name it still retains today. The confined entrance that can be identified on the 1884 map, has been retained, but now leads through to a bright courtyard containing refurbished properties.

A similar narrow passage at 111 Magdalen Street, still leads into Zipfel's Court. The court is named after a family of prestigious watchmakers who first traded on Magdalen Street in the 1830s. It is a bit of a hybrid. The properties adjacent to Magdalen Street and the entrance have been restored and retained, but the buildings at the rear have been demolished, and the area has been remodelled to provide a light airy living space. In the same way, a tunnel-like entrance leads to Twinemakers' Row, a very pretty courtyard development. This used to be Paradise Place (139 Magdalen Street), part of which was demolished in the 1930s.

*Twinemakers' Row, 2009*

*Boswell's Yard containing what was a bombazine factory complete with weavers' windows, 2009*

Unlike the earlier examples, a very wide entrance leads through to Boswell's Yard (24 Magdalen Street). Originally it mainly contained commercial buildings which had a variety of uses. Visiting today, one can clearly see that the top floor of a converted three-storey building in the yard contains weavers' windows (designed to let in the maximum amount of light). These may relate to the time that the building housed a bombazine (twilled fabric used for dresses) factory. In the latter part of the 20th century the buildings were converted for residential use.

Elsewhere, although yards have been totally demolished their names live on in new developments. Originally Cross Keys' Yard was located at 104 Magdalen Street, behind the Cross Keys' pub, which was closed in 1907. The photograph in the photo gallery shows that it was wide and far from airless.

By then it also seems to be the location of the car and cycle park for the Magdalen Street Cinema. The site of the yard is now covered by the EPIC studio, previously the home of Anglia TV. However, a new Cross Keys' Yard is now accessed through 'The Archway' at 120 Magdalen Street. On Fishergate Thompson's Yard may have been demolished but the name was subsequently given to new council flats built in the same vicinity in the 1930s.

Finally, along the street are signs which used to lead to yards, where buildings were demolished many years ago. Examples include Barnes' Yard, 87 Magdalen Street, which now lies under Roy's shop, and Loose's Yard, 41 Magdalen Street, which was demolished in the 1930s. They may be long gone, but the signs ensure they are not forgotten.

*Cross Keys Yard, 2009*

## Many entrances to yards still exist on Magdalen Street (all photos taken in 2009)

Boswell's Yard, 24　　　　　Gurney's Court, 31　　　　　Key and Castle Yard, 120

Hartley's Court
(White Lion Yard), 135　　Abel's Yard (Court), 65　　King's Head Yard, 40　　Thoroughfare Yard, 11

Webb's (Foulger's)Yard, 140　　Two Brewers' Yard,151　　Red Lion Yard, 19　　Twinemakers' Row
(Paradise Place), 139

118

# Poverty and Lawlessness: Cowgate and Pockthorpe

Yards identified in this section of the City include:

**Barrack Street**

- Rock Yard (34, N)
- Nickall's Yard (36, N)
- Say's Yard (40, N)
- Stewardson's Yard (42, N)
- Wrestler's Yard (54, N)
- Dove Yard (62, N)
- Bird in Hand (74, N)
- Griffin Yard (86, N)
- George Yard (92, N)
- Green Yard (96, N)
- Baker's Yard (116, N)
- Butcher's Yard (43, S)
- Mace's Yard (43, S)
- Nickall's Square (63, S)
- St James' Palace Yard (81, S)
- Water Lane (85, S)
- Fairman's Yard (101, S)
- Little Dial Yard (109, S)
- Big Dial Yard (121, S)

- Black Boy Yard (127, S)
- Sportsman's Yard (141, S)
- Seven Stars' Yard (143, S)
- White Horse Yard (147, S)
- Dun Cow Yard (149, S)
- Boddy's Yard (155, S)
- Light Horseman Yard (161, S)

**Bull Close**

- White Entry Yard (15, E)
- Friar's Yard (24, W)

**Bull Close Road**

- Burners' Row (96, E)

**Cowgate**

- Chapel Yard (39, E)
- Finch's Yard (61, E)
- Hartley's Yard (65, E)
- Phoenix Yard (75, E)
- Beckham's Yard (93, E)
- Priory Yard (121, E)

- Factory Yard (141, E)
- Bennett's Yard (100, W)
- Ship Yard (106, W)
- Pestell's Yard (110, W)
- General Windham's Yard (122, W)
- Brigg's Yard (128, W)
- Brettfield's Yard (134, W)
- Gaol Yard (121, E)

**Fishergate**

- Staff of Life Yard (53, N)
- Fleece Yard (63, N)

**Peacock Street**

- Harvey's Yard (21, E)
- Webster's Court (12, W)

> Please note that between 1884 and 1908 St James' Street was merged into Barrack Street. The addresses give the approximate entrance to individual yards based on Kelly's 1908 Directory.

*St James' Street (Barrack Street), c.1900*

Cowgate and
Barrack Street
clearance area

Peacock
Street Section A
clearance area

Bayfield Yard
clearance area

Peacock
Street – Cowgate
redevelopment
area

Peacock
Street Section B
clearance area

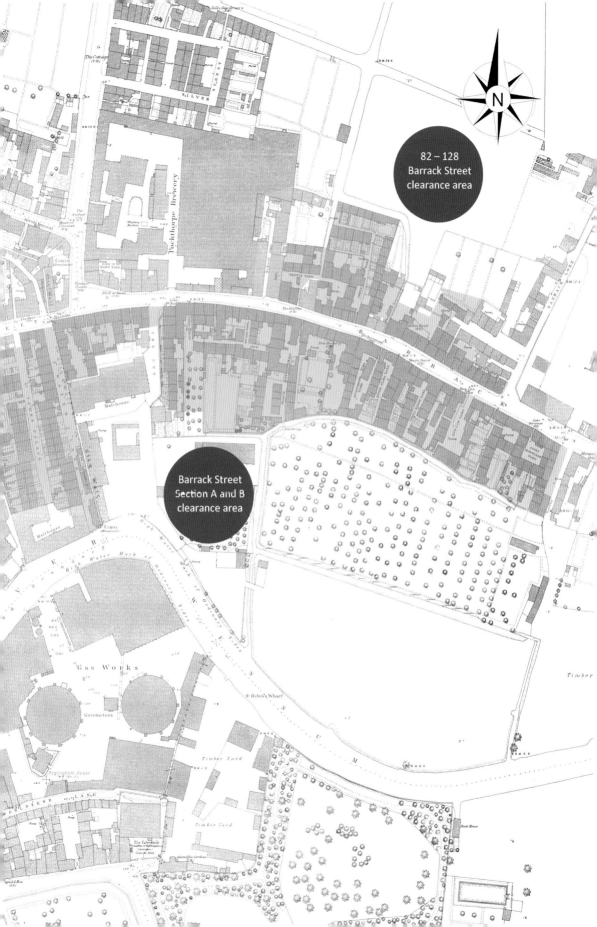

N

82 – 128
Barrack Street
clearance area

Barrack Street
Section A and B
clearance area

# Historical Background

*St Paul's Square with St James' Church in the background, 1962*

This area incorporates parts of the parishes of St James Pockthorpe, St Paul and St Edmund. In William Lee's Report to the General Board of Health (1851) the surgeon responsible for these areas commented: 'My official duties take me among the poorest of the people. The cottages are generally dirty and ill-ventilated and the supply of water is bad.' It was additionally noted that along Cowgate: 'There is no sewer and the semi-fluid refuse is almost stagnant in the rough pebble side-channels of the street for its whole length.' Hochstetter's map, produced in 1789, shows that by the end of the 18th century the area was settled, and that the yards adjacent to properties that lined the street were already being filled with buildings. By the time we reach 1884, this trend is even clearer. The street map clearly shows that yards, particularly those adjacent to pubs, e.g. Griffin Yard, Dun Cow Yard and Seven Stars' Yard (all on Barrack Street), have been populated. In the light of this it is not surprising that in 1898 both Cowgate and Pockthorpe were highlighted by the new Courts and Yards Committee as areas where old yards were rife. This point is particularly illustrated along the combined length of St James' Street and Barrack Street (by 1908 the two roads had merged) where in 1884 some 20 yards led from this one stretch of road.

Contemporary social commentators perceived Pockthorpe (a suburb immediately outside the Pockthorpe Gate to the east of the City) as rough and lawless, C. B. Hawkins going so far as to comment in 1910: 'To a Londoner, accustomed to what Norwich people no doubt refer to as East End slums, it is still something of an adventure to go through the unlighted nooks and corners of Ber Street or Pockthorpe after dark.' It is no wonder that it was rumoured that policemen always went around in pairs.

Two buildings dominated the area. The largest industrial site was occupied by Steward & Patteson's Pockthorpe Brewery, whilst the extensive Cavalry Barracks, later the Nelson Barracks, provided accommodation for 500 men and 340 horses. Unfortunately the latter put a strain on the local infrastructure, as explained in Lee's Report: 'There is a very bad ditch on the outside of Pockthorpe, immediately under the houses...that receives the refuse of those and other houses; it is the same ditch that received refuse from the barracks, containing when full from 200 to 300 persons, and probably 200 horses. The refuse lies stagnant in that ditch for a distance of above a quarter of a mile....Pockthorpe is not lighted or supplied with water. There is a drain

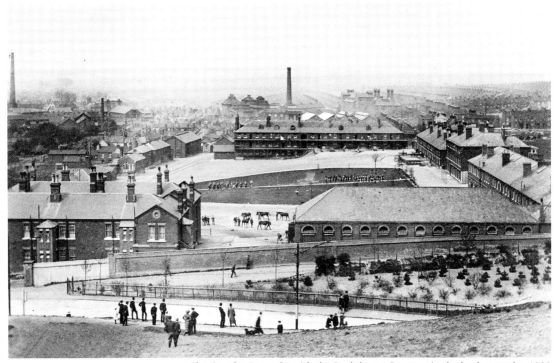

*The Cavalry Barracks with the Pockthorpe Brewery in the background, c.1900*

running through the whole length of it, and passing into the ditch of which I have been speaking. I think that the foul state of the surface in that district, and of the drains is from the want of water.'

Today, as a result of the combined effects of slum clearance, war damage and road widening, very few of the buildings, or even streets, that are shown on the 1884 map remain. Not only are the brewery and barracks no more, Cowgate has been severely shortened, whilst the medieval St Paul's Church was a victim of WWII. Amongst the few recognisable survivors are the medieval church of St James (now the Puppet Theatre) and parts of the City wall; leaving us to rely on memories, photographs, paintings and maps to discover its past.

## The Pockthorpe Guild

Although the residents of Pockthorpe were poor, they had their pride and a strong sense of local identity. They could not see why Norwich should have a mayor and sheriff when they did not. This was rectified in 1772, when the 'Pockthorpe Corporation', also called the 'Pockthorpe Guild', was set up. By the early 19th century the guild was flourishing. Annually, on a day of festivities, a 'Mayor of Pockthorpe', together with a sheriff and officers, was appointed; they even had a 'snapdragon', a reminder of the medieval Guild of St George. The pubs, of which there were many in the area, played an important part in the proceedings. In particular, the Dun Cow Hotel doubled up as the 'Guildhall', and after a sumptuous banquet, participants processed along Barrack Street to take part in 'convivial proceedings and sports' in the gardens behind the Cellar House.

In 1823 when John Patteson was elected Mayor of Norwich the Pockthorpe Guild made a special effort in honour of their distinguished neighbour, after all the Patteson family did own the Pockthorpe Brewery. The games in the Cellar House gardens were particularly splendid. They included wheelbarrow races for blindfolded septuagenarians, to the tune of 'Now Speed Ye Well My Brave Old Boys', and the chance to climb an 80-feet-high greasy pole which apparently commanded an excellent view of Norwich.

Until the 1930s two independent schools operated in this area.

The Anguish School was located at 61 Fishergate. Although officially named after its founder Thomas Anguish (Mayor in 1611), it was more popularly called the 'Bluecoat' or 'Bluebottle' School (the colour of the uniform). The school occupied a house and other property bequeathed by the founder for the education of boys and girls 'who have not friends to help them'. By 1885, the endowment had been redirected, and a 'school of housecraft' had been established for girls, whilst boys received help with secondary education and apprenticeships. Following the instigation of these initiatives the school was closed. The building was included in the 'Peacock Street – Cowgate redevelopment area'.

In 1842 Norman's Endowed School was constructed at the corner of Cowgate and Little Bull Close. The building was financed by an endowment made by Alderman John Norman. His intention was for the school to provide a grammar level of education for both his and his first wife's descendants. By 1933 the number of pupils had fallen, and so the school closed and the name transferred to a new elementary school opened on the Mile Cross Estate. The building has since been demolished (date unknown), although descendants of the Alderman still receive scholarships and other allowances.

*The former Anguish's School, 61 Fishergate, 1935*

*Alderman John Norman School, Cowgate, c.1930*

124

# Major Clearance Schemes

By 1884, in significant contrast to the rest of the area, the streets around St Paul's Church – bounded by Cowgate, Back Lane and St Paul's Street – were comprised of uniform rows of terrace houses separated by a traditional back alley. It was very different some 15 years earlier, when this two-and-a-half-acre site contained some of the worst housing in Norwich, resulting in it being the subject of one of the City's earliest slum-clearance programmes. The scheme ran into a number of difficulties and it eventually cost the Council around £11,000 (approximately £870,000 in today's money) to purchase 144 dwellings from some 38 owners. In White's Directory of 1883 the Council received praise for the scheme: 'A rookery of disgraceful tenements in St Paul's has been demolished under the Artisans' Dwelling Act, and a colony of trim cottages erected in their place.' However, writing some 30 years later it is clear that a Mr F. Hibgame, a local historian, did not share this view: 'The most picturesque square in the whole City at that time [*Norwich Fifty Years Ago*] was St Paul's, which showed a complete square of singularly quaint half-timbered houses. It looked very much then as no doubt it did in medieval times; but alas the jerry builder came along, down came all the old houses and in their place arose dozens of hideous red-brick cottages, all exactly like one another.' It is interesting to note that these arguments, for and against slum clearance, dogged such schemes through the 20th century. We have no images of the original properties, but numbers 25 – 33 Barrack Street bordered the square on the south side, and give some idea of the style of property which was demolished.

It says something about the state of this area that the Priory Yard Estate was one of the few slum-clearance programmes undertaken by the Courts and Yards Committee (See Clearance Case Study 1) and subsequently vast swathes of property were demolished. Areas effected included :

- **Barrack Street**: A combination of schemes in the mid-1930s (see Clearance Case Study 3) followed by the widening of Barrack Street resulted in this area being decimated, and by 1940 Pockthorpe was changed beyond recognition. Literally in one decade the vast majority of yards and older residential properties in this area were annihilated.

*25 – 33 Barrack Street, 1936*

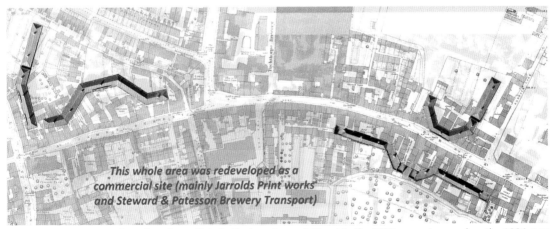

*This whole area was redeveloped as a commercial site (mainly Jarrolds Print works and Steward & Patesson Brewery Transport)*

*Location of new flats built along Barrack Street in the 1930s superimposed on the 1884 map*

- **The area bound by Peacock Street, Barrack Street, Cowgate and Fishergate**: In 1936 plans were afoot to clear the 'Peacock Street – Cowgate redevelopment area'. The subsequent intention was to widen and improve the streets, build 74 council flats and four council houses whilst retaining a selection of commercial premises and public buildings. Although clearance was well underway in 1939, WWII brought a halt to the project; in particular the housing scheme was suspended. Post-war the entire area was designated for industrial use and today it is the site of the vast Norwich Corrugated Board Ltd factory.

In total, interwar clearance schemes undertaken in this section of the City affected around 40 yards, 320 properties and 750 people. They included the clearance and demolition of Palace Yard (called St James' Palace Yard in 1884) which contained some 45 properties and more than 160 tenants making it, by both measures, the largest yard in the City cleared during this period.

Following demolition, in response to public demand, the Council utilised part of the land to build council housing. This mainly took the form of two and three-storey flats. More than 200 such apartments were built on developments around Bull Close, Cowgate and Barrack Street, most of which survive.

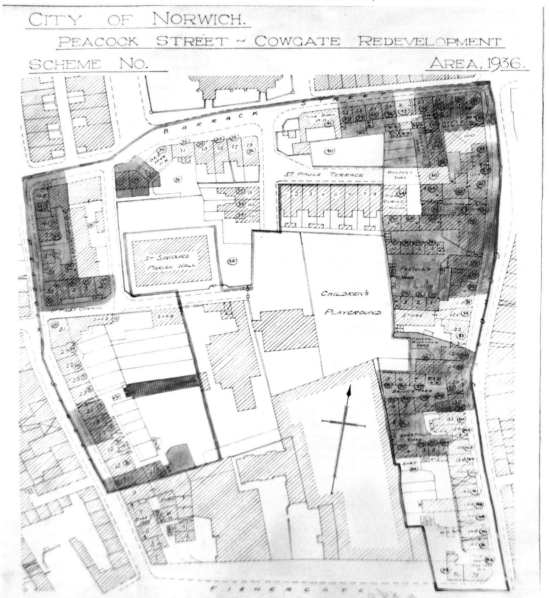

*Plan of the 'Peacock Street - Cowgate redevelopment area', 1936*

# Yards of Note

In 1884 more than 45 yards were located in the area highlighted on the map. There are few photographs of them, but both William Lee and a journalist from the *Norwich Mercury,* visiting in 1851 and 1897 respectively, do provide some vivid descriptions. In the late 19th century yards located in this area included the following:

## Beckham's Yard (93 Cowgate)

This yard featured in William Lee's report. At the time it was noted that the yard had no drainage, nor any water supply, either by pump or tap. Lee visited one dwelling which consisted of a single room for which the rent was 1s. per week. It contained 'only one wretched bed, and scarcely a vestige of furniture' for use by the occupant, his wife and eight children. When the yard was cleared in 1935, as part of the 'Cowgate and Barrack Street clearance scheme', it contained six properties with 18 occupants.

## Bennett's Yard (100 Cowgate)

When visiting in 1897 the *Norwich Mercury* reporter noted that the yard had a narrow entrance and, unusually, was paved. It had two divisions. In the first was a midden and privy whilst the second one seemed 'very cleanly and open'. When it was cleared in 1938, it contained just three properties occupied by six tenants.

## Black Boy Yard (127 Barrack Street)

The yard originally took its name from the Black Boys' pub, which stood near its entrance before losing its licence in 1867. The name is a reference to Dominican friars who wore a black cloak over their white habits, hence the nickname.

In the 1890s the yard was entered by a narrow entrance tunnel some four feet wide and 15 feet in length. It was split into two sections and the *Mercury* journalist was clearly impressed by the drain in the first, which he described as: 'The best drain I have yet seen in Norwich having only been laid down the previous week.'

In 1934/5 the yard was cleared of 14 houses and 36 residents.

*Mid-18th-century Cowgate, with St James' Church, by David Hodgson, painted c.1830*

## Burners' Row, also known as Pipe Burners' Row (96 Bull Close Road)

This was a hotchpotch of buildings, with all the characteristics of an old yard. In 2009, the Norwich Living History Group recorded the memories of Cyril Stamp who was born here in 1926: 'There was one outside tap between each of two houses in the yard and just at the bottom was a wash house and the house itself, that was three rooms on top of each other. There was no kitchen, no bathrooms, no toilets, nothing.' The row was subject to clearance in 1935, when Cyril and his family moved to a parlour house on the Mile Cross Estate, and had the luxury of an inside bath which was located in the kitchen! When not in use the bath was covered by a lid, and it doubled up as a table, but they weren't complaining.

## Dove Yard (62 Barrack Street)

The yard lay adjacent to the Dove public house, which was closed under compensation in 1907. At the time the pub premises were described as being in bad repair whilst the police reported that they found it difficult to supervise. However, maybe surprisingly, the yard itself was spacious and although the entrance looked narrow, uniquely for the district, it was uncovered overhead. In 1897, the privies, midden and drains were all in 'good condition'. It was cleared in 1935.

## Fairman's Yard (101 Barrack Street)

This was a small yard with a narrow entrance. Joyce Wilson, who lived in the yard in the 1930s, recalls it was 'quite pleasant'. There were only two houses in the yard, which meant that her family only had to share the loo, which was 10 yards from the house, with one other household. The only water supply came from a pump in the yard. Joyce's house was below pavement level which made it very dark; it consisted of three rooms on three floors, although the top room was only a small garret it provided welcome extra space.

Inside the facilities were very basic: 'The only light we had was a gas bracket on the wall in the living room. The mantle was always blowing out and we had to run across the road to buy another one which cost one penny. In the bedrooms there were no lights whatsoever. We used to carry up a candle or night light in a saucer. Our heating was one little black fireplace in the living room. Of course in the wintertime there was often ice on the inside of the window panes. The other thing, being so damp, so old and so cramped the white-plaster walls in the bedroom gave off a strange smell. It was almost like almonds. Later on I found out it was the bugs in the wall; I suppose that the soft plaster was a haven for them.'

The yard was demolished c.1935.

## George Yard (92 Barrack Street)

The yard was named after the George & Dragon public house. Despite the pub closing in 1869 the name was retained.

The seven properties in the yard were demolished in 1936.

*Entrance to George Yard, Barrack Street, 1936*

## General Windham's Yard (122 Cowgate)

The yard took its name from the neighbouring public house which traded here from around 1857 to 1908. In 1897 the *Mercury* reporter seemed reasonably impressed and observed: 'Seems cleaner and better than many and is the most airy yet visited while the midden and privies are unusually removed from the houses. The entrance passage is narrow. The yard is partly cobbled paved and the inhabitants have piped water. A respectable garden, mainly taken up with dog kennels and a henhouse, is at the rear.'

*General Windham's Yard, Cowgate, c.1938*

## Nickall's Square which became Priory Square (63 Barrack Street)

In the early 1960s an entrance located in the vicinity of 63 Barrack Street led to Priory Square which, as far as we can tell, was made up of houses which previously formed part of Nickall's Square. In the early 20th century, Nickall's Square had been included in the Priory Yard Estate and destined for demolition. However, plans had been abandoned and what remained was renamed Priory Square (see Clearance Case Study 1).

Dorothy Dugdale remembers the area well: 'My husband's family lived in Priory Square, along Barrack Street. I first visited there around 1944. You'd pass a fish shop and Mr Cannell's butcher's shop [71 – 75 Barrack Street] and then you'd come across a narrow passage leading to a yard. You'd turn left and see a house which I was always told belonged to a Mrs Willis [65 Barrack Street], then I came to my mother-in-law's house. When I knew it, it was quite a nice little house. There was an inside toilet and bathroom. It was rather unusual to me as all of the rooms fronted onto the square. They always said that when they papered the back wall, they were papering on sack, not a properly plastered wall. It had two "front doors", and so you could go upstairs and nobody knew you were there, or you could go in the other door and walk through the downstairs rooms until you again came to the stairs. Possibly it used to be two separate flats. It was convenient for my sister-in-law to creep in when she came home late from a night out. There were houses around all three sides of the square; they all had little gardens. My father-in-law had a greenhouse in his where he grew grapes. The Priory Gym was at the end of the gardens.'

## Pestell's Yard (110 Cowgate)

In the late 19th century the yard consisted of three sections. In 1897, the journalist from the Norwich *Mercury* seemed almost relieved to report on something other than drains, paving and middens, when he noted: 'Sundry hens were wandering about, a baby was screaming, and a lady was warbling (not very sweetly) of a maiden who dwelt by the riverside.'

In 1938, 47 tenants were cleared from 13 properties.

*Pestell's Yard, Cowgate, 1938*

## Ship Yard (106 Cowgate)

*Fastolf's House, 106 Cowgate, 1936*

Ship Yard was situated to the rear of a 15th-century building, part of the Norwich home of Sir John Fastolf.

Sir John, whose family owned Caister Castle, was a knight in the 100 Years' War and is believed to have been the prototype for Shakespeare's character, Sir John Falstaff. Francis Bloomefield (1795 – 1752), the historian, records visiting the property early in the 18th century: 'His [Fastolf's] great hall is now a baking office; the bow-window is adorned with the images of St Margaret, St John the Baptist in his garment of camel's hair, the Virgin Mary, St Blase holding a wool comb, and St Catherine. In a large north window are ten effigies of great warriors and chiefs, as David, Sampson, Hercules etc., holding bows, swords and halberds etc., ornaments suitable to the taste of so great a warrior as Sir John was.'

Between 1830 and 1907, 106 Cowgate was the home of the Ship public house, which gave the yard its name. In 1906 the Chief Constable objected to the renewal of the Ship's licence. It is sad to think that by then this once great house was registered as a common lodging house with 16 beds. As there were 15 other licensed premises within 200 yards, the premises was considered superfluous to requirements and it was closed under compensation in 1907.

In 1897, the *Mercury* reporter visited the yard. He noted it had three houses, was paved and the houses were 'not bad', although he did observe an open drain

'full of liquid matter'. The yard was cleared in 1938. At this time it contained four dwellings occupied by 16 individuals.

Along with the adjoining Ship Yard, the property was caught up in the 'Peacock Street – Cowgate redevelopment area' and was demolished *c.*1939.

*Entrance to Ship Yard, Cowgate,1938*

## Sportsman's Yard (141 Barrack Street)

This is another of the many yards in the area which derived its name from the adjacent pub. In 1897 the *Mercury* journalist entered the yard through a narrow tunnel and along a passageway of similarly narrow width, which together amounted to some 40 feet. The yard itself was paved with cobbles, and its six (maybe seven) properties were serviced by two privies and one midden; the filth and sewage were described as terrible. Conditions were probably worsened by the fact that the properties were: 'One-room tenements (furnished), generally let to members of the travelling fraternity, hawkers and the like, here today and gone tomorrow.'

In 1933, clearance records prepared by the Council show that the seven properties were occupied by 23 adults and nine children. Number 3, a one-up one-down property, was occupied by William Seeley, an unemployed wherryman, his wife and five children. To gain much-needed extra space the family sub-let an additional bedroom at number 6. They were hoping to be moved to a four-bedroomed property. Henry Olley, who rented both 4 and 5 Sportsman's Yard, for himself, wife and four children, was similarly unemployed, and obviously didn't think much of his neighbours, as council records indicate that after clearance he wanted 'to get away from other tenants in Sportsman's Yard'.

The yard was demolished *c.1934.*

# A Walk Down Memory Lane with Philip Armes

*Cowgate looking towards St James' Church, 1938*

'When I was a boy I lived with my family at 117 Cowgate in one of the letting properties originally owned by my grandfather. It was scheduled for compulsory purchase in the 1930s, when it was part of the City's slum-clearance programme.

'Our house was a three-storey building. Next door was empty, it had a room on the top floor which had very big windows; I've got an idea that it was used by weavers who worked at home and needed a lot of light for their work. After my grandmother died her three boys came to live with us. So in our house were my two sisters and myself, my mum and dad and my three uncles, and so it was a bit cramped. When you went out the front door there wasn't a garden, but for some reason there was a step that led straight onto the pavement. Both Scales, the grocery shop next door, and the rag-and-bone shop next to it had steps in as well. There was a difference in the level of the house from the front to the back. Downstairs we had a front room, a back room where we had an old-fashioned fireplace with an oven at the side. Although we didn't have a kitchen we did have a scullery with a butler's sink and a copper which mum used to do her washing on a Monday. We had a very small garden at the back. Next door was empty, the back wall was bulging, and so it was shored up with timbers.

'My mother worked hard in the house. She bought us up and also looked after her three stepbrothers. I don't think she saw it as a particularly hard life, I think then you were more accepting of what you had. Later when we moved to Bull Close Road she took in washing; when the weather was bad she used to hang it out across the living room to dry.

'We lived next to Scales [119], a little grocery shop. The thing I still remember quite clearly, is on a Sunday in the summer time they made ice cream to sell. I can see them now churning the ice-cream in the back yard. Of course they always had a cat sitting in the shop's front window, they never seemed to show any products in that window. Instead a representative from the Imperial Tobacco Company would come with loads of flat cigarette cartons. He'd set them all up with a little tube of glue and pins and he'd make a wonderful display of Players or Goldflake packets, and these would occupy most of the window. They'd stay there for weeks, then he'd come along, take down the old display and put up another one. I imagine they had some income from that.

'Mrs Porter across the road, opposite us, was a widow. She had a convenience store [110] where she sold everything. I always remember a leg of ham on the counter; it was there all day long. we didn't have refrigeration in those days. She even sold elastic by the length. She'd measure it against a brass ruler attached to the front of the counter, we always joked that when she measured it she used to stretch it a bit! On a Saturday the cattle came through Cowgate on the way to the market in the centre of the City. Mrs Porter had two doors in the front of the shop and it was quite common when they were open in the summer time that a cow would poke its head through the door and come half way in. She just took it in her stride.

'At 118 Cowgate there was Flowerdew's fish and chip shop. In those days the common order was a "two and a one", which was tuppence worth of fish and a penny helping of chips. Then came Wards, a shoe repairer. Going up the street was Cable the dairyman [136]. He had a large container of milk on the counter, he didn't seem to have much else in the shop. He went out delivering milk, but also people came into the shop with a jug and he'd ladle the milk into it – it wasn't in bottles. Jex was the greengrocers [138]. Then on the other side to the entrance of Jarrolds' print works was another shop also owned by Mrs Porter [143], but run by her daughter. It also sold cigarettes and sweet, but being next to the print works it was a little goldmine.

'There was a rag-and-bone man's shop on Cowgate Street, run by a Mr Cullum. I can still smell the dusty sacks I associate with him. He used to give sixpence for a rabbit skin – which wasn't bad.

'I remember visiting Ship Yard [106], it seemed to me that nobody lived there, but I can quite definitely remember once seeing a man slaughtering a pig. He poleaxed it, shoved something into his brain, slit its throat, squeezed it to get the blood out and then scrubbed it in one of those huge galvanised washtubs that all of the women had. I think his name was Bridges.

'I can clearly recall crossing a yard near to Blackfriars' Bridge which had a communal wash and toilet area in the middle. Once when I was walking across I heard a girl shout across the yard: "Mum, I want a piece of paper to wipe my bum!" I think water was laid on. We had water at number 117, and so I imagine it would be flush.

'I remember playing with my friends in Brigg's Yard [128] and Pestell's Yard [110], which were near us. The girls always wanted to get a concert together. One of them said I could be a cowboy, and so I went back home and told my mum who made me a felt hat. We always made our own entertainment. Another thing we always knocked up was a den.

*Playing cowboys, Philip Armes (top right), c.1935*

'We used to play on the street. It was quite safe because there was very little traffic and mum would be in the back room. When a horse and cart came through some of the more adventurous boys would try and get a ride on the back axle. The other thing I can recall is the water cart coming along on a hot summer's day. It was a waggon with sprays out of the back, a bit like an agricultural fertiliser, it was meant to lay the dust and stop it blowing around. It didn't do much good, but as kids we loved to run in and out the cold spray. Those were the days!'

*Bradfield's (Brettfield's) Yard, 134 Cowgate, 1938*

*Robert and Elizabeth Frewer with their son William in the Fountain (Shell) Garden, c.1875*

It is hard to imagine that this wonderful garden was located in one of the poorest and most notorious areas of Norwich. Known as either the Fountain or Shell Garden, it was the creation of Robert Frewer. Jenny Sumser-Lumpson, Robert's great-great-granddaughter, takes up the story: 'Robert and his family were based in Brandon where he worked as a flint knapper. As the trade died out he moved to London and entered the shoe industry. He eventually moved back to Norwich to work at Southalls and found a house in St James Palace Yard, better known as Palace Yard, off Barrack Street.'

*The Fountain (Shell) Garden visible on the 1884 OS map*

Containing around 45 houses, Palace Yard was one of the largest yards in the City. As elsewhere, residents shared inadequate washing and toilet facilities. Houses were crammed together; in fact, this was one of the few places in Norwich containing back-to-backs. Despite such conditions, Robert created this delightful garden decorated with mollusc shells in the area behind number 18. Jenny explains: 'I think the shells came from a fish shop on Barrack Street, possibly George Ramsay's who traded at number 62. My great aunt used to tell of people coming from miles around to see the garden.'

It is remarkable that the layout of the garden, which can be clearly seen in the photograph taken in the early 1870s, matches the outline on the 1884 map. Sadly, in 1912 the garden was swept away in the floods which devastated the City. Luckily the photograph survives; it is a testament to Robert's creative ability and determination. A reminder that many yard dwellers may have been forced to live in poverty, but they took pride in their homes.

133

Today, apart from the 19th-century terrace houses around St Paul's very little survives of the old houses and yards which characterised this area at the beginning of the 20th century.

Almost all that remains of the housing that once dominated the landscape is a cobbled entrance that once led into one of the largest yards in the City, Palace Yard (also known as St James' Palace Yard) and the opening to Water Lane (also known as River Lane).

Although we can decry the loss of so much history, we should not forget that as a result of slum clearance many people had the opportunity to improve their living standards almost beyond recognition. As local journalist, Jonathan Mardle observed: 'You can photograph picturesque streets...but you cannot photograph smells...the effluvium of the tannery that pervaded Barrack Street. These were superimposed upon the characteristic smell of the yards themselves – a smell like stale cabbage, that was compounded of overcrowded humanity, bad drainage, and the row of privies that served all the families in the yard.'

*Former entrance to Palace Yard, 81 Barrack Street, 2014*

*67 – 79 Barrack Street, amongst the few properties on Barrack Street that survived the 1930s, 2014*

# Pubs, Shops and Churches: St Benedict's Street and Pottergate

Yards identified in this section of the City include :

**Lower Westwick Street**

- Waterman's Yard (52, N)
- Holmes Yard (58, N)
- Cowling's Yard (68, N)
- Barker's Yard (72, N)
- Little Eagle Yard (108, N)
- Eagle Yard (112, N)
- Peel's Yard (69, S)
- Pipe Yard (75, S)
- Alefounder's Yard (83, S)

**Pottergate**

- Cott's Yard (21, N)
- Cook's Court (25, N)
- Whiting's Yard (43, N)
- Baker's Yard (57, N)
- Playford's Court (65, N)
- Bagley's Court (6, S)
- Wood Entry Yard (34, S)

**St Benedict's Alley**

- Jermy's Yard (1, W)
- Neale's Square (16, W)

**St Benedict's Street**

- Self's Yard (33, N)
- Queen of Hungary Yard (47, N)
- Reeve's Yard (49, N)
- Beehive Yard (65, N)
- Crown Yard (71, N)
- Mulberry Yard (77, N)
- Fountain Yard (85, N)
- Brown's Yard (4, S)
- Lord Howe's Yard (6, S)
- Green's Yard (8, S)
- Gaffer's Yard (20, S)
- Hannant's Yard (24, S)
- Turner's Court (30, S)
- Prince of Wales' Yard (32, S)
- School Yard (36, S)
- Grigg's Yard (40, S)
- Three Kings' Yard (44, S)
- Little Plough Yard (56, S)
- Plough Yard (58, S)
- Hinde's Yard (70, S)
- Cardinal's Cap Yard (84, S)

- Adam and Eve Yard (88,S)
- White Lion Yard (104, S)
- Little White Lion Yard (108, S)
- Griffin's Court (114, S)

**St Swithin's Alley**

- Hampshire Hog Yard (10, W)
- Clarke Yard (20, E)

**Ten Bell Lane**

- Trowse Yard (14, E)
- Browne's Court (18, E)

**Three King Lane**

- Hipper's Yard (1, W)

**Wellington Lane**

- Wellington Square (20, E)

Between 1884 and 1908 Lower Westwick Street was renamed Westwick Street. House numbers were unchanged.

On St Benedict's Street, house numbers changed at the end of the 19th century when part of the thoroughfare was demolished to accommodate trams. All house numbers relate to 1908.

*Holmes Yard, 58 Westwick Street, c.1930*

Westwick Street and St Benedict's clearance area

Neale's Square and 104 – 113 Pottergate clearance area

Ten Bell Lane St Benedict's clearance area

Three King Lane St Benedict's clearance area

Self's Yard
St Benedict's
clearance area

Playford's
Court and St
Lawrence School
Yard
clearance area

St
Lawrence
Lane St Benedict's
clearance area

Pump Yard
Pottergate
clearance area

# Historical Background

In days gone by Norwich was said to have 'a church for every week and a pub for every day of the year'. If anybody thought this an exaggeration (it was actually an understatement) one look at this area would disabuse them. Here you would have found around 30 pubs and five medieval churches. In fact the name of the Ten Bell's pub (78 Pottergate) is believed to allude to the fact that at one time you could stand on this stretch of street and clearly hear the bells from ten different churches. During the 19th century St Swithin's Lane, which joins Pottergate to St Benedict's Street and lies adjacent to the pub, was renamed Ten Bell Lane. Similarly a number of yards take their names from neighbouring hostelries, including Queen of Hungary Yard (47 St Benedict's Street), Waterman's Yard (52 Westwick Street) and Cardinal's Cap Yard (84 St Benedict's Street).

This area's links with beer and alcohol extended to producing it, and amongst the breweries located here was Bullard & Sons' massive Anchor Brewery. As early as 1837 the brewery had been established in premises near St Miles' Bridge. It was subsequently extended and by the end of the 19th century covered seven acres. The site was ideal for brewing not only because it was adjacent to the river but also because it was built over an artesian well dug deep in the chalk under the brewery. The water from the well was of a very high quality which gave the beer its excellent flavour. As late as 1960 Bullards was one of the City's leading companies, but in 1963 it was taken over by Watney Mann and in 1966 the *Eastern Evening News* announced that brewing was to cease. In 1972 the

## St Benedict's Street

St Benedict's Street (often known simply as St Benedict's) has been a principal thoroughfare since medieval times. For many years it was known as Upper Westwick Street, but in the mid-18th century it was rechristened after the medieval church of St Benedict's. The body of the church was destroyed during the Baedeker air raids in 1942, although the distinctive round tower has survived.

*St Benedict's Church, 1934*

site was sold and it is now a residential development known as Anchor Quay.

Although not renowned in the same way as Barrack Street for having poor-quality housing, it is clear from the 1884 map that in this section of the City numerous yards were slotted behind properties lining the main

*Charing Cross towards St Benedict's Street, c.1900*

*Bomb damaged Westwick Street, 1942*

streets. They were typical of the old yards found throughout Norwich, as recalled by Joan Banger who visited here as a girl in the 1930s: 'When I went up St Benedict's I can remember women standing in the narrow entrances that led to the yards. They had their arms folded and were chatting away. I suppose it was because the sun would never shine beyond where they stood. So they would come out for a little air. Sometimes people were inclined to laugh at them because they looked so dirty and the women used to swear back.'

Back in 1851, William Lee included descriptions of two yards from this area in his report to the Board of Health. In Bailey's Yard (West Pottergate, exact location unknown) he discovered: '16 houses have only two privies, and they are under the bedroom of two houses. The tenants adjoining the privies complained much of the stench.' Meanwhile he reported that in Armes' Yard (St Benedict's Street, exact location unknown) amongst the houses was 'an establishment for bones and rags...the bones contained a large quantity of animal matter'.

Although during the 1930s numerous clearance schemes took place in this area, in general, as can be seen on the map, the properties fronting the street were excluded from demolition. Sadly, the Luftwaffe were not as understanding and during WWII this section of the City was badly bombed. In particular parts of both Westwick Street and St Benedict's Street were ravaged.

Despite these twin assaults, along St Benedict's Street and Pottergate many older buildings have survived. In particular, with the exception of St Benedict's, the medieval churches are largely intact, and although no longer used for worship, they still play a vibrant role in the community. As regards the yards, with a few exceptions, the original buildings have been demolished. However, what really stands out, especially along St Benedict's Street, are the number of named entrances to old yards which together with the churches and 'new yards' give a unique atmosphere to this part of the City.

## Pottergate

The name, which literally means street of potters, derives from its early association with pottery works. Saxon kilns excavated here date from before the Norman invasion (1066). Despite the trade not being practised in the City after 1300, the name has endured.

*Pottergate, 2014*

# Major Clearance Schemes

During the 1930s, more than 100 buildings in around 17 yards were cleared and demolished in this section of the City. As a result, more than 260 residents were displaced, with the vast majority moving to newly built council houses. Although the buildings in yards were demolished, the main thoroughfares remained largely unchanged: then came WWII.

In her book, 'Norwich at War', Joan Banger describes, in the words of an observer, some of the devastation wreaked during the Baedeker raids which took place in April 1942 (the bracketed numbers refer to addresses on St Benedict's Street which are given where known): 'But it is at the junction of Grapes Hill and St Benedict's Street that your eyes for a few seconds cannot accept the scene. The area of St Benedict's Gates has been torn from its foundations – the whole cross-road section is one enormous crater – gone are the premises of Bretts' the antique furniture dealers [75], the 18th-century posting tavern, the Fountain public house [89], Ashworth & Pike the bakers [87], the St Benedict's Post Office [85], Vittell's the grocers and Hicks the fishmonger [79]. Sections of the City wall are intact but stand perilously near to the crater. St Benedict's Church...has only one wall left standing, but the tower, apart from large holes torn in its side, is still standing. You walk up St Benedict's Street towards the City and see further devastation. The Crown [71], the Stag [65], and the Cardinal's Cap [86] are severely damaged and some eight houses have been totally destroyed, and as far as the eye can see there is no glass in any window-frame.'

*Junction of Grapes Hill and St Benedict's Street from Barn Road, 1942*

# Yards of Note

This section of Norwich was filled with yards. Entrances could be found on the main thoroughfares and also from the narrow lanes and alleys, such as Three King Lane. Yards of particular interest include the following:

## Cardinal's Cap Yard (84 St Benedict's Street)

*Cardinal's Cap pub and entrance to the yard, 1936*

The yard took the name of the adjacent pub which was so-called in honour of Cardinal Wolsey, who visited Norwich in 1517 and again in 1520, when he was accompanied by Queen Catherine of Aragon. The pub was badly damaged during the Baedeker raids in April 1942, although it continued to trade until 1960. The pub building has been renovated and the original yard entrance now gives access to a parking area.

*Cardinal's Cap Yard, 1937*

## Hampshire Hog Yard (10 St Swithin's Alley)

*9 – 10 St Swithin's Alley, 1938*

Unsurprisingly, the yard took its name from the nearby public house, which is assumed to derive from a poem by Drayton which contains the unusual line: 'Hampshire long hath had the terms of hogs.'

In the late 19th century the pub's landlord was the boxer John 'Licker' Pratt (1825 – 1903). In 1850 John had beaten the celebrated boxer Jem Mace, who later became the middleweight champion of England, in a memorable bare-knuckle fight that lasted over two hours. The Hampshire Hog's other claim to fame is that it was the last pub in Norwich, and possibly East Anglia, where logats, which was similar to skittles or 'Aunt Sally', was played.

From the clearance map produced in 1937 the yard looks to have been quite spacious. It contained eight houses, which appear to have had gardens. Over 1937/38 it was cleared of 21 residents and demolished. Numbers 9 and 10 St Swithin's Alley, which stood near the entrance to the yard, were saved. In 1975 these 17th-century properties were restored as one unit by the Norwich Preservation Trust. It is one of the few ancient buildings within the old City walls which has retained its thatched roof.

*9 – 10 St Swithin's Alley, 2014*

## Hipper's Yard (1 Three King Lane):

*East side of Three King Lane, 1936*

Hipper's Yard was very typical of an old Norwich yard. The clearance map, drawn up in 1934, clearly illustrates how it was crammed into a tiny space behind houses directly on St Benedict's Street. The houses along one side of the yard faced Three King Lane, itself an excessively narrow thoroughfare, whilst on the other they overlooked Little Plough Yard. Muriel Chilvers knew the yard well in the 1930s: 'My grandmother [Harriet Lansdell] lived at number 2 Three King Lane. Her house was located on one side of Hipper's Yard. She lived in four rooms. There was no water inside the house, to get water she used a communal tap and also shared a communal toilet in Hipper's Yard, which was a big wide yard. The one thing I think was marvellous was despite such limited basic facilities, nearly everyone who lived in the main yard took in washing. Just think what you had to do just to earn a few pennies? One of her neighbours was a little old lady called Mrs Powell, for some reason we all called her Nanny Powley....The house where she lived with her husband was even more of a slum than my grandmother's, not because she was dirty, but because her house had nothing. She didn't even have a gas light; the house was lit by an oil lamp which she kept in the middle of the table. I can't recall that she had anything to cook on, she lived next door to her daughter, a Mrs Cann, and so possibly they shared something.'

The area was cleared in 1935 and the properties demolished in 1936. George Plunkett's photograph (above) was taken after Harriet's house had been knocked down. It gives an impression of how claustrophobic Three King Lane would have been when the properties on the west side, which made up one side of Hipper's Yard, were still standing.

## Neale's Square (16 St Benedict's Alley)

*Muriel (left) with her cousin Lennie, 1927*

From the map Neale's Square appears to be spacious with a number of houses even having gardens.

Muriels Chilvers visited the yard in the 1930s: 'My Aunt Mabel [Mrs Palgrave] lived in Neale's Square, between St Benedict's and Pottergate; you got there from St Benedict's Alley. I can remember being horrified when I visited in the 1930s, because it was so different to my house in Ripley Close [off Elizabeth Fry Road]. My cousins' house consisted of two rooms, one room down and one up. I admit that they were quite big rooms, but in the bedroom there was one double bed where three sons slept, one single bed for the eldest daughter, one cot for the recently born baby and one double bed for mum and dad. There was a reasonably large space outside and a communal wash house which was shared with the neighbours, and so you had to sort out your wash day with them. The water supply and toilets were in the yard, and were also shared.'

Although Muriel's family lived in cramped conditions, overcrowding was not endemic. Clearance registers show that in 1937 (when residents were moved out) 69 people occupied 22 properties. The yard was demolished in 1938.

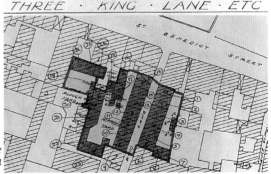

*Plan of the 'Three King Lane Etc. clearance area', 1934*

## Plough Yard and Little Plough Yard (58 and 56 St Benedict's Street)

*Plough Yard, St Benedict's Street, undoted*

The entrances to these two yards are located at either side of the Plough public house which can trace its licence back to 1822. The main pub building, which fronts directly onto St Benedict's Street, dates from the 17th century, when it was a merchant's house. The entrance to Little Plough Yard is integrated into the main building, and led into the courtyard of the original house. The opening to Plough Yard is much wider and would have been for horse-drawn vehicles. According to Nikolaus Pevsner (the architectural historian) the flint rear wing, which still runs at right angles to St Benedict's Street, pre-dates the main building, and was built in the 16th century.

Little Plough Yard was cleared of its three properties and 11 residents in 1935 and demolished the following year (at the same time as Hipper's Yard). The site of the yard is now the location of the pub's beautiful beer garden.

By 1937 the main buildings in Plough Yard appear to have been demolished. The yard itself has survived, where the 16th-century wing with its impressive eleven-light mullioned window can still be seen.

## Trowse Yard (14 Ten Bell Lane)

This small yard could have been named after Christopher Trowse, a tailor, who is recorded as living at 14 Ten Bell Lane in Kelly's 1908 Directory.

John Curson recalls visiting the yard in the 1930s: 'Years ago if you lived in a six-roomed house, and maybe fell on hard times you'd let two of the rooms and give use of the kitchen, that's how my uncles lived on Trowse Yard. They rented a little living room and bedroom and shared the kitchen. They didn't have their own furniture. In the bedroom they had a double bed, a wardrobe and a wash table with a jug. Everything was very basic, but they were always spotless. When they came to visit us on a Friday night, my uncles were always sparklingly clean. The facilities weren't there, but the effort was. We lived on Northumberland Street, where we had our own toilet, but on Trowse Yard they had a communal toilet stuck in the middle of the yard. I think there were two toilets and a wash house and it was up to the people who lived there to keep them clean.'

Trowse Yard was cleared of five houses and 13 residents 1938/39. Demolition is believed to have been completed by 1940.

## Wellington Square (20 Wellington Lane)

The square was described in William Lee's 1851 report when he noted: 'The cottages look comfortable as they have gardens at the front. However, the back premises of the houses are not more than three-or-four feet wide, and those I inspected hemmed in with high buildings. I examined the privy cesspools and found them very offensive. There is no drainage whatever, and, as the ground is inclined, the houses on the lower side of the square suffer.'

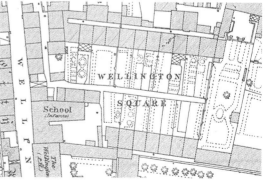

*Plan of Wellington Square, 1884*

# Muriel Chilvers remembers St Benedict's Street in the 1930s

'I particularly remember coming out of Three King Lane and turning right down St Benedict's. After passing Green's, which was an upmarket gent's outfitters [42 and 44], you'd come to a special sort of butcher's called the British & Argentine Meat Co. Ltd [40]. As far as I could make out, it didn't sell anything else apart from English or Argentine beef and so if you wanted pork you went to Thirkettle's [29].

'Moores, on the other side of the road [21-23], were drapers and sold all sorts of things like clothes, curtains and linen. Jarvis's [55], sold similar things, but they were bigger. You almost went into the shop then you turned a corner and there was another little alley with an arcade – we thought it very posh.

'The baker's shop was called Lemmon. They were on the corner with St Benedict's Alley [96]. On Sundays, families in the St Benedict's lanes and yards that didn't have cooking facilities used to take their meat and potatoes in baking trays to Lemmons, to be cooked in ovens there.

'The number of pubs along St Benedict's always fascinated me. My mother worked in a pub until she was married. It was the Fountain [89]. My Aunt Mabel cleaned at the next but one pub up, the Stag. There was a pub every three or four shops. My father didn't have a lot of money but on a Saturday night he'd have his *Pink 'Un* delivered, and so he was happy and quite prepared to stay home and look after me whilst my mother went to visit grandma in Three King Lane. He'd give her a shilling which was enough to pay for her bus fare and two glasses of stout at the Three Kings [46].'

*Muriel's parents, George and Ida Pratt, 1924*

*Aunt Mabel, c.1935*

*St Benedict's Street, c.1935*

# Photo Gallery of the Yards on St Benedict's Street and Westwick Street

*Alefounder's Yard, 83 (Lower) Westwick Street, 1937*

*Beehive Yard, 65 St Benedict's Street, 1937*

*Gaffer's Yard, 20 St Benedict's Street, c.1910*

*Hannant's Yard, 24 St Benedict's Street, 1937*

*Little Plough Yard, 56 St Benedict's Street, 1938*

*Little White Lion Yard, 108 St Benedict's Street, 1937*

*Peel's Yard, 69 (Lower) Westwick Street, 1937*

*Pipe Yard, 75 (Lower) Westwick Street, 1937*

*Queen of Hungary Yard, 47 St Benedict's Street, 1937*

*Reeve's Yard, 49 St Benedict's Street, 1936*

*St Lawrence School Yard, 36 St Benedict's Street, c.1910*

*Self's Yard, 33 St Benedict's Street, 1937*

*Turner's Court, 30 St Benedict's Street, 1937*

*Waterman's Yard, 52 (Lower) Westwick Street, 1937*

*White Lion Yard, 104 St Benedict's Street, 1936*

# The Yards Today

St Benedict's Street is still lined with numerous openings, often intriguingly named. Some lead to ancient yards now renovated, others lead to new yards containing modern buildings, many lead... nowhere.

Take for example the short distance between St Swithin's and St Margaret de Westwick Churches. The first opening, Reeve's Yard, leads to the Norwich Arts Centre. Although the Queen of Hungary pub hasn't traded since 1913, the neighbouring yard bearing its name has survived. The ten properties at the far end of this yard were demolished in 1939, but it is still possible to reproduce George Plunkett's 1937 photo taken inside the yard looking back at the entrance (below). Although the 'cricket stumps' are no more, the location is still clearly recognisable. On the other side of the road the entrances to Little Plough Yard and Plough Yard, with its 16th-century building, still flank the Plough public house. Further along, at number 70, a narrow gated entrance indicates the location of Hinde's Yard.

Modern courts along St Benedict's Street include Woolgate Court and Maude Gray Court. The latter hit the headlines in 1987 when *Eastern Evening News* readers were asked: 'Who is Maude Gray?' Suggestions put forward ranged from an American Liberator bomber to a ghost. Eventually Mike Fox, who developed the yard, solved the mystery when he explained: 'I couldn't think of a name until I was talking to a friend one day and suddenly realised her name was Gray and her dog was called Maude...it was as simple as that.'

In contrast few entrances to old yards remain on Pottergate. One of the exceptions is Playford's Court, although little survives of the original buildings which were demolished in 1935. Modern developments include Colman Court, which incorporates Colman House. In its long history this Georgian property has housed many organisations, including the Norwich Sports Club and the shoe manufacturers Shingler & Thetford. Further along, Damocles Court, is a new 1970s development in the vicinity of what was Wellington Square. Interestingly, like an old yard, this attractive development is located behind ancient buildings, namely 98 – 104 Pottergate, all of which are listed properties. However, the design is miles removed from its predecessors; 19th-century cottages have been combined with modern buildings to create an attractive space in the heart of the City.

*Colman House, Pottergate, 2012*

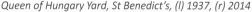

*Queen of Hungary Yard, St Benedict's, (l) 1937, (r) 2014*

*The former Queen of Hungary pub, St Benedict's, 2009*

The old yards which lay on Westwick Street have long since been demolished. In the early 20th century those lying between Westwick Street and the River Wensum would have suffered from their proximity to the waterway. In particular they would have experienced increased dampness and been badly affected by the disease and smells generated by the river. Today, as a result of improved sanitation and building regulations, such problems have been rectified. Of course, a riverside location is now a desirable one and Westwick Street is the home of several modern residential developments, including the conversion of the old Bullard's Brewery and a modern Waterman's Yard, located in a similar vicinity to its predecessor.

Interestingly many of these attractive, airy new complexes are built as cul-de-sacs around courtyards, but, we are very glad to say, this is where the resemblance to the old yards ends.

*Waterman's Yard, Westwick Street, 2015*

*Bullard's old Anchor Brewery is now the site of Anchor Quay, 2015*

*Brown's Yard, 4*　　　*Gaffer's Yard, 20*　　　*Hinde's Yard, 70*

*Little Plough Yard, 56*　　　*Lord Howe's Yard, 6*　　　*Maude Gray Court, 25*

*Plough Yard, 58*　　　*Turner's Court, 30*　　　*Woolgate Court, 55*

# Georgian Norwich: Bethel Street and St Giles

Yards identified in this section of the City include:

## Bethel Street
- Blazeby's Yard (26, N)
- Jay's Court (30, N)
- Austin's Yard (21, S)
- Bell Yard (27, S)
- Coach and Horses Yard (51, S)
- Watts' Court (55, S)
- Master's Court (63, S)

## Cow Hill
- Chestnut's Court (5, W)
- Little Cow Yard (14, W)

## Fisher's Lane
- Roaches' Court (10, E)

## Guildhall Hill
- Woburn Court (8, N)

## St Giles' Street
- Chesnutt's Court (15, N)
- Freeman's Court (29, N)
- Mayes Court (85, N)
- Tuck's Court (24, S)
- Rigby's Court (52, S)
- Fox's Court (72, S)
- Cock Yard (80, S)
- Gunn's Court (84, S)

## Grapes Hill
- Lincoln's Court (11, W)

## St Peter's Street
- Pope's Head Yard (7, W)
- Bennett's Court (9, W)
- Day's Court (23, W)
- Mancroft Yard (33, W)

## Theatre Street
- Chantry Court (8, S)
- Butcher's Court (9, N)

## Upper Goat Lane
- Malthouse Yard (8, W)
- Warners Yard (14, W)

## Wellington Lane
- Bell's Yard (6, E)
- Baker's Yard (12, E)

> Please note that between 1884 and 1908 St Giles' Hill was renamed Grapes Hill. The addresses give the approximate entrance to individual yards based on Kelly's 1908 Directory.

*6 - 22 St Giles' Street, 1934*

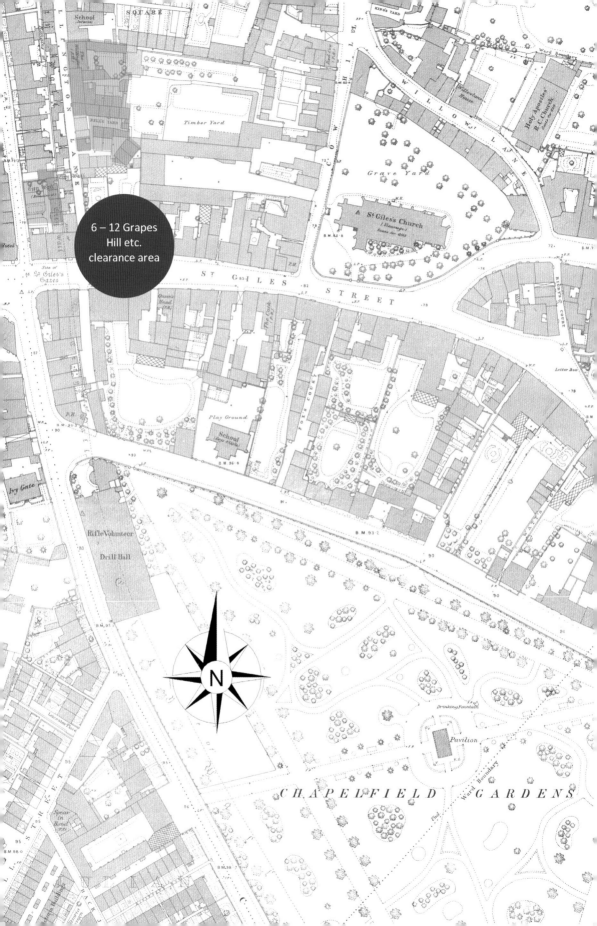

6 – 12 Grapes Hill etc. clearance area

Roaches' Court, Fisher's Lane and Freeman's Court clearance area

Fire Station

City Hall

The Forum

Mancroft Yard St Peter's Street clearance area

# Historical Background

Although not renowned for its old courts and yards it is still worth having a short review of this area.

Reporting in 1851 William Lee noted that 'the health of the poor in St Peter Mancroft and St Giles is relatively good'. This was partially put down to the fact that both parishes were supplied with water from the public works and there were few pumps. However, all was not rosy: 'These taps for the poor are outside the houses, each family having a key. I should think that on average there would be one tap per 20 dwellings of the poor.'

It was also observed that the parishes contained many large houses. This is clearly illustrated along St Giles' Street which has been a major thoroughfare since late medieval times; even today many impressive buildings line the street. A large number of the houses are either Georgian, or had Georgian facades applied to earlier structures.

Buildings of earlier origin include 74 St Giles' Street, parts of which date from the 16th century. At one time it was the home of the Black Swan public house. To the left was a narrow entrance to Fox's (later Hales) Court. The court was one of a number leading through to Chapelfield North which should more accurately have been described as thoroughfares. In a similar fashion both Watts' Court and Master's Court (later Ninham's) linked Chapelfield North with Bethel Street.

Since 1930, as a result of slum clearance, war damage and changes in road networks, many buildings have been demolished in this area. However, one major project had a bigger effect in this section of the City than all of the other factors combined: constructing the new City Hall and associated buildings (outlined on the 1884 map, page 153).

It was in 1931 that Charles Holloway James and Stephen Rowland Pierce won a national competition to design the City Hall. Seven years later, on the 29 October 1938, at its official opening, King George VI declared the City Hall to '...be worthy of the past and equal to the demands of the present and future'. Despite this it did not win universal approval, with the well-known artist John Piper going so far as to scathingly remark that 'fog is its friend'. Notwithstanding such criticism the architectural historian, Nikolaus Pevsner, describes it as 'the foremost English public building of between the wars'.

In April 1938 that the City Council first announced their plans to compulsorily purchase land lying between Bethel and Theatre Streets to facilitate the construction of a new library. However, it was not until 1961 that the site was finally cleared. Two years later, in January 1963, the Central Library was officially opened by the Queen Mother. Disaster struck on 1 August 1994 when the building was devastated by fire. Subsequently, The Forum, a building designed by Sir Michael Hopkins and costing £65 million, was built on the site (which is outlined on the map, page 153) to mark the Millennium in the East of England. Historically, three yards were located under the building: Bell and Austin's Yards, entered at 27 and 21 Bethel Street respectively, and Mancroft Yard which was accessed from 33 St Peter's Street.

*Bethel Street rooftops, view from tower of St Peter Mancroft Church, 1933*

# Major Clearances

Few would argue that the construction of the City Hall and associated buildings in the 1930s was the biggest single development in the centre of Norwich of the interwar years. In preparation for this momentous event, for a number of years Norwich Council had been acquiring property in the area bound by Bethel Street, St Peter's Street and St Giles' Street. It was early in 1933 that they began the first phase of the project, the construction of the fire station, which was deemed the most urgently needed of the civic buildings.

The footprint of the fire station has been marked on the map. It resulted in the demolition of numbers 20 to 36 Bethel Street, together with the appropriately named Blazeby's Yard (26) and Jay's Court (30) to the rear. The yards had been located behind houses built in the Tudor period, of which George Plunkett observes: 'Their history appears to have been uneventful. All were in a very rundown condition at the time of their disappearance.' The new fire station, which remained operational until 2014, was opened on 8 November 1934 by the Lord Mayor, Mr F. C. Jex. The following year work began on clearing the remainder of the site for the new City Hall.

As can be seen from the map, and photographs, the site encompassed a huge block covering numbers 2 – 18 Bethel Street, numbers 1 – 25 St Peter's Street and numbers 2 – 22 St Giles' Street, together with all land in between. Yards which were demolished included Tuck's Court (24 St Giles' Street) and Pope's Head Yard, Bennett's Court and Day's Court (7, 9 and 23 St Peter's Street).

Slum clearances were not a major feature in this part of the City. Yards that were cleared as slums in the 1930s included Bell Yard, 6 Wellington Lane, which featured in Lee's 1851 report when it was described as: '...a very close ill-ventilated place. The refuse of 13 or 14 houses flows along the surface, and then passes under a house. I examined the floor and walls of the house and found them damp.' It was demolished, together with Baker's Yard (12 Wellington Lane), in 1937/8.

*28 - 34 Bethel Street, 1933*

*The site of the new City Hall has been cleared. The new fire station has been built and is located to the left. Mancroft Yard can be seen directly below the tower of St Peter Mancroft, c.1935*

## Mancroft Yard (33 St Peter's Street)

*Mancroft Yard, 1938*

This yard, which was located close to St Peter Mancroft Church, had all the characteristics of a typical Norwich yard. In particular, large buildings had been sub-divided into 'squalid tenements', it was made up of ancient buildings which could be dated back to the 15th century, and it was divided into two sections which meant that ventilation and light would have been an issue for the residents.

On the 29 May 1873, a Mr Rayment from the Sanitary Inspector's Office completed a report on the yard. From this we can determine that 61 tenants lived in 14 properties. There were communal privies, bins and wash houses. The inspector's report indicated that some properties were sub-divided, but there is no evidence of overcrowding.

In 1904 the City's Courts and Yards Committee reported that Mancroft Yard was under review. In January 1907 it was reported that 'private street works' (e.g. repaving) had cost £92 3s. 5d. whilst the cost of installing sanitary conveniences amounted to £50 10s. 5d.

Local historian George Plunkett both photographed and described the yard: 'There were in fact two yards here, one behind the other, with a gabled timber-framed building lying between the two. At the street

entrance was a small wooden arch bearing the grocer's arms and a merchant's mark in one spandrel and a merchant's mark and the initials "M.B." in the other. These could be the initials of Margaret Barnard who lived here in 1626, or those of Michael Beverley, mayor in 1692.'

Donald Read recalls the yard in the 1930s:

'I lived in Mancroft Yard on the right-hand side as you went in from the St Peter Mancroft end. There were one or two steps up from the yard into the front room, which I used to sit on. There were wash houses on the other side and the toilets for the houses were outside where the tap water was. Although we did have a sink and a cold-water tap indoors, my mother did her washing in the communal wash houses.

'There were seven of us living there, my parents, myself, two brothers and my two sisters. I believe we had two bedrooms upstairs. I remember playing hopscotch and skipping in the yard, all sorts of things like that. We weren't allowed to play outside the yard, in fact I never realised how close the yard was to the church, I can't believe that it was only a road's width.

'One of the people in the yard was my uncle, he didn't have any children. Two other families I remember were the Budds and the Wards. There was also a music teacher called Miss Nightingale.'

In 1936/37 Mancroft Yard was cleared of 26 residents, and was demolished *c.*1940

*Mancroft Yard from St Peter Mancroft tower, c.1935*

## Master's Court (63 Bethel Street)

*Ninham's (Master's) Court, 1928*

Master's, now Ninham's, Court still runs from 63 Bethel Street to 10 Chapel Field North. By 1908 it had been renamed in honour of Henry Ninham (1796 – 1874), a member of the Norwich School of Artists. In 1911, whilst resident in the court, Walter Nugent Monck, a theatre director, founded the Norwich Players. His company first performed in the drawing room of his home, which was obviously very large as there was room for a small stage and an audience of about 70 people. As the group's popularity grew they needed more space and eventually Monck purchased and restored what is now the Maddermarket Theatre.

Numbers 6, 9 and 10 Ninham's Court are listed buildings with parts believed to be from the 16th century. Under them is a 15th-century undercroft.

*Ninham's (Master's ) Court, 1950*

## Watts' Court (55 Bethel Street)

*Watts' Court, 1935*

Watts' Court lay between 55 – 57 Bethel Street. Its entrance was spanned by a carved wooden archway of Tudor origin.

The court was named after John Langley Watts, a merchant, who lived at 61 Bethel Street during the 18th century. He was sheriff in 1771 and mayor in 1774, dying during his mayoralty.

The court together with 53 – 57 Bethel Street was destroyed by incendiary bombs during air raids on the night of 27 June 1942.

### Bethel Street

The street took its name from the Bethel Hospital. When opened in 1713, the hospital was the first purpose-built asylum in the country. By 1995 the hospital had been closed. The buildings, which lie just behind the Forum, have now been converted for residential use.

*Coach and Horses Yard, 51 Bethel Street, 1936*

*Cock Yard, 80 St Giles' Street, 1937*

*Cow (Little Cow) Yard, 14 Cow Hill, 1937*

*Hales (Fox's) Court, 72 St Giles' Street, 1936*

*Hales (Fox's) Court, 72 St Giles' Street, being demolished to make way for Cleveland Road, 1969*

*Tuck's Court, 24 St Giles' Street, 1938*

*Pope's Head Yard, 7 St Peter's Street, c.1935*

*Hales (Fox's) Court entrance (left), St Giles' Street, 2015*  *Gunn's Court entrance, 2015*

Despite the major developments which have taken place in this section of the City, there is still evidence of old yards, particularly in the area around Upper St Giles' Street.

Although Hales (Fox's) Court now lies under Cleveland Road a sign alongside Hales House (74 St Giles' Street) indicates its former entrance. Moving westwards one comes across the entrance to Cock Yard, which took its name from the adjacent pub and which was renovated in 1974. Next comes the entrance to Gunn's Court, now accessed by way of a gate which leads through to another refurbished development. Across the road is a gated entrance to Mayes Court.

Just around the corner on Cow Hill a sign denotes the entrance to Cow Yard. The yard took its name

from the Red Cow public house which could trace its licence back to 1760. Sales particulars for the pub, produced in 1851, list the property as including a large yard complete with extensive stables and a cow shed. George Plunkett noted that at one time properties in the yard included a little cottage and garden. All were cleared away under an improvement scheme (date unknown). The entrance now leads through to modern houses. Another modern development, Watling's Court, stands on the former stables of Norwich's first horse-drawn omnibus. The land was subsequently owned by the Watling family and it was from here they ran their haulage company. The yard is named after the family. Geoffrey Wattling (1913 – 2004), is well known as a long-time chairman of Norwich City FC and benefactor to many good causes.

*Cock Yard, St Giles' Street, 2015*   *Watling's Court, Cow Hill, 2015*   *Cow Yard, entrance, Cow Hill, 2015*

*Britons Arms, Elm Hill, Henry Ninham, c.1830*

# The Historic Heart: Elm Hill and Quayside

Yards identified in this section of the City include:

## Elm Hill

- Norris Court (37, E)
- Wright's Court (45, E)
- Monastery Court (10, W)
- Dutton's Court (18, W)
- Crown Court (22, W)
- Towler's Court (28, W)
- Roache's Court (34, W)

## Palace Street

- College Court (21, N)
- Chiddick's Court (35, N)

## Quayside

- Cock and Pie Yard (6, S)
- Beckwith's Court (13, S)

## St Martin-at-Palace Plain

- Pye's Yard (8, N)
- Beehive Yard (18, N)

## Wagon & Horses Lane

- Spark's Yard (6, N)

## Wensum Street

- Flower's Court (13, E)
- Barnard's Yard (20, W)

*Elm Hill, c.1895*

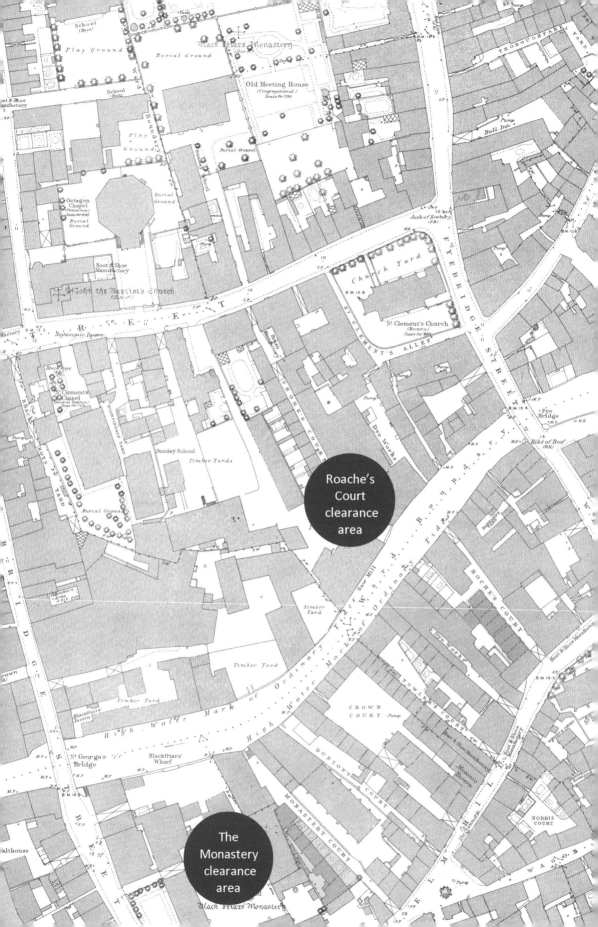

School
(Boys)
Play Ground
Burial Ground
Black Friars Monastery
Old Meeting House
(Congregational)
Seats for 700
School
(Girls)
Boot & Shoe Manufactory
Boundary
Play Ground
Burial Ground
Sunday School
Octagon Chapel
(Unitarian)
Seats for 600
Burial Ground
Burial Ground
Boot & Shoe Manufactory
St John the Baptist's Church
(Site of)
STREET
Nightingale Tavern
Factory
Black Boys
Clements Chapel
(General Baptist)
Seats for 700
NIGHTINGALE YARD
Sunday School
Timber Yards
Burial Ground
BLACK BOYS YARD
Clothier's Arms
Timber Yard
Blackfriars Tavern
Timber Yard
St George's Bridge
Blackfriars' Wharf
BLACKFRIARS BRIDGE
Crown
Malthouse
STREET

Church Yard
St Clement's Church
(Rectory)
Seats for 500
ST CLEMENT'S ALLEY
FYEBRIDGE STREET
Jack of Newbury
(P.H.)
Bull Inn
Pump
THOROUGHFARE YARD
Pump
Fye Bridge
Ribs of Beef
(P.H.)

SHORES COURT
Dye Works

Roache's Court clearance area

Boundary Ward of Ordinary Tidal
High Water Mark of Ordinary Tide
Saw Mill
Timber Yard
Timber Yard

FOWLERS COURT
Dye Works
Boot & Shoe Manufactory
ROCHES COURT

CROWN COURT
Pump
DUXTON'S COURT
Masonic Tavern
ELM HILL
WAGON
NORRIS COURT
Boot & Shoe Manufactory

The Monastery clearance area

MONASTERY COURT
Black Friars' Monastery

**2 – 12 Bedding Lane C.P.O.**

**10 – 24 Quayside clearance area**

**7 – 13 Pigg Lane clearance area**

**Pye's Yard & St Martin-at-Palace Plain**

**9 – 13 Palace Street clearance area**

# Historical Background

Most visitors to Norwich will find their way to these picturesque streets which lie adjacent to the City's magnificent cathedral. It is hard to believe that in the interwar years much of this area was designated for slum clearance.

Elm Hill, which acquired its name from the elm tree which was planted here in the early 16th century, is believed to have been in existence since the 13th century. In 1507 most properties were destroyed by a fire which swept through the area; these were subsequently rebuilt by prosperous merchants, craftsmen and civic dignitaries. Because of their proximity to the River Wensum, a major transport route, the houses on the north of the thoroughfare were particularly popular with merchants, many of whom owned their own quay and ran workshops behind their houses. However, from the end of the 18th century, as Norwich went into decline, so did Elm Hill. The land to the rear of the once grand buildings fronting the street was a perfect space for speculators to haphazardly erect poor-quality housing, and by 1884 seven courts and yards had entrances leading from the main thoroughfare. By the early 1920s Elm Hill had degenerated, and rather than be synonymous with wealth it was now associated with poverty and squalor. As a result the City Council planned to demolish the north side of the street and build a swimming pool. In response, in 1924 the Norwich Society began the fight to preserve Elm Hill. As part of their campaign they prepared a report which made it clear that despite the abysmal state of the area it still retained buildings with historic and architectural merit. Their recommendation for partial clearance of slums combined with a sympathetic renovation of the more important buildings was accepted and passed by just one vote. As a result Norwich still contains one of the 'best-preserved Tudor streets in England' (Norwich Preservation Trust).

The area bordered by the River Wensum, Whitefriars' Street, Palace Street and Wensum Street also contains buildings and yards with fascinating histories. The area was subject to a number of clearance schemes during the 1930s which were generally small scale and uncontroversial – with one major exception. In 1937 plans were made to demolish, Tudor and Georgian properties on St Martin-at-Palace Plain (Palace Plain). As with Elm Hill, it took a massive campaign to save these wonderful properties, which included the former home of the celebrated Norwich artist, John Sell Cotman (see Clearance Case Study Four, page 34).

This area provides a perfect example of what can be achieved by selectively demolishing poor-quality buildings whilst retaining those of historic interest.

*The thatched Britons Arms, probably the only house on Elm Hill to escape the fire of 1507, 2014*

# Major Clearance Schemes

As previously noted, unlike other parts of the City, wholesale clearance did not take place in this area. Instead the worst yards were demolished but the properties that fronted the street were retained. In this respect the clearance schemes, especially the work done on Elm Hill in the 1920s, could be considered to have been some of the most successful undertaken. Here, poor-quality housing was removed without razing an entire area: effectively a win-win situation. This outcome was not achieved because of the foresight of the Council, instead it took major campaigns to save Elm Hill and the vista on Palace Plain.

Today these areas are very important to the City's tourist trade. Whilst applauding Norwich City Council's achievements in improving living standards in the 1930s, one can't help but wonder how the cityscape would have been enhanced if buildings in areas such as Cowgate had also been preserved.

The major clearance schemes proposed in the 1930s are outlined on the main map, including the Pye's Yard scheme. This clearly illustrates the devastating impact it would have had on Palace Plain if it had gone through without amendment.

Another reason that this area avoided wholesale clearance, is that it has not been subject to any major road building programmes – this is not totally by chance. After WWI a traffic scheme was proposed which involved the demolition of one side of Elm Hill, the City walls and the medieval Cow Tower (Riverside). Again these important buildings were only saved after a vigorous campaign.

*Crown Court and Towler's Court after clearance. The Tudor houses on Elm Hill remain untouched, c.1938*

# Yards of Note

At the end of the 19th century this section of Norwich contained around 18 courts and yards. Unlike other parts of the City few were adjacent to pubs, with many lying in what would once have been the courtyards of grand houses. The following are of particular interest:

## Beckwith's Court (13 Quayside)

The yard was named after John Christmas Beckwith (1750 – 1809), who conducted at the Norwich Festival and was organist at both St Peter Mancroft Church and the nearby Cathedral.

In the photograph (below) we can clearly see the three-storey late-Georgian houses which stood at the entrance of the original yard. The attic-storey has the type of casement windows usually associated with weaving, because they were designed to let in the maximum amount of light.

By the early 20th century the main properties had been sub-divided into houses of multiple occupation. The yard's eight houses were cleared of 29 residents in 1937 and were demolished in 1938. A modern court, with the same name, now stands on a similar footprint to its predecessor.

## Crown Court (22 Elm Hill)

Numbers 20 – 26 Elm Hill were originally a single quadrangle house which was entered through what is now Crown Court. The house was built by Augustine Steward after the 1507 fire on the site of Paston Place, the home of the Paston family, authors of the famous letters. Steward was a leading City merchant who served as both sheriff and mayor. The front elevation of number 20 was practically rebuilt around 1650, and it no longer matches that of the rest of the original house. Numbers 22, 24 and 26 include the archway which leads to Crown Court. They were renovated as a single property in 1927 when the properties in the yard behind were demolished, by order of the Council. A gentlemen's club, 'The Strangers Club', moved in the following year and is still there.

The carved wooden beam over the archway (an integral part of number 22) which leads to Crown Court still bears Augustine Steward's merchant mark, (incorporating his initials) on the right. The arms of the mercers' guild are on the left. The yard took its name from the Crown pub, which was located on the opposite side of the street at number 29. The hostelry could trace its licence back to 1760 and was closed under compensation in 1927, one cannot help but wonder if the withdrawal of the licence was linked to improvements to the street.

From the 1884 map we can see that Crown Court was quite spacious, and so was it a pleasant place to live? Not according to William Lee, who reported in 1851:

*Beckwith's Court, c.1930*

*Crown Court, c.1910*

'[It] is a wide place and has recently been paved, but it contains about 155 persons, when all of the houses are filled. There are four privies for the whole, and two of them situated under a bedroom, empty directly into the river, not more than a yard above the place where the people take water.'

Although the properties in the yard were demolished in 1927 the entrance from Elm Hill has survived.

## Dutton's Court (18 Elm Hill):

This long narrow court (erroneously named Dunton's Court on the 1884 map) was squeezed between Augustine Steward's house and what was once another single house (now 12 – 18 Elm Hill). By 1783, number 18 (which lay on one side of the entrance) had been divided from the main building and it became a retail outlet. Subsequently the Tudor frontage was given a Georgian and then a Victorian makeover, also a third floor was added. At one time the entrance to the living accommodation, which was located behind the shop, was in Dutton's Court. Although properties in the yard were demolished in the 1920s, the red brick building which lay between Dutton's and Monastery Courts, was retained and is now owned by the Norwich University of the Arts.

Since 1990 18 Elm Hill has been the home of the wonderful Bear Shop. The entrance to Dutton's Court now leads into a beautiful secret garden based on a design by Gertrude Jeckyll, the Edwardian writer and garden designer.

*Dutton's Court, Elm Hill, c.1890*

*Dutton's Court, Elm Hill, c.1930*

## Monastery Court (10 Elm Hill)

Monastery Court was once known as De Hagues' Court after the family who owned it in the late 18th century. It was renamed when an Anglican Churchman, the Revd J. L. Lyne known as Father Ignatius, settled on Elm Hill and attempted to revive a form of monasticism. A plaque over a door between numbers 14 and 16 records where Father Ignatius lived. Although he collected funds to build the red-brick Chapel of St Mary and St Dunstan, behind these buildings, Father Ignatius never occupied it, and like the Court It became known as the Monastery.

The buildings forming numbers one to five Monastery Court were cleared in the late 1930s, but the former Chapel still survives and is now part of Norwich University of the Arts.

### The 'Monastery'

In the mid-20th century the Priory Chapel, better known as the 'Monastery', was owned by Norwich City College. It was set up for training purposes as a small shoe factory. Many of the City's shoe workers came here on day release to learn their trade.

*Former Chapel of St Mary and St Dunstan, 2012*

## Pye's Yard (8 St Martin-at-Palace Plain)

*Pye's Yard, St Martin-at-Palace Plain, 1936*

The yard (referred to as Pye's Court on the 1884 map) was entered through a covered archway between numbers 8 and 9 Palace Plain. It mainly consisted of 19th-century buildings which formed a long row of small dwellings joined by inner yards filled with even smaller tenements. In 1937 the council made orders to clear and compulsorily purchase Pye's Yard (previously Court), together with adjoining properties, with the aim of replacing them with 38 flats for the working classes. As outlined in Clearance Case Study Four, the scheme (which included the demolition of Cotman House) fell through.

In 1938 Pye's Yard was eventually cleared of 57 residents and its 17 properties were demolished. In 1961 the derelict site was opened as the City's first 'Pay and Display' car park. It was not until 1982 that new houses were built here. Unlike the proposals made in the 1930s, the attractive new development has been slotted between existing buildings; a good example of how to meld old and new architecture. Pye's Yard has been rebuilt on a similar footprint. It is still surrounded by Tudor, Georgian and 19th-century properties, but now it is an attractive place to live in the centre of the City.

*Rowe family, Pye's Yard, c.1906*

The Rowe family lived at 4 Pye's Yard in the early 20th century. This wonderful photograph was taken in the yard. The family are all dressed up in their Sunday best for the christening of baby Sarah, who is held by her mother Amelia. The family's patriarch, Nathaniel (Big Nat), sits next to his wife and daughter. Big Nat worked at the City Gasworks, although family members believe that at one time he was a scavenger, who drove a 'honey cart' around the City, collecting effluent from privies. In the mornings, before he set off on his rounds, he would go round and warn people of his impending arrival so that they could close their windows!

*Pye's Yard entrance (l), interior (r), 2014*

## Roache's Court (34 Elm Hill)

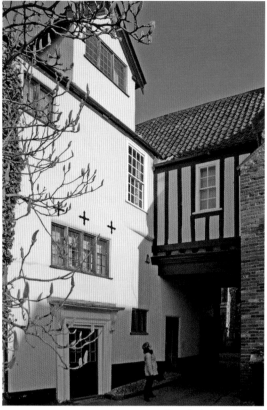

*Roache's Court, 2015*

## Towler's Court (28 Elm Hill)

*Towler's Court, c.1920*

Numbers 34 and 36 Elm Hill were built in 1540. They originally comprised a substantial merchant's house and premises which extended down to the river. The central courtyard was entered through the archway which now separates the two premises, which was eventually developed to form Roache's Court (erroneously labelled as Roche's Court on the 1884 map). During the 16th and 17th centuries the Suckling family lived here. John Suckling achieved the position of sheriff in 1566 and mayor in 1584. Although the premises were renovated in Georgian times, the original flint construction can still be seen in the lower floors.

The court was partially cleared of buildings in the late 1920s. In 1937 a further seven cottages were cleared of 27 residents, and were demolished the following year. The court entrance survives and now leads through to gardens and the river.

In the early 20th century Towler's Court was home to both commercial and residential buildings. In 1908 many of the businesses were linked with the shoe trade, including A. Chittock & Co., W. E. Scarlett, and John Miller, who all manufactured boots.

The buildings were of poor quality and were demolished as slums in the 1920s.

## Wright's Court (45 Elm Hill)

The Pettus family were prosperous merchants. John Pettus was knighted in 1603 and elected mayor in 1608. Their house and business premises originally extended from number 41 to St Simon and St Jude's churchyard. Number 41, a half-timbered building, was part of the original building.

What is now Wright's Court was the central courtyard entrance to their house. On the right of the court is a studded-oak door, believed to have been one of the original doors leading to their mansion. At the end of the court is a seven-mullioned window above a first-floor jetty dating from the 16th century which would have formed a link between the two wings of Pettus's premises.

The yard was renovated in the 1960s and now contains a variety of properties.

# The Yards Today

The area around Quayside has been attractively developed. The old entrance to the modern Pye's Yard is clearly marked whilst the new Beckwith's Court is located in the same vicinity as its predecessor.

Meanwhile one suspects that few visitors come to Elm Hill to visit its courts and yards, but it really does retain brilliant examples of how they have evolved. In particular, it is amazing to think that so many of the yards were built as the courtyards of grand 16th-century mansions; few would have realised then that they would evolve to contain the houses of the poor.

Wright's Court, in particular, is one of the few remaining examples in the City of a renovated yard which used to be the courtyard of an ancient house. Although it is now very pretty, and a perfect place to enjoy a cup of tea, you can easily get an idea of how airless such a space would have been when many families lived there in unsanitary conditions.

Today, everything has gone full circle. The slums have been demolished, but the Tudor houses and yard entrances survive. Now, when you wander through the openings you may come to a car park (Crown Court) or a garden (Roache's Court), in either case be sure to look back at the wonderful architecture which could so easily have been lost.

*Wright's Court, Elm Hill, 2014*

*The lovely garden based on a design by Gertrude Jeckyll, the former Dutton's Court, Elm Hill, 2013*

*Crown Court, 22 Elm Hill*

*Norris Court, 37 Elm Hill*

*Roache's Court, 34 Elm Hill*

*Towler's Court, 28 Elm Hill*

*Wright's Court, 45 Elm Hill*

*Impressive roof lines, a rear view of Elm Hill, 2015*

# The Commercial Centre: Around St Stephen's Street

Yards identified in this section of the City include:

## Red Lion Street
- Peacock Passage (2, E)
- Orford Yard (9, E)
- Birds' Court (13, E)

## St Stephen's Street
- Barwell's Court (12, N)
- Stocking's Court (24, N)
- Unicorn Yard (28, N)
- King's Head Yard (34, N)
- Wellington Yard (42, N)
- Wade's Yard (52, N)
- Shoulder of Mutton Yard (54, N)
- Lock's Court (60, N)
- George Yard (64, N)
- Mansfield's Court (39, S)
- Crown and Angel Yard (41, S)

- Andrew's Yard (47, S)
- Wheatsheaf Yard (51, S)
- Rose Yard  (59, S)

## Surrey Street
- Boar's Head Yard (2, E)
- Anchor Yard (18, E)
- Miller's Court (22, E)
- Bignold's Court (13, W)

## Timber Hill
- Osborne Square (10, E)
- Mounser's Yard (14, E)
- Star and Crown Court (20, E)
- Palmer's Yard (19, W)
- Lion and Castle Yard (25, W)
- Scott's Court (31, W)

*St Stephen's Street looking towards Orford Place, 1895*

175

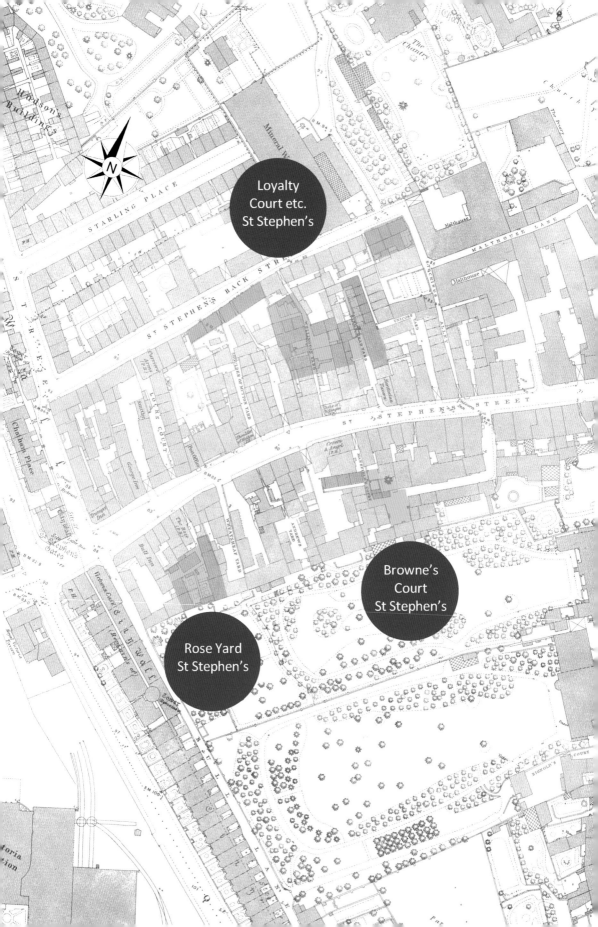

Loyalty
Court etc.
St Stephen's

Browne's
Court
St Stephen's

Rose Yard
St Stephen's

All Saints' Alley

# Historical Background

This section of Norwich is dominated by St Stephen's Street. As early as 1285 the gated entry – which was located in the vicinity of the present-day roundabout at the junction with Chapelfield Road – marked the principal route into Norwich. The gate was on the main road from London and the street now known as St Stephen's at one time ran directly from the gate to the castle. Therefore it is of no surprise that in 1578, when Queen Elizabeth I visited Norwich, she entered the City through this entrance, which had been richly decorated in honour of the occasion. Unfortunately, in 1793 the gates and walls were considered a hindrance to trade and health and were destroyed.

At the turn of the 20th century St Stephen's was still one of the busiest thoroughfares in the City. Pubs and shops lined the pavements, whilst behind them were residential yards. It was also very narrow, and not at all suited to the age of the motor car. In the 1930s the Council began their quest to widen the road, but could not decide which side of the street should be set back. They had a conundrum. On the east stood two medieval buildings: the Boar's Head Inn and Crown & Angel public house. To the west were Buntings and Curls, both very popular department stores (now the location of Marks & Spencer and Debenhams respectively). The problem was solved, somewhat drastically, in 1942 when the Luftwaffe intervened. During the Baedeker Raids, three of the four buildings were destroyed: only Buntings survived.

As a result St Stephen's has changed beyond recognition, not because of slum clearance, although this did take place, but as a result of war damage and urban planning. The writing was on the wall when the *City of Norwich Plan* (1945) reported that the street had 'few buildings of outstanding merit' and proposed that the road should be designed as a dual carriageway and pavements be 15 feet wide. In 1953 a start was made by widening the east side at the City-centre end. The entire scheme was completed in the early 1960s.

Other major routes in this section of the City include Surrey Street and Timber Hill.

At the turn of the 20th century the northern end of Surrey Street was dominated by impressive offices and mansions, many built by renowned Norwich architects, which stood in contrast to the somewhat humbler buildings found in the yards. Although the yards have been demolished, the grand buildings remain. Of particular note is Surrey House, an outstanding example of Edwardian architecture designed by Edward Skipper and built in the early 20th century for the Norwich Union Life Insurance Society (now Aviva) on the site of the 16th-century home of Henry Howard, the Earl of Surrey. Further

along the street, numbers 29 – 35, a four-storey terrace designed in 1761 by Thomas Ivory, have been restored.

From the beginning of the 16th century Timber Hill was known as 'Tymbermarket Hill', for the simple reason that wood was sold there. By 1884 a number of yards were located behind the ancient houses which lined the street. These included the Star and

## Daphne Way recalls St Stephen's Street in the 1930s

'We used to shop on the old narrow St Stephen's; it was lovely. We loved going to the Co-op, my mother was a real Co-op lady; I went there until it closed [48 – 62, 49, 51, 59 & 71]. Over the top was the Co-op social club. At the top of Bull Lane [71 St Stephen's] was their butchers, they even killed animals there. Procter's the butchers was further down St Stephen's [35], they used to sell lovely sausages, and we used to get delicious cakes from Ashworth's [74] who were bakers. Then there was the Maypole Dairy [30], who sold butter, they'd make butter pats with wooden paddles.'

*Procter's, St Stephen's Street, 1936*

*Timber Hill, 1936*

Crown Yard, which was located next to the pub of the same name. Along with many other buildings on the east side of the street, the pub was destroyed in an air raid on 27 June 1942. Writing in 1987, George Plunkett observed that many of these buildings had not been replaced. Not so today. The street still contains more than 20 listed buildings, but now, alongside these are modern retail units, including the entry into the Castle Mall Shopping Centre (opened 1993). When the Mall was built great care was taken to retain the character of Timber Hill, as explained by architect Michael Innes: 'We wanted the new properties that we built on the east side to reflect the style and character of the historical west side but not to copy it. To achieve this we introduced different roof levels for the new buildings each of which had its own features, including unique window designs. This has given a feel of individuality to the modern shops whilst enhancing the street frontage.' A perfect example of how old buildings can prosper alongside new developments.

> ### Rampant Horse Street
>
> The thoroughfare took its rather strange name from an inn, originally known as the Ramping Horse Inn, which was located in the vicinity in the 13th century. In turn, the hostelry got its name because of its proximity to the City's horse market which was held in the area outside St Stephen's churchyard.

## Clearance Schemes

Although this area was subject to several clearance schemes in the interwar years, none were extensive. The slum clearances that did take place were behind the street line, thus not impinging on its character. Yards affected on St Stephen's Street included Browne's (previously Mansfield's) Court where 29 people were cleared from 11 buildings which were subsequently demolished, and Rose Yard where 25 tenants were rehoused and nine buildings demolished.

However, a combination of war damage and the subsequent widening of St Stephen's has resulted in the street changing beyond recognition and, of course, the demolition of many of the old yards.

# Yards of Note

Although at the turn of the 20th century more than 20 yards were located in this section of the City, they were not a dominant part of the landscape. The following are of particular interest:

## Bignold's Court (13 Surrey Street)

The court was named after the Bignolds who founded the Norwich Union Insurance Company. The yard differed significantly in both stature and quality from other properties in the street associated with the family, including Bignold House and Surrey House. By 1936 it had been demolished to make way for the new bus station.

*Bignold's Court, Surrey Street, c.1910*

## Peacock Passage (2 Red Lion Street)

The yard was flanked by two public houses, the Coach & Horses and the Peacock. In 1955 the *Eastern Evening News* printed Arthur Spencer's reminiscences. Arthur was born in one of three small cottages situated in the yard which he believes were demolished around 1938. He recalled that it was a narrow red-paved yard where he spent happy childhood days. For a spot of entertainment, Arthur and his friends would venture onto the busy shopping area outside to ask passers-by: 'Have you any cigarette cards, please?' He particularly remembered one of his neighbours, a chimney sweep called Billy Blake: 'Although Billy had a reputation for being a grumbling, grunting old fellow, this hid a kinder side as he always brought nuts, sweets or fruit back for us children. On his early morning rounds as a chimney sweep Billy was reputed to tell every householder that he'd had no time for breakfast, with the result that by the time he finished work around midday he did not want a lot more food!'

## Pipe Burners' Yard (42 St Stephen's Street)

This narrow alley was originally called Wellington Yard after the Duke of Wellington pub which traded at 42 Stephen's Street from 1822 to 1908. It was one of a number of very cramped lanes lined with buildings which linked St Stephen's with St Stephen's Back Street, others included Lock's Court (60), Shoulder of Mutton Yard (54) and King's Head (later Loyalty) Yard (34).

Sometime between 1911 and 1931 Wellington Yard was re-christened Pipe Burner's Yard. In 1951 the *Eastern Evening News* ran an article after the death of Joseph Browne in which they recalled: 'Mr Browne was the last member of the family of Norwich pipe burners who practised the craft in the old workshops in Pipe Burners' Yard. As a boy he worked there himself, but even at that time clay pipes were losing popularity. He was chiefly employed on the delivery of the clay pipes, and used to say that at one time he knew every public house in Norfolk.'

In 1936/7 the yard was cleared of 14 tenants and subsequently eight properties were demolished. In 1953 a public notice announced the intention of 'stopping up' the yard for the purposes of traffic. It now lies under the entrance to the Chapelfield Shopping Centre.

## Scott's Court (31 Timber Hill)

Around 1910 Sidney Harvey, who died in 1985 at the age of 81, moved to 3 Scott's Court with his mother, Ada, and grandparents, Emma and Henry Harvey. He left notes to his son, Paul, in which he explained: 'The court consisted of dwellings three-storeys high. Some had access to the court whilst others led to both the court and All Saints' Alley. They had one bedroom and one living room and kitchen combined. The water supply was in the court and was shared by all. In winter when it, and the one lavatory, froze up the first person using it had to defreeze it; this was always honoured by the residents. The rent for these dwellings was 1*s*. 6*d*. per week.'

The court was cleared of five properties and 10 residents in 1938, along with properties on All Saint's Alley, which George Plunkett described as being: 'A row of quaint gabled houses...mainly of the 17th century, brick built, but mostly faced with cement.' The date of demolition is unknown, but probably predates 1940. Number 31 Timber Hill has survived, as has the original entrance. Parts of this attractive building date from the 16th century, and it is now Grade II listed.

# Photo Gallery of Old Yards in the 1930s

*Browne's (Mansfield's) Court, 39 St Stephen's Street, 1937*

*George Yard, 64 St Stephen's Street, 1936*

*Loyalty (King's Head) Court, 34 St Stephen's Street, 1936*

*Wade's Yard, 52 St Stephen's Street, 1937*

# The Yards Today

*Lion and Castle Yard, 2015*

A combination of bombing, street widening and commercial development means that few of the yards which were located here in the late 19th century have survived. Those that have include Palmer's Yard and Lion and Castle Yard, located at 19 and 25 Timber Hill respectively. The former has a gated entry to the left of a late 18th-century listed building (not open to the public). All that remains of the original Lion and Castle Yard, which previously lay behind a public house of the same name, are two 17th-century weavers' cottages. In 1993, when they were totally dilapidated, they were taken over by the Norwich Preservation Trust which has attractively renovated them; one has been restored with is original roof of reed thatch. In 2014, as part of the renovation of Westlegate Tower, new apartments and retail units have been built opposite the cottages to form a new, modern-day Lion and Castle Yard.

*The modern east side (right) of Timber Hill designed to reflect the character of the west side (left), 2015*

# 'Blood and Guts' Street': Ber Street Neighbourhood

In 1884 there were more than 40 yards along Ber Street alone, giving it one of the highest densities in the City. The following were amongst those located in this section of Norwich in the late 19th century:

## Ber Street
- Emm's Court (4, E)
- White Hart Yard (6, E)
- Cannell's Court (10, E)
- Mason's Yard (14, E)
- Lamb Yard (28, E)
- Twitters' Court (34, E)
- Flecked Bull Yard (38, E)
- Boarded Entry Yard (54, E)
- Royal Oak Yard (64, E)
- George IV Yard (74, E)
- Greyhound Yard (102, E)
- Knight's Yard (114, E)
- Bayfield's Yard (150, E)
- Paul's Yard (154, E)
- Field's Yard (162, E)
- Bakers' Arms Yard (9, W)
- Brooks' Court (13, W)
- Jubilee Yard (21, W)
- Black Swan Yard (23, W)
- Crawfoot's Yard (43, W)

- Berry's Court (49, W)
- Houghton's Yard (61, W)
- Till's Court (71, W)
- Lock and Key Yard (89, W)
- Kahler's Yard (95, W)
- Fiddy's Yard (101, W)
- Hewitt's Yard (103, W)
- Scott's Yard (119, W)
- Jolly Butchers' Yard (125, W)
- Bull's Head Yard (137, W)
- Cobb's Yard (147, W)
- Turrell's Yard (147, W)
- Fox and Hounds' Yard (151, W)
- Little Fox and Hounds' Yard (153, W)
- Wordingham's Buildings (157, W)
- Hodd's Yard (165, W)
- Grimmer's Yard (167, W))
- Hayward's Yard (171, W)
- Jeckell's Yard (175, W)
- Clarke's Yard (183, W)

## Golden Ball Street
- Dawson's Yard (5, E)
- Woolpack Yard (9, E)
- Grout's Thoroughfare (14, W)

## Market Lane
- Paradise Place (16, N)

## Mariners' Lane
- Old Friends' Yard (1, S)
- Wood's Yard (7, S)

## Scholes Green
- Bedford Yard (17, N)
- Globe Yard (21, N)
- Wilde's Yard (2, S)

## Thorn Lane
- Toper's Square (8, N)
- Bacon's Square (18, N)
- Middle Square (20, N)
- Lower Square(22, N)
- Commerce Court (28, N)

*Cattle being driven down Ber Street, 1908*

Thorn Lane Etc. clearance area

Black Swan Yard Etc. Ber Street clearance area

Bennett's Yard, Foulger's Yard Etc. Ber Street clearance area

90 – 104 Ber Street clearance area

Wood's Yard, Mariners' Lane, Lily Terrace, Ashbourne Street clearance area

Hayward's Yard Ber Street clearance area

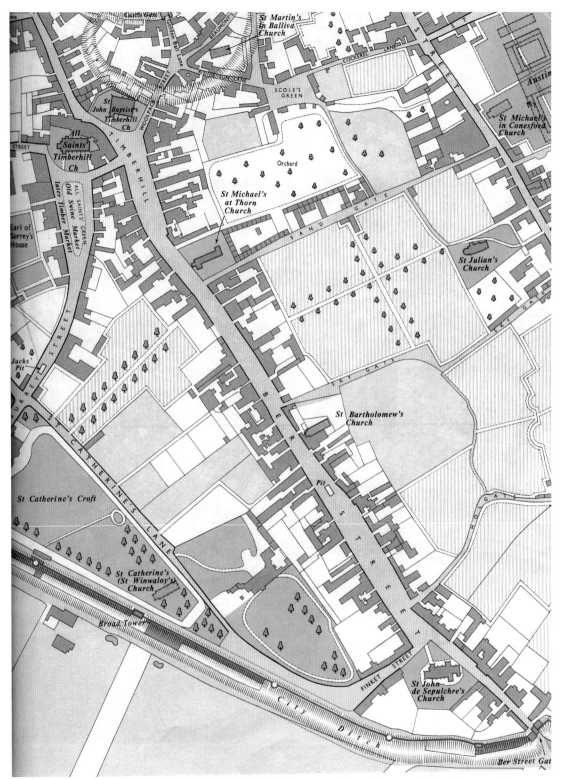

*Ber Street, detailed map produced by the Historic Town Trust adapted from Hochstetter's original plan, 1789*

*Ber Street, c.1920*

Ber Street, meaning 'Hill Street', owes its name to its situation on a long chalk ridge. There is some debate as to whether its origins can be traced back to Roman times, but it is generally agreed that the thoroughfare was in existence during the Norman settlement of the City. Further proof of its early development can be found in the enrolled deeds for Norwich (a type of land register covering the period from the height of medieval expansion to the Black Death) which clearly show that during the period 1285 – 1340 Ber Street was occupied.

Cunningham's Plan of 1558 reveals that Ber Street was built up as far as the City gates, whilst the map (left) clearly shows that by 1789 there were buildings along its length. Behind many were gardens, but some of these had already been filled, and by the time the 1884 map was produced, the area behind the street was packed with courts and yards. Photographs taken of Ber Street in the 1930s show that a number of timber-framed jettied buildings had survived from the 16th and 17th centuries, and that small cottages had been crammed into the spaces behind. Examples include Greyhound Yard, which stood to the rear of 102 – 104 Ber Street, and Paul's Yard, which stood behind 156 – 160 Ber Street.

Ber Street was a thriving area long associated with butchers, slaughterhouses and allied trades. It became an adjunct to the Cattle Market which was held in the centre of Norwich from at least the 17th century until the 1960s (today it is the site of the Castle Mall shopping centre). Until the early 20th century, every Saturday morning, and at the great Christmas and Easter fairs, animals were driven up the thoroughfare, which was one of the widest streets in Norwich. R. H. Mottram (the local historian) describes the street becoming: 'A "parking" place for drove after drove of frightened, fidgeting, lowing beasts, rounded up and kept together by drovers and dogs until a place could be found for them in the iron-fenced pens in the Cattle Market.' Such activity led to the street's nickname: 'Blood and Guts Street'.

Ber Street also provided stabling and sustenance for the many visitors who travelled to the market. Not surprisingly it contained a number of drinking establishments beside which yards developed, including, the Bakers' Arms (9), the Jubilee (21) the Lock and Key (89) and the Fox and Hounds (153).

During the late 19th and early 20th centuries, a number of Italian immigrant families settled

*'Big Peter Chiesa', said to be the first ice-cream seller in Norwich, Ber Street c.1910*

here, including the Parravanis (ice-cream makers) and Marcanonios (confectioners). R. H. Mottram eloquently explains: 'Men, small and dark, found some sort of work. The women, their abundant hair bound with richly coloured scarves, trundled piano organs, with a baby slung across the shafts, into the better residential districts and turned the crank-handle.... Scanty as their rags might be, and penurious their lot, those women had magnificent headpieces, each one worthy of copying on a bronze medallion.' Although this Italian community has long since moved on, Ber Street still plays host to a range of nationalities who trade their wares in its many shops and restaurants.

A number of factors contributed to the changing ambience of the area. Not least was the livestock market moving out of the City in 1960. Even before this, as transport improved country people visiting the Cattle Market no longer needed to stay for the night in the hostelries on Ber Street. As a result the fortunes of the many public houses on the street – in the 1880s there had been more than 20 – declined.

Then of course came the slum clearances of the 1930s, swiftly followed by war damage. Change continued after the war. In particular, in the 1950s and 1960s both Ber Street and the land between here and King Street were significantly redeveloped. Ber Street is still a busy thoroughfare lined with a combination of commercial and residential buildings, but there are now very few ancient structures.

It is very easy for us to decry the loss of so much history, but what did people think at the time? Writing in 1953, Mottram made the comment that since 1914 Ber Street had changed 'utterly'. Interestingly, he did not mourn the loss of the old houses which gave the street so much character, instead he wrote that it proved that 'poverty, hopelessness and helplessness' had been slain. That slum clearance and the introduction of the welfare state meant that tenants no longer needed to live in those 'unlighted, unpaved yards in which they had existed, often in single rooms, with a fine view of the common privy and single tap that served them.' In fact for him the changes proved that 'fairy tales...could come true'.

# Major Clearance Schemes

During the 1930s the yards in this area were extensively cleared. Altogether, more than 35 yards containing around 295 properties and 900 tenants were dealt with.

One of the largest programmes, affecting 11 yards, more than 100 houses and 316 tenants, was the 'Thorn Lane Etc.' clearance scheme. Amongst the yards affected were Twiddy's (Twitters') Court, Flecked Bull Yard and Lamb Yard.

As a result of slum-clearance programmes by the end of the 1930s the yards were no longer prevalent in this section of the City. Although during WWII the area was bombed, and buildings such as Bonds, the popular department store, and St Michael at Thorn Church, were destroyed, residential property was not badly affected.

Then in the late 1950s, the area was again subject to extensive clearance when it became part of a large redevelopment scheme which incorporated the building of Rouen Road (1962) and the redesigning of the area between the east side of Ber Street and King Street. This resulted in the demolition of many 19th-century buildings which were replaced by both low-rise homes and one of Norwich's few tower blocks: Normandie Tower. One wonders what early yard dwellers would make of this 16-storey edifice, so far removed in design from the buildings that dominated this area for so many years.

*Plan of 'Thorn Lane Etc. clearance area', 1937*

## Normandie Tower

In 1962, when Rouen Road was created, the Council planned to build three tower blocks on the side of the Ber Street slope. In the event, tunnels in medieval chalk workings put paid to this scheme and instead only one tower block was built together with the low-rise 'village on the hill'.

When Normandie Tower was officially opened on 21 May 1966 it was heralded in the *Eastern Evening News* as an interesting counter-movement to the construction of council estates on the outskirts of Norwich. However, this statement was not strictly accurate. During the interwar slum-clearance programme, the City Council built a number of flats in the centre. Unlike these earlier developments, which were a maximum of three-storeys high, the 95 apartments in Normandie Tower were distributed over 16 floors. In 1963 the City architect assured the housing committee that no damage would be done to the City skyline: 'It will be seen against the background of trees on the hills and it will not even overshadow the tower of St John de Sepulchre.' The initial intention had been to build a 21-storey block of flats, but this had been considered too high.

By the end of the 1960s high-rise apartments were no longer de rigueur, and Normandie Tower had the distinction of being only one of two high-rise flats erected within the City: the other was located on Vauxhall Road.

# Yards of Note

In the late 19th century this area was riddled with yards. The following yards are of particular interest:

## Fox and Hounds' Yard and Little Fox and Hounds' Yard (151 and 153 Ber Street)

*The little girl (to the left) stands at the entrance to Little Fox and Hounds' Yard. The wide entrance (on the right) leads to Fox and Hounds' Yard, 1936*

*Fox and Hounds' Yard, Ber Street, 1936*

These two yards lay either side of the Fox and Hounds public house which could trace its licence back to the 1760s. On Hochstetter's map of 1789 it is clear that there were already properties in both yards.

With so many people not only living in a confined space, but also next door to a pub, these would undoubtedly have been rowdy places to live; a fact confirmed by a police report produced in 1908. At this time the Fox and Hounds was a difficult pub to supervise, not least because there were a further 13 licensed houses within 200 yards. A number of rooms in the pub were let to lodgers, and sad to say there had been complaints of singing and shouting carrying on at 4 o'clock in the morning. The police explained that it was impossible to tell if the commotion was caused by 'bona-fide loafers or others'. They were particularly concerned that the house was frequented by 'poachers and other low-class customers'. In his defence the landlord explained that the establishment was of a higher quality than a 'common' lodging house, but he did give shelter to 'broken-down gentlemen'.

Between 1936/37 around 30 tenants were cleared from the two yards and ten properties demolished. At the same time the pub was finally closed.

## Greyhound Yard (102 Ber Street)

*92 – 104 Ber Street, 1938*

*Corporal Sidney Day VC, c.1918*

The yard was located behind the former Greyhound public house, sometimes known as the Greyhound Pleasure Gardens. In its heyday the pub had extensive grounds and many attractive features, as described in sales particulars produced in 1835: 'A large parlour, club room, roomy bar, tap room, six bedrooms, extensive cellars, bottling house, stabling for 50 horses, playground and convenient outbuildings attached. Gardens of upwards of three-quarters of an acre with a well-frequented bowling green.' By 1871 the pub had closed whilst by 1884 the extensive gardens had been replaced by nine properties, which were reached through a very narrow entrance. The properties were cleared of 29 residents c.1939.

## Jolly Butchers' Yard (125 Ber Street)

The yard lay adjacent to the former pub of the same name. It was in 1935 that landlady Antoinette Hannent (née Carrara), better known as Black Anna because of the colour she habitually wore, took over the helm of the Jolly Butchers, and here she reigned supreme until her death in 1976. Anna was the daughter of one of the Italian families who migrated to Norwich in the late 19th century. Anna's mother, Elizabetta, hired out piano organs from a depot in Newman's Yard (95 Ber Street, also known as Kahler's Yard) and earned the soubriquet 'queen of the organs'. Anna was a consummate performer and even as a girl she sang the same Italian operatic airs that rang out from the piano organs. However, jazz became her real love and she became known as Norwich's Sophie Tucker. Jazz at the Jolly Butchers, led by Anna, became legendary.

Out the back of the Jolly Butchers, leading down the yard, is an annexe built around 1850 specifically as a lodging house. It became known as Day's Lodging house, after the family who ran the pub from 1902 until 1922. Corporal Sidney Day, is remembered for his valour during WWI when he was awarded the Victoria Cross. The ground floor of the lodging house contained one huge, tiled kitchen with a big cooking range that used to be kept alive day and night. Upstairs were dormitories. It was rumoured that at one time the Jolly Butchers had 76 beds.

The pub was converted to offices in 1989. The building, including Day's lodging house, is now commercial premises. The yard still exists.

*Black Anna and the Jolly Butchers, c.1960*

## Lock and Key Yard (89 Ber Street)

*Lock and Key Yard entrance, 2014*

The yard's somewhat unusual name derived from the adjacent public house which was so-called because the cattle drovers who were herding their beast to market considered this a safe place to leave their money and valuables. Although the pub's licence was withdrawn under compensation in 1913 the yard's name remained unchanged.

Chris Farrow's family lived in the yard in 1901, she explains: 'Unfortunately, my family's story of life at number 2 Lock and Key Yard is not a pleasant one. In October of that year my grandfather [George Farrow] was witness to his father [Alfred] striking his mother [Sarah] during an argument whilst they were both the worse for drink; she died from bleeding to the brain three days later. Grandfather had to be a witness at court, where his father got two years hard labour. This caused a family rift as the siblings felt they had already lost one parent and did not want to lose the other. I suppose he could have been hung in those days. They tried to reason it was an accident, but grandfather could not lie under oath, it caused a huge rift in the family.'

In 1935/6 the eight properties in the yard were cleared of 33 residents. A door and plaque between 87 and 89 Ber Street still marks its original entrance.

*Ber Street, painted by Alfred Munnings, c.1925*

## Old Friends' Yard (1 Mariner's Lane)

*Mariners' Lane. The Old Friends is on the right, and the entrance to Wood's Yard was through the arch at the bottom of the slope, 1936*

The yard was located behind the public house of the same name. Andy Anderson recalls visiting it: 'In 1940 my family came to live in Norwich and I became friendly with the sons of the licensee of the Old Friends public house, Charles Dixey. There were the remains of a Norwich yard behind the Old Friends where we played cricket. A lady we called Miss Smith kept a milliners shop in Ber Street [140]. Behind the shop was an enclosed garden with a door in the wall which gave access to the yard. Quite disgracefully, in retrospect, we used her door as a wicket, and she used to periodically come out and remonstrate with us. In the centre of the yard was a water pipe and tap, and I remember on many occasions seeing a gentleman who lived in one of the remaining houses in the yard return from the pub at Sunday lunchtime and clean his potatoes very methodically and carefully. I didn't think about it very closely then, but it must have been his only water supply. By then most tenants had been moved out.'

The yard had been included in the 'Wood's Yard Etc. clearance area'. Although the order was passed in 1938, the war intervened. Eventually all properties included in the scheme were demolished (date unknown) and the area became the premises of the metal merchants, A. King & Sons.

## Paul's Yard (154 Ber Street)

*156 – 160 Ber Street, 1939*

The yard was located behind 156 – 158 Ber Street. Together with 160, they still form a row of three houses facing the east end of the medieval church of St John de Sepulchre.

Number 158, called Ber House, was built in the late 18th century. It is flanked on either side by numbers 156 and 160, which are of Tudor origin and are believed to have once been the wings of a building known as Black's Hall, the central part of which is now covered by Ber House. Although it would be lovely to believe the legend that the Black Prince (1330 – 1376, the eldest son of King Edward III) once distributed largesse to the poor of the City from here, it is more likely that the hall's name is derived from that of William Blackamore, who is recorded as the owner during the reign of King Edward III (1327 – 1377).

By the 1940s, numbers 156 and 160, which were late additions to the original hall, had fallen into a deplorable condition. Fortunately, in 1949 they were restored by Christopher Perks and Sidney Glendenning. At the time of the restoration it was discovered that number 160 was built c.1450, with the upper part added about 1590 and the dormer a few years later. Despite its age, the structure was found to be in excellent order, and even the main roof beams were intact.

It is assumed that the four buildings in St Paul's Yard were demolished at the time of this renovation.

*156 – 160 Ber Street, 2015*

*Boarded Entry Yard, 54 Ber Street, 1937*

*Field's Yard (note Tudor archway), 162 Ber Street, 1935*

*Lamb Yard, 28 Ber Street, 1938*

*Lower Square, 22 Thorn Lane, 1938*

*Middle Square, 20 Thorn Lane, 1938*

*Mason's Yard, 14 Ber Street, 1936*

*Twiddy's (Twitters') Court, Ber Street, 1938*

*Wood's Yard, 7 Mariners' Lane, 1938*

Looking at Ber Street today it is hard to believe that it was once riddled with old yards. The sparse evidence of their earlier existence includes the renovated Jolly Butchers' Yard and the entrance to Lock and Key Yard.

However, at 101 – 103 Ber Street there is a very appropriate memorial to the old yards. This is the location of Fiddy's Yard, a modern semi-sheltered housing scheme, built and managed by the Norwich Housing Society. It has taken the name of the original yard, which in turn was probably named after local grocer Robert Hicks Fiddy who traded in the vicinity in the 1870s. Back in 1936 the original yard was cleared of its eight residents, and it was subsequently demolished.

One wonders what the old tenants would think if they came back today and saw the lovely new development. Instead of a wash house, a laundry room is available along with a social room. But one of the biggest changes is the yard itself, no longer a place which is smelly and dark but a lovely bright area: an ideal place to sit and enjoy the sun.

*Fiddy's Yard, Ber Street, 2009*

*Frances outside Jolly Butchers' Yard, Ber Street, 2014*

*125 – 129 King Street, 1946*

# The River and Trade: King Street

Yards identified in this section of the City include:

## King Street

- Allcock's Yard (43, E)
- Murrell's Yard (53, E)
- Obey's Yard (61, E)
- Watson's Yard (73, E)
- Lifford's Yard (77, E)
- Lewis Yard (85, E)
- Old Barge Yard (123, E)
- Greenman Yard (131, E)
- Websdale Yard (137, E)
- Cockey Lane (139, E)
- Wickham's Yard (193, E)
- Half Moon Yard (241, E)
- Ferry Yard (247, E)
- Three Tuns' Yard (60, W)

- Watson's Court (64, W)
- Swan Yard (68, W)
- Raven Yard (86, W)
- Strike's Yard (116, W)
- Watson's Court (118, W)
- Waterman's Yard (146, W)
- Baxter's Court (158, W)
- Little Ship Yard (166, W)
- Big Ship Yard (168, W)
- Lincoln's Court (184, W)
- Barber's Yard (186, W)
- Rayner's Yard (194, W)

## Rose Lane

- Turner's Square (17, S)

*86 – 90 King Street. The entrance to Raven Yard is on the right, 1935*

Turner's Square, King Street clearance area

92 – 96 King Street clearance area

St Ann's Lane
Etc. King Street
clearance area

Abbey Lane
Etc. King Street
clearance area

Rayner's Yard
King Street
clearance area

# Historical Background

*River Wensum, view from Carrow Bridge, undated*

King Street's history is inextricably linked with its location next to the River Wensum. The river provided an essential trading route linking Norwich to the ports at Yarmouth and thence overseas. Even before the Norman Conquest, King Street enabled merchants to transport their wares from the riverside staithes to the old Tombland market.

The trading links were attractive to merchants who, along with the county's landed aristocracy, built fine properties here. However, as time moved on, more tradesmen and industrialists settled along the thoroughfare, and the elite moved out to more salubrious dwellings.

King Street's most impressive building typifies this progression. It was in the early 15th century that Robert Toppes (*c.*1405 – 1467) built his magnificent trading hall here. Being a rich merchant the main hall, on the first floor, was built to impress. It was 88 feet long. Its crown-post roof was made using expensive oak timbers and incorporated 14 carvings of dragons. Although only one of these mythical creatures survives, the building is now known as Dragon Hall. Until the mid-16th century the building served as the town house of wealthy citizens. After they left, the hall was divided into tenements, eventually

numbered 113 – 123 King Street. The ground-floor rooms housed many businesses, including a variety of shops and ale houses. Meanwhile, extra floors, staircases, windows and chimney stacks filled the Great Hall, and the yard at the rear, known as Old Barge Yard, was crammed with poor-quality housing. Most of the properties in the yard were demolished in 1937, but Dragon Hall survived and in 1954 it was listed as a Grade I historic building. It has since been restored and now looks magnificent.

Another survivor is Jurnet's Hall, also called the Music House. Parts of the building, including the vaults and northern gable, are believed to be Norman. It is thought that they were built by Isaac the Jew, a financier, who constructed the cellars as a semi-fortress to store his coin and bullion. From the 13th century it was the home of a string of noble families, including the Pastons and the Cokes. Like Dragon Hall, during the 18th century the house was subdivided into tenements, and by the late 18th century it contained a pub. In 1865 the building was bought by Youngs, Crawshay & Youngs, who incorporated it into their brewery. Today, the building is part of the Wensum Lodge Adult Education Centre.

By the late 19th century King Street was a hive of industry and commerce. From the 1884/5 map we can clearly discern the following characteristics:

- Brewing is a major activity in the area.
- Behind the properties lining the street there are a large number of yards containing buildings. Many are built adjacent to pubs, which give them their name, e.g. Three Tuns' Yard (60 King Street) and Old Barge Yard (123 King Street). Others are associated with what were once fine houses e.g. Murrell's Yard (53 King Street) and Raven Yard (86 King Street – please note that on the 1884 map Raven Yard is erroneously located at 70 King Street).
- Many of the street, yard and pub names are derived from their proximity to the river. Examples include Waterman's Yard (146 King Street) and Ferry Yard (247 King Street).

In the 20th century King Street continued to be a centre for trade. In the 1930s George Plunkett described it as 'a street of small shopkeepers' who were perfectly placed to serve both the local community, and the many brewery workers who converged there daily. Although as the century progressed the area suffered through a combination of slum clearance, bombing and the closure of the breweries, it is now benefitting from something of a renaissance. Today, most visitors go to see the wonderful medieval and Tudor buildings, but a brief wander along the street also gives an opportunity to see a variety of yards, including good examples of how they have evolved.

## Brewing in King Street

By the late 19th century, two major Norwich businesses, both brewers, dominated the street: Morgans, and Youngs, Crawshay & Youngs.

Morgans owned the Old Brewery, which could trace its origins back to 1563, when it was known as the Connisford Brewery. In 1942, the building suffered extensive bomb damage. Although it was rebuilt, in September 1961 Morgans went into voluntary liquidation. The brewery was purchased by Watney Mann Ltd, before eventually closing in 1985. By 2005 the site had been cleared, and has since been redeveloped with residential properties.

Around 1807 John Youngs established his Crown Brewery on King Street. Beer was brewed here until 1958 when the business was taken over by its rival, Bullards, and the brewery was closed. In 1961 the site was purchased by the Norfolk Education Committee and it is now the Wensum Lodge Adult Education Centre.

*Youngs, Crawshay & Youngs' Brewery, c.1900*

*King Street, view from the River Wensum, c.1890*

# Major Clearance Schemes

King Street was not selected for special attention in William Lee's 1851 *Report to the General Board of Health*. We cannot take this to mean that the area was particularly hygienic, it rather suggests that other places were worse. Similarly, although in the 1930s it was subject to five major clearance schemes, they were not particularly focussed around the yards, and only around 50 buildings in yards, occupied by approximately 100 tenants, were demolished.

During WWII sections of King Street were badly bombed. In particular, both Morgan's Brewery and St Julian's Church were demolished; after the war both were rebuilt. The same cannot be said for either Strike's or Watson's Yards, which lay between these two sites. In fact the land was taken over by Morgan's

and it was incorporated into their new, state-of-the-art brewery.

Further major changes occurred in 1958 when, along with neighbouring Ber Street, King Street became part of a redevelopment area. Yards which were demolished as a result of this scheme included Little Ship Yard (166) and Baxter's Court (158). More recently, King Street has seen the demolition of Morgans' Brewery and the construction of many new homes.

Despite all of the above, it has avoided the wholesale clearance which affected neighbouring Ber Street, and as a result still has an eclectic selection of buildings and yards.

# Yards of Note

In the late-19th century more than 25 yards were located in this relatively small area. They came in all shapes and sizes. Many were long and narrow, with all that implied for the quality of air and light, whilst those on the east side often led down to the river, the source of much disease and stench. The following yards are of particular interest:

## Murrell's Yard (53 King Street)

*Murrell's Yard, King Street, 1936*

In 1890 the yard was approached through an opening spanned by a wooden archway. At this time within the yard stood another doorway with spandrels containing both the arms of East Anglia and a bell in a letter 'R', the rebus of Robert Bell who was admitted to the freedom of the City in the reign of Henry VII (1485 – 1509).

Murrell's Yard lay behind 47-51 King Street. Writing in 1916 Walter Rye noted that these buildings were 'noticeable for having portions of some of the original open shop fronts and a little late-Gothic window upstairs...I should date the block about 1450'. All three shops have since been swept away. Number 45, a separate structure to the north, has survived. It is timber-framed (as were its neighbours) with a plastered upper front which jetties out slightly over the pavement. George Plunkett believed that part of the building dates from the 16th century.

The main houses in the yard were built in the 17th century. George Plunkett's photo not only shows that they were constructed of brick together with lath and plaster, but also that in the late 1930s they were in a terrible state of disrepair. The yard was cleared and demolished in 1939. Prior to this, five of the seven houses in the yard had already been vacated.

A modern housing development, called Murrell's Court, is now located in the same area as its predecessor.

## Old Barge Yard (123 King Street)

*Old Barge Yard (l to r): c.1850 by Thomas Lound, 1935, 2014*

The yard took its name from the Old Barge pub, part of the Dragon Hall building. It was one of the many along King Street that led down to the river. The inhabitants had many occupations. There were small shopkeepers, cow keepers who grazed cattle in the fields over the river, and brewery workers. By the 1930s Old Barge Yard contained a mix of residential and commercial buildings, including a coal yard, an ice store and stables. When it was cleared, c.1937, 38 people lived in 14 houses. Only one cottage survived the slum clearance. Today it is part of the Dragon Hall complex.

## Raven Yard (86 King Street)

The yard still lies behind three, early 17th-century houses. All the buildings are two-storeys high with an overhang. They have timber frames and are made of brick and flint. The houses would have originally been a single unit, which is believed to have been the residence of the Berney family (a rich influential dynasty). Richard Berney's tomb (died c.1623) can still be seen in St Peter Parmentergate Church.

The yard now contains modern flats and garages.

(Please note that on the 1884 map Raven Yard is erroneously located at 70 King Street).

*Raven Yard, King Street, by Holmes Edwin Winter, 1878*

## Ship Yard (168 King Street)

Ship Yard (called Big Ship Yard on the 1884 map) and Little Ship Yard were located either side of the Ship Inn, which could trace its licence back to the late 18th century. Somewhat misleadingly a lintel above the yard entrance proclaims it as the 'Princes In'. It is thought that this could be a piece of memorabilia retrieved from a hostelry of that name which was located on Tombland in the late 14th century.

Youngs, Crawshay & Youngs' brewery was located on the opposite side of the street. By the early 20th century the six houses in the yard were all owned by the brewers, who let the houses to their workers. There was even a 'breakfast room' at one end of the yard for the men who worked in the tun room (where barrels were washed).

The yards lay behind a range of old houses, including numbers 170 – 180 King Street (believed to date from the 16th century). Around 1964, these buildings together with 182 (a tall Victorian house), were converted into three flats and five cottages, and at the same time what was described as 'an accreditation of old rubbish at the back', encompassing sculleries, sheds, old buildings and outhouses, was removed. In 1969 the pub closed, and the following year this was also purchased by the council and converted into two dwellings.

During the various renovations, the dilapidated cottages in the yard were demolished. However, the buildings which faced the street, a space behind and the entrance to Ship Yard have survived.

*Ship Yard, King Street, 1938*

*Entrance to Ship Yard, King Street, 2015*

# Irene Foster Recalls Life in Ship Yard

'I first moved into Ship Yard when I was just four years old [c.1928], when my father started a new job at Youngs' Brewery. When we arrived, the only house that was free was number 1, next door to what was called the breakfast room. This was used by men from the brewery who'd had an early start. I don't remember much about it, but I know there was an oven in the corner of the room and you'd hear the men coming across at around 9 o' clock to have a meal.

'The yard was clean enough. There were six families there. They were alright; people made it nice.

'On Saturdays cows were herded down King Street on their way to the cattle market. They very often used to find their way into Ship Yard. When we lived at number one, a cow got into mother's wash house. I don't know what she did to get it out, but it gave her a bit of a shock.

'There was a little tiny shop run by a Mrs Swoish, just next to the entrance of Little Ship Yard [166 King Street]. Mrs Swoish was a funny little lady and when she couldn't reach the counter she used to stand on an old bag of spuds or something. It was a general store, and she used to sell things like fruit and vegetables and sweets. When mother used to pay her bill, once a week, she used to give us kids a little bag of sweets. I particularly remember that she used to sell piccalilli and red cabbage that she kept in big jars. You'd go in with a basin or cup and she'd weigh you out however much you wanted; in those days it tended to be two penn'th. I used to love this cabbage, and once when I had tuppence to spend I bought some pickle just for myself, and afterwards was I ill!

*Irene, aged 18*

'We eventually moved to a house on King Street, but in 1947, after I was married, I moved back. This time I lived in number two, which was next door to the one I'd lived in as a child. It was fine and we even had a big wash house all to ourselves. It contained old-fashioned boilers which you'd have to light to heat water; we used to keep our bikes and everything in there. All the others had to share another wash house. Even then the house didn't have electricity, and when my first son Stephen was born the room was lit by a gas light. We cooked on an old gas stove. Later on number six became available which was bigger and had electricity, and so we moved again.

'In the summer my next door neighbour used to sit on the doorstep enjoying a ciggie and my toilet was right opposite, but as by then my mother lived on King Street, I went around the back way and used hers. I didn't feel comfortable sitting in my loo, with the neighbours just a few yards away.

'I put in for a new council house, and in 1953 we moved to Theobald Road in Old Lakenham. The house we left at Ship Yard had electricity, but even then we only had an outside loo and no bathroom – we still used a tin bath in front of the fire. The new house was a lot better!'

## Three Tuns' Yard (60 King Street)

The yard is located behind numbers 56 – 60 King Street which were originally built in the 17th century. Although the buildings' distinctive dormer gables were rebuilt in 19th-century brick, it is believed they represent the original design.

The yard took its name from the neighbouring public house (which stopped trading in 1969). Below the building, lies a 15th-century vaulted undercroft. Unlike many City yards, the entrance to Three Tuns' Yard is wide. This was because it also led to the pub stables. As confirmed by a sales document for the pub, produced in 1888, which stated: 'The Tuns Yard includes stables, a cart shed, closets and bins.'

The buildings in the yard, along with neighbouring Watson's Court, were subject to a clearance order c.1938, at which time it contained four properties. It is unclear when the properties were demolished.

The entrance to the yard can still be seen today. In 1985 the rear of number 60 was extensively renovated. Modern properties have since been built to replace the original yard houses. A modern Three Tuns' Court, now stands in the same area as its predecessor.

*Three Tuns' Pub and entrance to yard, 1936*

*Renovation of Three Tuns' Yard, 1985*

# Photo Gallery of King Street Yards in the 1930s

*Entrance to Barber's Yard, 186 King Street, 1936*

*Entrance to Buxter's Court, 158 King Street, 1939*

*Entrance to Rayner's Yard, 194 King Street, 1936*

For anyone interested in the City's yards, a visit to King Street is an absolute necessity. It is almost like a living museum, containing, as it does, examples of yards through all their reincarnations.

Of particular interest is Swan Yard, which is located at 68 King Street (note it is wrongly located next to the Nelson Monument on the 1884 map, it is the yard to the immediate south, labelled Raven Yard). In 1998 Swan Yard was fully renovated. Despite the fact that it has been attractively updated, you can get an idea of what it would have been like living here in the past, when sanitation was poor. It still has many of the characteristics of an old yard, in particular it retains the long, narrow tunnel-like entrance which was typical of many yards and it has also been fitted into a space behind old houses which front the street.

Further along King Street a good example of new houses built in an ancient yard can be found at Raven Yard, which now contains modern flats and garages. On the other side of the road Lane's Yard (called Lewis Yard on the 1884 map) lies behind a run of Georgian buildings (83 – 89). In 1977 a £50,000 restoration scheme was begun, with the aim of converting the houses into flats and cottages. As part of the renovation garage doors which had led through to a workshop were removed to create a wide entrance. The yard is now something of a hybrid, containing an attractive mixture of old and new buildings, together with a parking area.

Old Barge Yard was not so lucky. After being subject to slum clearance in the 1930s, the yard still remains. However, apart from the one cottage which forms part of the Dragon Hall complex, all other buildings have been destroyed

Finally, the street also contains many modern yards. Following the demolition of Morgans (later Watney Mann) brewery on King Street, the site has been redeveloped with new residential properties. These have been built in cul-de-sac formations which have been designated as courts and yards. They differ significantly from the City's 'old yards' in that they are not 'infills' crammed into spare space behind older properties but were carefully designed as part of the new development. The yards bear such names as Maltsters, Dray and Polypin – all reminders of the brewing industry which played such an important part in the street's history.

*Swan Yard, King Street, 2014*

# Outside the City Wall: Heigham

Yards identified in this section of the City include:

## Heigham Street

- Shuttle's Yard  (10, N)
- Globe Yard (14, N)
- Brett's Yard (1, S)
- Weston Square (3, S)
- Flower in Hand Yard (9, S)
- Clarke's Yard (13, S)

- Blake's Yard (20, S)
- Crocodile Yard (27, S)
- Bridge's Yard (39, S)
- Allcock's Yard   (43, E)

## Barn Road

- Baldry's Yard (71, W)
- Cooper's Yard (61, W)

# Historical Background

Brian Ayers observes that historically Norwich was noted for its lack of suburbs and that Heigham 'was essentially created when it was left outside the City walls', which were completed by the mid-14th century. The early village settlement clustered around the medieval church of St Bartholomew, which lay just beyond the crossroads now formed by Heigham Street and Mile Cross Road. The church was bombed in 1942 and only its tower survives. Other ancient buildings in the same vicinity which withstood the hostilities include the Dolphin Inn, parts of which dated from the 16th century, and a nearby 16th-century timber-framed building, which is better known to many as the Gibraltar Gardens pub.

During the late Tudor age the suburb expanded. This was for two main reasons: firstly the walls no longer had a military purpose, as in these more peaceful times citizens did not require the protection they afforded; secondly, the City was becoming very crowded. New buildings erected in this period included 12 Heigham Street, which had flint walls and long weavers' windows. (It was unfortunately bombed and destroyed during WWII.) Expansion continued and by the end of the 18th century, buildings lined Heigham Street immediately outside the City gate.

However, it was in the 19th century that Heigham grew significantly, as described in detail in William Lee's 1851 report. Lee noted that in 1842 Heigham

*Dolphin Inn (Bishop's Palace), 1937*

91 – 127
Midland Street
clearance scheme

Brett's Yard Etc.
Heigham Street
clearance scheme

Globe Yard
Heigham Street
clearance scheme

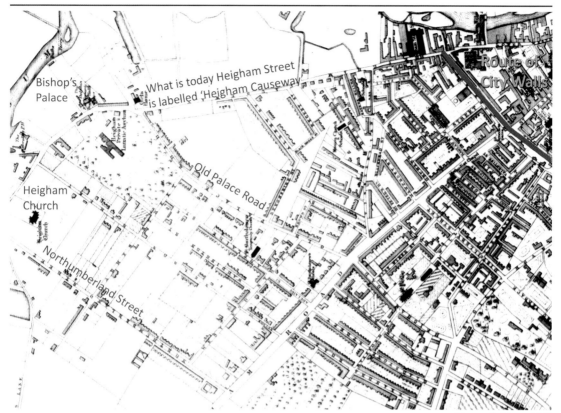

*Morant's Map, 1873*

*Flint walls and long windows, 12 Heigham Street, 1937*

had 15 streets containing around 1500 properties, whilst by 1851 there were 22 streets with around 1850 properties. Over the same period the suburb's population grew by about 16% to 7,000. Sadly the infrastructure could not cope with the rapid expansion: 'Heigham Street, as it is called, which is 150 – 200 yards in length [we assume that this refers to the area immediately outside Heigham Gate] has an open central channel which receives the outpourings from all of the yards on the left-hand side of the street. And the refuse that is swept off those yards into the central channel by the inhabitants of the courts, containing very many cottages, remains stagnant. On the right-hand side of the street there are three or four yards which are drained into the central channel in the same manner. This central channel, through its entire length has but one reservoir or receptacle, namely a grating, that is called a cockey – a sort of cess pool for solid matter.'

On the 1884 map we can clearly see the difference between the 'old yards', such as Flower in Hand Yard, which were inserted behind older houses lining the street, and the 'modern' 19th-century terrace developments on newly planned roads, such as Ely Street and Canterbury Place. By then 'old Heigham' formed just a small part of the suburb as, unlike areas in the City centre, the suburb could spread ever outwards.

214

# Yards of Note

*The ladies of Globe Yard, c.1916*

As elsewhere, a number of yards in Heigham were named after pubs, including Flower in Hand Yard, Crocodile Yard and Shuttle's Yard. One yard, more than any other, stands out in this area. Not because of its conditions, but because of a single photograph. Brian Hollings explains: 'If you look at the photo of Globe Yard [taken between 1914 – 1918] there are no men in the picture because they were all away fighting in WWI. I understand Marie Lloyd, the famous music hall star, was appearing at the Norwich Hippodrome, and she heard about this and paid them a visit. She also went to the school, where she had her photo taken. It appears she did not have a picture taken with the ladies, but then with her finery I can see why. The reason I have an interest in this photo, is because my mother is the little girl standing by the baby chair on the right of the picture, and my grandmother, is the tallish lady behind carrying the young baby, my uncle. My grandmother died at 33, but my mother reached the grand age of 92.'

## Clearance Schemes and the Yards Today

Although the old yards in Heigham, including Globe Yard, Brett's Yard and Blake's Yard, were subject to slum clearance in the interwar years, the programmes were as likely to encompass non-yard developments, such as Sayers Buildings and Coleby Place.

It was during WWII that many buildings were destroyed. Heigham was particularly targeted because of its proximity to the City Railway Station.

The area has subsequently been redeveloped and the old yards lost.

### Heigham Street Gate

Heigham Street Gate, was also known by the rather macabre name of 'Porta Ubfern' or 'Hell Gate'. There are a number of explanations for this. It could be because it was both the lowest lying Norwich gates and near a swampy, unapproachable river bank. Alternatively it was on Lower Westwick Street which was possibly one of the City's 'bad streets'. Finally 'hell' could be a corruption of 'holl' or 'hole', the Norfolk dialect for a ditch.

*Heigham Street Gate, by Henry Ninham, c.1830*

# Joyce's Story – Born in the Yards

**Joyce Wilson (1924 – 2015) with her husband, Don**

Joyce loved to talk about her life. Here she vividly explains what it was like living in the old Norwich yards and moving to the council estates. We have spoken to Joyce many times over the years, and in 2014 she added extra reminiscences to our earlier interviews.

She makes it very clear that living in the Pockthorpe yards was tough, but her account covers more than the hard physical conditions, it is a tale of resilience, cheerfulness and pride.

Joyce passed away on 1 January 2015 after a short illness...this is her story.

# My House

'The yards in Pockthorpe where I was born were absolutely notorious at the time. Nobody had an indoor toilet, nobody had water inside.

'We lived in a little yard called Fairman's Yard [101 Barrack Street] which was situated opposite Steward & Patteson Brewery. Early memories, it was quite pleasant as far as we were concerned, but that was unusual. Some of the neighbouring yards further up the road were in very bad condition. Some of the houses didn't even have a window. There was a door, which led down into these little dark hovels. There was very often filth in the yards, drains got blocked, refuse was just thrown about and on really wet days it was horrendous. But, people on the whole did make the best of the situation, but sometimes it was just a battle against all of the odds. We were fortunate, because there was just one other house in our yard, and so we just had to share our loo, which was perhaps 10 yards from the house, with one other family. But in the main yards up the road, like Palace Yard, where we weren't allowed to visit, there was perhaps a dozen families sharing one loo, which sadly very often…well to say unclean was a euphemism, it was absolutely appalling.

'Mother had to go across the flagstones to reach the pump to get water. Obviously there was no electricity. As far as our house went we had a living room which had red flagstones on the floor, the only floor covering we had were "piece rugs", which my mother made by knotting old rags: they were in front of the hearth. The other thing of course, we always had crickets in the hearth. We heard them chirruping, but we never took any notice of them. It was just one of those things.

'Many of the houses had just a door and tiny window, and were just "one up and one down". We had three rooms because we had an extra little one in the garret where I used to sleep with my sister Hilda.

'Our house was below pavement level, which made it very dark. The only light we had was a gas bracket on the wall in the living room. The mantle was always blowing out, and we had to run across the road to buy another one which cost one penny. In the bedrooms there were no lights whatsoever. We use to carry up a candle or night light in a saucer. Our heating was one little black fireplace in the living room. Of course in the wintertime there was often ice on the inside of the window panes. The other thing being so damp, so old and so cramped the white-plaster walls in the bedroom gave off a strange smell. It was almost like almonds. Later on I found out it was the bugs in the wall; I suppose that the soft plaster was a haven for them. We slept in proper beds with straw mattresses. If any of us came down with a little red bump on our skin, my mother used to take a little bowl of water up and she used to search for fleas which she'd catch and squash and put in the bowl. She was scrupulously clean, but it was a real battle. When she hung her washing on the line it was pure white: nobody's looks like that today. Despite having to pump every drop of water she used to change all of the beds every week.'

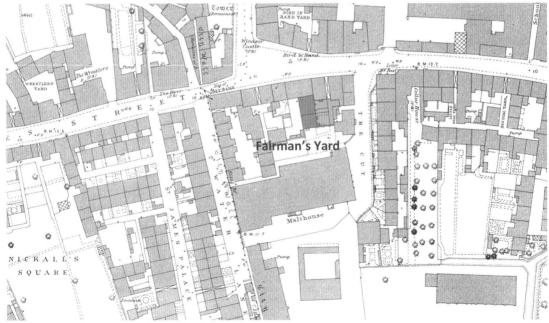

*Location of Fairman's Yard, highlighted on OS Map, 1884*

# My Family

'I lived with my parents, four sisters and brother. Hilda was born in 1916, Dorothy in 1920, Marjorie in 1922. I came along in 1924, Olive in 1926 and John in 1929. Then in 1931 mother had her final child, a baby girl, who only lived four days. Mother was 44, and relieved that her child-bearing years were over.

'At one o' clock the horn went off at Steward & Patteson Brewery to tell the brewery workers it was dinner time. My mother used to tell the story of when she was having me. She heard the horn go and she said to the midwife "there goes one", and the midwife replied "...and here comes one", and I was born.

'When we were kids there wasn't a happier crowd. My mother didn't allow us to mix. We thought because we weren't in a big yard and didn't have to share facilities, that we were a little bit better than them. This meant that we were very close. In our summer holidays from school, if the weather was good at all we spent our days on Mousehold Heath. I can still pick out the big hawthorn tree we sat under; we used to call it Hawthorn Cottage. We always took the latest baby in the pram. Mother used to send us out in the morning and tell us not to come back until tea time. We always took sandwiches but never any money. I knew the heath like the back of my hand.

We used to collect blackberries, and wild flowers for school. I'd go in on a Monday, and other girls brought in a buttercup and daisy but I'd produce around 23 varieties of flower, all pressed and labelled. The houses on Mousehold Estate hadn't been built then and it was all heath.

'We all had to go to church and Sunday school. We went to St Paul's, which was a lovely little church, but that was destroyed in the Blitz. We all ran down to see it ablaze. St James was nearer, it's still there, but now it's the Puppet Theatre.

'We all had our own jobs and personalities. Hilda was the eldest and motherly one, she had to grow up quickly. Dorry was the naughty one, she always had a very quick wit and made up lovely stories. The only thing was that the heroine was always called Dorothy, and so we'd have tales such as "Dorothy Saves the Day" or "Dorothy to the Rescue", and I used to get so annoyed because just once couldn't it be "Joyce"? She was also responsible for seeing after the latest baby. Marjorie was domesticated, and so she had to dust. I had to run the errands, because they reckoned that I had plenty of cheek. I was busy all of the time. We never got smacked, but we always obeyed my mother.'

*Joyce (l) with brother John and three of her sisters, c.1980*

# My Mother

'My mother's father was an invalid and so she had left school at 12. Thinking back, despite her limited education she was a very able lady and she'd often sit and help us with our school work. Her first job was at Chamberlin's, a tailoring factory in St Augustine's. She was a wonderful seamstress. Later on when we were all little, on top of looking after us and the house, after tea she was always doing sewing and it wasn't just for us, it was also for other people. She rarely worked with new material. As often as not she'd be given an old piece of adult clothing, such as a coat, and she'd be asked to make a child's coat or jacket out of it. She did the most beautiful hand sewing. She'd charge half-a-crown to make a coat. Often she'd be presented with a pair of large trousers where the knees and seat where gone, but she could salvage enough material from the legs to make a new pair of trousers for a kiddy: she'd charge around a shilling or one-and-six for all of that work. Her work was beautiful; I don't take after her!

'Like other women who lived in the yards, life was very hard for my mother On wash days at about 5.30 a.m. she would light the coal fire under the copper [large metal pot] which was in the corner of the wash house which was found on the other side of the yard beyond the pump. There was no water supply there, mother had to get it from the pump in the yard and then transport it across in buckets. On top of normal clothes because my father worked as a butcher he had seven aprons, one for every day, and each evening when he came home they would be covered in blood and grease, but every day he had a clean one. Overnight she would have been soaking all these aprons in a bath of salt water. On top of all that she changed all the beds every week and washed every scrap of linen. It was a mammoth job. First everything had to be soaked, then scrubbed, then it was put in the copper where it was boiled. Next it was transferred to another bath of cold water where it was rinsed, then she squeezed a packet of "Reckitt's Blue" in it to make the washing look whiter. When all that was done, all the aprons had to be starched. She finished around 6 p.m. then the water left in the copper was used to wash down all the things she'd used. So without fail she had a 12-hour stint every Monday. It was alright when the weather was good, but when it was bad she had to hang it on lines across the room...and didn't that use to smell and steam! When I think now, I don't know how she did it. On washdays we always had cold meat for dinner and a big suet pudding and blue peas, which were dried peas soaked overnight. I was always sent down the shop to buy two penneth of pickled onions or pickled cabbage. We never had jars and used to get it in a basin we took from the house. Of course if it was piccalilli I used to dip my finger in it and nibble it all the way home...so there was always less of that! Then Tuesday was ironing day, and you've got to remember there were no electric irons. Irons had to be heated on the fire, you'd spit on them and if they sizzled you'd know they were hot enough! There was a day for everything. The only day I can remember my mother not working was a Sunday afternoon. She'd cook a big Sunday dinner, then she'd wash, put a clean blouse on and then sit and read the *News of the World*. She never went out: we did the shopping, she just gave the orders and kept working. But she did live to be 93, after all they do say hard work doesn't kill you. What's more her face never lined, when people asked her how she managed it she always said: "Plenty of good living, hard work and a contented mind".'

*Joyce's mother aged 93, c.1980*

## Health

'When I was a child many people seemed to have lung troubles, whole families. I suppose that today it would be called tuberculosis, but then we called it consumption. It went through whole families. Then there was diphtheria. Lots of people were going down with it, and they went into the school to take samples and discovered that my brother John was a germ carrier. Yet although we lived in very cramped conditions none of the rest of the family caught it. John was taken into an isolation ward at the hospital until he was clear of it. If you were ill you'd never call a doctor in, unless you really were desperate. My sister Marjorie got rheumatic fever, and a doctor visited her once, I think it cost 2s. 6d. but for things like measles, mumps or whooping cough, we just got on with it. There were lots of lame children wearing leg irons and built up boots, which is something you don't really see today, it came from polio.'

# I Loved School

'We went to school at Bull Close, which is now St Augustine's. That was a good school. I remember the day I started, I was four. Mother wanted me to go because she had another baby on the way. I remember the headmistress was called Miss Green, and I met a perky little girl called Vera Carver who became a very good friend. Then when we were 11 we took the scholarship and the lucky ones were allowed to go to grammar school. The shame is that Hilda, myself and my sisters, Ollie, Dorry and Marjorie were all awarded scholarships. We brought the letters home saying that we were entitled to go to grammar schools, but my father just refused to have anything to do with it. He said that he left school at 12 and he didn't see why he should keep us, what was good enough for him should be good enough for us, and so we continued at Bull Close. We all really enjoyed school. We all loved stories and drawing pictures. We didn't have notebooks or paper, instead we used to go to the corner shop run by an old boy called Billy Royal and asked him if he had any Woodbine [cigarette] boxes. They were white cardboard, which when flattened were about 12 inches by 8 inches. One of my sisters had a terrific imagination and wrote poetry. We had a very full life and I never envied anyone.

'I didn't want to leave and work in a factory because I loved school, especially when I became head girl which made me feel important. I used to stand every morning and read a piece out loud from the Bible, and it was "Joyce this" and "Joyce that".'

# We Ate Well...

'Because my father was a butcher we ate well; he used to bring meat home in his pocket. Not steaks or chops or anything like that, but something like breast of mutton or sweetbreads; luckily my mother was a wonderful cook. For tea [evening meal] we'd always have a new 2lb loaf from Taylor's Bakery at the bottom of Silver Road and we'd have it sliced with either half an egg or half a banana, but my mother always prepared something special for father such as smoked haddock or ham. As the man of the house he expected it, and that was the general attitude in most households. We never expected much, in fact I don't think that I ever had a whole egg until I was in my teens.

'You mustn't forget that very few of our neighbours had ovens, so they were really restricted in what they could cook. Generally you had a fireplace with a few little trivets outside, where people always had a saucepan cooking some cheap bit of meat and as many rough vegetables you could get in and maybe some sort of suet pudding. Then on Sunday I used to love coming home from church, because we walked by Taylors, the bakers. You could always see the women coming across wearing sack aprons and carrying big baking trays with some sort of meat in it and packed with potatoes and onions. On the top was a sheet of greaseproof paper with their names on it. They took it to Taylors, and after he took his bread out of the oven, these trays all went in. Then about 1 p.m. you'd see all the same ladies coming back to collect their cooked food, but by this time they'd finished their chores, and so they'd taken out their curlers and were wearing their Sunday-best aprons. It smelt lovely. That was the main meal of the week, because otherwise everything was cooked on the trivets in the fireplace. At Christmas, most people made a Christmas cake, but no one cooked them. Instead the women always took them to the bakers who baked them for you, I think he also rented out his tins. My mother used to make four. I can't remember how much the baker charged to use his ovens, but I think ordinary Sunday dinner was about tuppence each. My mother took her cakes across, but normally she was able to cook our Sunday dinner at home, because we had a back oven in the wall which was heated by the fire.

'We never had holidays. Occasionally we had a half-day outing to Yarmouth by train. Father used to go into work first, and then we'd set out with a big old pile of sandwiches. One loaf would be spread with dripping; we always had dripping because father bought the fat home from the slaughter-house and mother'd cook that up with onions and a squeeze of Bisto and so forth. The other loaf would be spread with jam. We then put two pennyworth of sherbet in two empty bottles which we'd fill with water and they were our drinks for the day.'

*Joyce with husband Don, c.1970*

# Work

*Joyce's father, c.1931*

'We all had to leave school at 14 which was a shame. My sister Hilda was the eldest one and in her first job straight from school she started on eight shillings a week. It was a family joke that on her first day at work she wore a borrowed pinafore and patched knickers! It was really as bad as that. We all started in the shoe factories. My first day was a real let down when they sat me on the work bench with a pot of solution and a brush and told me to stick labels in shoes, but I was only there a year, 'cos I left school in 1938 and in 1939 the war started and I had a complete change and started working with my father, a butcher. This change occurred because rationing was introduced and my father's boss said that they would have to get someone in to organise things. So my father said: "I've got a daughter who'll do that". I was responsible for making registers of all the customers, removing coupons, cashiering and doing the wages and the book work: I loved my new job. Later, when supplies became limited, my work expanded and I started making sausages, preparing mince and serving customers. Officially I was called a clerk/butcher, it was my introduction to the clerical work I did later in life.

'There was a great deal of unemployment at times. The main employers were the shoe factories and others included the breweries, the Carrow works and Caley's Chocolate factory – it used to smell lovely when we went by there! Of course there was much more manual labour, and the men worked very hard for their wages. I think that's why so many of them drank, because that was all there was in their lives. My father always stopped for a drink on the way home, and arrived in about eight, by which time we were all in bed. My mother then did him something special for his tea.

'But for the men it was just a question of working from one week to the other. Especially in the shoe factories where work was uneven. Some weeks there'd be plenty of work, in others they'd be on slow time and only go in for two or three half-days. Because wages were so low they didn't have a chance to put anything away or prepare for holidays. They just worked to live.'

## The Spirit of Dunkirk

'When you get this sort of situation when things are really bad and depressing, I do think that people try and stick together, and there was a terrific community spirit. The women didn't stand about a lot, there wasn't time, but especially in the yards where they had to share a copper to do their washing, and there'd be Mrs Jones waiting for Mrs Bernard to get her washing done, they had to get on. There was quite a lot of domestic violence, it didn't apply in my family. I can remember people saying a couple were fighting again. But the women would get together and try to help some poor helpless wretch who was getting a battering, I don't know why, she'd probably spoken out of time or hadn't got the meal ready, but violence was apparent. It was almost like the wartime spirit. When you're all in it together, you had to make the most of a bad job. I've known women to interfere and stick their necks out just to show solidarity.

'We didn't feel deprived by any means. We didn't have a great deal, but we didn't expect a great deal. People living in the yards did struggle, but it was funny they had a certain pride. They were dark little houses with one door, but it was so strange often the door step outside was whitewashed and the door knobs were "Brassoed" [polished]. So, on the outside you had a shiny door knob and a gleaming white doorstep, which we were told to walk over and not to stand on, we had to stretch over it so we didn't leave a footprint. But I think that the whitewashed step was a little bit of defiance, it was if the women were saying: "Look it's not too bad after all."'

## The Yards Came Down

'The big change when the yards started to come down was in the early 1930s, I was still in the infant school. I clearly remember a man coming to the door with a book under his arm and saying: "Well Mrs Aspland I must condemn this house." He then turned and looked at us lot of rosy-cheeked kids and added, "...but I can't condemn these children". She thought that was a huge compliment and repeated it often with a great deal of pride.

'But that was the beginning. As the time drew nearer to our leaving Fairman's Yard we were very aware of something happening. We could see families leaving to go to their new homes. Today when people move house we're used to seeing a van take furniture and carefully packed crates. All I can recall is men with their shirt sleeves rolled up, sporting belts and braces, pulling along handcarts which they'd hired from Tom Spauls. There was very little furniture, just the inevitable iron bedstead lying flat with rolled up mattresses, usually tied with the ropes from orange boxes, on top. Additionally there'd probably be two or three wooden chairs or stools and sometimes a chest of drawers...but nobody had a sideboard or occasional furniture. Then there would be a few saucepans strung together, which clanged together as the cart was pushed along. Families had few possessions then.

'We weren't displaced to one of the new council estates. My mother had a stepfather who lived on Mousehold Street. He was due to go to what was the old-people's hospital, known as the workhouse [now the site of the West Norwich Hospital], and so we took over his house. When we moved we were all involved each carrying boxes full of brushes, dusters, crockery or cutlery. We made many trips walking to Mousehold Street. It was a new chapter in our lives. We were now living in a six-room terraced house with three bedrooms. The toilet was just outside.

Although we didn't have a bathroom, the tin bath just hung outside the back door ready to be brought in on bath night, but it was far better than what we had been used to. For a start there were three bedrooms, but best of all we'd finished with the necessity of a pump. It was heaven to turn on a tap, in fact when we first moved in it was such a novelty I used to love just turning it on and watching it.

'Many houses and yards were pulled down around Barrack Street. You have to remember, these were dreadfully put together hovels and so when they were demolished there were huge clouds of dust. Many of the houses were badly infested, and as the wood was pulled away they almost crumbled. I still remember the rats. Talk about the Pied Piper of Hamelin, there were rats everywhere...black rats, grey rats, white rats, even ginger rats. I remember people throwing sticks at them. Afterwards there was rubbish left about, water stood in green puddles and the stench was awful; it's a wonder there wasn't more disease. As houses were pulled down the people who remained would go and gather old gate posts and other bits of unwanted wood which they could put on their fires.'

*Nos 25 – 33 Barrack Street, 1938*

## Moving to the Council Estates

'People who lived in the yards on Barrack Street moved to the new council houses. I think that some went to the Plumstead Estate, others to the Drayton Estate or Mile Cross. Often people were simply shifted out together, and of course that did mean that you didn't do away with the community spirit, because so many of the people who lived in the yards found themselves moved to areas where they were still with each other; your old neighbours still lived around the corner. As such although the yards were done away with, I think that spirit did go with them.'

## Changes on Barrack Street

'After the demolition they built a lot of new flats in Barrack Street across the road from us, and in many ways it then lost its character. It was strange to us because we'd never seen flats before. When I was a little girl there were shops along the main road. There was a shop called Ketteringham's [32 Barrack Street], he always had a bitch that sat in the window. It kept producing pups, and so you'd often see a notice in the window announcing that these were for sale. He used to sell records and comics and papers, and other things like that. There was also a rag-and-bone man just around the corner from us, on Cowgate next to the Priory Gym. We often visited there because when my mother did her sewing she saved every spare scrap of material which was put in a "rag bag". Every couple of weeks or so when the bag was full, two of us would take it down there. The rag-and-bone man would weigh the bag and depending on how heavy it was he'd pay us up to four pennies for it. Then on the way home we always had instructions to buy something extra for tea, like a jar of jam. Many of the new flats have now been condemned and demolished. It's strange to think that it all happened in my lifetime.'

## Chamberlin Road

'I now live at 72 Chamberlin Road in a house that was originally occupied by my mother-in-law. She moved here in the late 1920s. The Wilsons were Freemen of the City of Norwich. Don's father worked at Greens, who were high-class gents' outfitters on the Walk, he was a porter or something like that. He wasn't anything important, but it was just a slightly elevated position. After the war, in 1946, when Don was sent back from Italy there was a housing shortage in Norwich because of the bombing, and my mother-in-law said we could have the rooms upstairs; I've been here ever since.

'In the early years, the tenant in the house across the road from here was a Mr Vines who had a thriving shoe repairing business in Pitt Street, on the other side of the road was the manager of Sainsbury's. A few doors down was the manager for the Trustees Savings Bank even the mayor, a Mr Cutbush, lived a few doors down. Across the road was a man who had a flourishing tobacco business on Stump Cross, Policeman Dockra lived at the bottom of Blythe Road, he was an inspector at the finish. Don used to tell me that two teachers lived opposite at one time. Down the road was Mr Sabberton, who owned a jewellers business. When you think that people with important jobs, bank managers and the like, were allocated these council houses. They were all middle-class people, not working class; you had to be somebody to live on Chamberlin Road.'

## A Long and Happy Life

'Although I have had few regrets in my life, I had always wished I could have had more education, and so at the age of 70, with my four grandsons all at university, I enrolled at night school. Under the enthusiastic guidance of an inspirational teacher, Chris Napp, I successfully completed 'O' Level English. Two years later, at the grand age of 73, I took and passed my 'A' Level.

'I feel life has been kind to me. My 90 years have consisted of a magical childhood followed by a happy and busy working life. I am supported by a wonderful family, lovely neighbours and loyal friends. My crowning glory is my great-grandchildren: I feel truly blessed.

'It's been a long journey from those early days in the yards to a house in one of the new council estates. By some strange coincidence I can see that the circle is almost completed, and I feel privileged to have been part of the new Norwich.'

# Additional Information
## Bibliography

**Anderson, A. P. and Storey, N. R.** 'Norwich, Eighty Years of the Norwich Society', Sutton Publishing, 2004.

**Archant Publications** including the *Eastern Daily Press* and the *Eastern Evening News*, various dates.

**Atkin, M.W. and Sutermeister, H. et al,** 'Excavations in Norwich, 1977/8: The Norwich Survey – Seventh Interim Report', Norfolk Archaeology, 37, Part 1, 1977/8.

**Ayers, Brian '**Norwich, A Fine City', Tempus Publishing Inc, 2003.

**Barringer, Christopher** 'Norwich in the Nineteenth Century', Gliddon Books, 1984.

**Brooks, Pamela** 'Norwich Street by Street', Breedon Books Publishing, 2006.

**Courts and Yards Committee**, 'Reports to the Council', 1898 – 1911.

**Carter, Harold and Lewis, C. Roy** 'An Urban Geography of England and Wales in the Nineteenth Century', Edward Arnold, 1990.

**Corfield, Pamela** 'The Social and Economic History of Norwich, 1650 – 1850', University of London, PhD Thesis, 1976.

**Daunton, M.J.** 'House and Home in the Victorian City', Edward Arnold, 1983.

**Dennis, Richard** 'English Industrial Cities of the Nineteenth Century', Cambridge University Press, 1984.

**Digby, Anne** 'Pauper Palaces', Routledge & Kegan Paul Ltd, 1978.

**Doyle, Barry M.** 'Mapping Slums in a Historic City: Representing Working-Class Communities in Edwardian Norwich', article in 'Planning Perspectives', 2001.

**Dragon Hall Research Group** 'The 19th-Century Residents of Dragon Hall', unpublished, 2010.

**Friends of Elm Hill '**Elm Hill**'**, Norwich Heart, undated.

**George, Ethel and Blackwell C.& M.** 'The Seventeenth Child: Memories of a Norwich Childhood, 1914 – 1934', Larks Press, 2006.

**Goreham, Geoffrey** 'Yards and Courts of Old Norwich', (no publisher recorded), undated.

**Green, Barbara and Young, Rachel M. R.** 'Norwich: The Growth of a City', Norfolk Museums Service, 1981.

**Gurney-Read, Joyce** 'Trades & Industries of Norwich', Crowes of Norwich, 1988.

**Gurney-Read, Joyce** Miscellaneous collection of information retained in the Local Studies Section, Norfolk & Norwich Millennium Library, various dates.

**Hannah, Ian C.** 'The Heart of East Anglia', Heath, Cranton and Ousley Ltd, 1914.

**Harman, Janet** 'An Introduction to Council Housing in Norwich', Thesis (M.A.), U.E.A., 1972.

**Hawkins, C. B.** 'Norwich: A Social Study', P. L. Warner, 1910.

**Hoskins, W. G.** 'The Making of the English Landscape', Pelican, 1955.

**Housden, Sarah** 'Norwich Memories', Norwich Living History Group, 2009.

**Johnson, Paul** '20th-Century Britain: Economic, Social and Cultural Change', Longman, 1994.

**Kelly's 'Directory of the City of Norwich'**, various dates.

**Kennett, Helen** 'Elm Hill, Norwich', unpublished.

**Lee, William** 'Report to the General Board of Health on a preliminary Inquiry into the Sewerage, Drainage and Supply of Water, and the Sanitary Conditions of the Inhabitants of the City of Norwich', 1851.

**Malpas, P. and Murie, A** 'Housing Policy and Practice', fifth edition, Macmillan Press, 1999.

**McLean, J. J.** 'A Fine City, Fit for Heroes', unpublished, 2011.

**Meeres, Frank** 'A History of Norwich', Phillimore, 1998.

**Meeres, Frank** 'The Story of Norwich', Phillimore & Co. Ltd, 2011.

**Meeres, Frank** 'Strangers: A History of Norwich's Incomers', Norwich HEART, 2012.

**Mile Cross History Research Group** 'Milestones to Mile Cross', Mile Cross History Research Group, 1995.

**Mile Cross Community Festival Committee** 'Mile Cross Memories: Moments from the Past', self-published, 1993.

**Ministry of Health Annual Reports,** various dates.

**Morning Chronicle** Letters XVI and XVII, printed 12 December 1949 and 15 December 1949.

**Mottram, R. H.** 'If Stones Could Speak', Richard Clay and Company Ltd, 1953.

**Nobbs, George** 'Norwich: City of Centuries', George Nobbs Publishing, 1978.

**Norfolk Archaeological Unit** 'An Archaeological Desk-Top Assessment on Lind BMW Ber Street Sites, Ber Street, Norwich', Report 1103, November 2005.

**Norwich City Council Planning Services** 'Conservation Area Appraisal: Mile Cross', HMSO, 2009.

**Norwich City Council** 'Housing of the Working Class Act 1890 – 1914. Rayner's Yard Improvements Scheme. Town Clerk's Brief', unpublished, 24/3/1914.

**Norwich City Council**, Reports of the Courts and Yards Committee to the Council, 1897 – 1911.

**Norwich HEART** 'Norwich 12', Norwich HEART, 2008.

**Norwich Heritage Projects** 'A Market For Our Times', Norwich Heritage Projects, 2010.

**Norwich Labour Party Housing Policy Group** 'Norwich Housing Report', self-published, c.1977.

**Norwich Mercury,** various dates.

**Norwich Town Planning Committee** 'Norwich Planning Handbook', self-published, 1968, 1972, 1982.

**Oldfield, T.H.B.** 'An Entire and Complete History…of the Boroughs of Great Britain', London, 1792.

**Perks, Christopher** 'Vanishing Norwich', article in The Norfolk Annual, 1936.

**Plunkett, George A. F.** 'Disappearing Norwich', Terence Dalton Ltd, 1987.

**Pound, John** 'Tudor and Stuart Norwich', Unwin Brothers Ltd, 1988.

**Rawcliffe, Carole and Wilson, Richard** 'Medieval Norwich', Hambledon and London, 2004.

**Rawcliffe, Carole and Wilson, Richard** 'Norwich since 1550', Hambledon and London, 2004.

**Royal Commission** 'Second Report of the Royal Commission for Inquiring into Large Towns and Populous Districts', Government Paper, 1845.

**Reed, Brenda** 'The Courts and Yards of Norwich', Norwich Heritage Projects, 2009.

**Zipfel, Alan L.** 'Zipfel and Sons', self-published, 1987.

## Websites

| | |
|---|---|
| **www.archives.norfolk.gov.uk** | Information about the archives relating to the history of Norfolk held at the Norfolk Record Office. Includes extensive material on the Norwich yards, particularly documentation and maps on the interwar clearance schemes. |
| **www.georgeplunkett.co.uk** | An outstanding collection of 20th-century photographs of Norwich. |
| **www.historictownsatlas.org.uk** | Owned by the Historic Towns Trust, the project has published an early map of Norwich based on Hochstetter's plan of 1789. |
| **www.norwich-yards.co.uk** | Our own website which contains a variety of information, including a yards' index with search facility based on the 1884 OS map, clearance and demolition details and a selection of recorded interviews. |
| **www.picture.norfolk.gov.uk** | A superb site operated by the Norfolk County Council Library and Information Service which contains over 17,000 images of people, places and events from across the country. |

## Norwich Heritage Projects

Norwich Heritage Projects is a voluntary organisation which is self funding. We are a small group of volunteers who aim to promote Norwich's rich past. Additional information, including audio and visual recordings can be found on our various websites:

**www.norwich-heritage.co.uk**

**www.norwichshoes.co.uk**

**www.norwichcathedrals-stainedglass.org**

**www.norfolkstainedglass.org**

**www.norwich-pubs-breweries.co.uk**

**www.norwich-market.org.uk**

# Acknowledgements

We are very grateful to all who have generously shared information with us. Without their help this book could not have been written.

Special thanks must be given to Penny Clarke for her advice and help in editing the book.

Philip Armes has greatly assisted by sharing his memories and giving us access to his photographic collection. We are again obliged to Jonathan Plunkett for allowing us to print so many of George Plunkett's historic photographs.

The staff at both the Norfolk County Council Library and Information Service and the Norfolk Record Office have given much guidance and also permission to use their archive material. Particular thanks to Clare Everitt, who looks after Picture Norfolk, for her help in locating photographs.

We are indebted to all who shared their memories with us and who allowed us to reproduce personal images. We are also grateful to Olwyn and Paul Venn together with Jude Sayer and Brenda Reed who helped with the original project back in 2009.

It is always useful to access newspaper reports, which really do give an insight into events as they happened. We extend our appreciation to Archant, in particular Rosemary Dixon, for allowing us to access their archive.

We have made much use of printed works; all publications and relevant websites are listed in the bibliography. Further information on photographic resources can be found on page ii.

Finally we apologise if we have inadvertently failed to acknowledge any of our sources. Anyone who has not been contacted is invited to write to the publisher so that full recognition can be given in subsequent editions of this book.

*George Plunkett, 1986*

## George Plunkett (1913 - 2006)

George Plunkett spent his life in Norwich where he worked first for the Norwich Public Health Department and then the Norwich Union (now Aviva).

George realised that the slum-clearance schemes were changing Norwich forever and he became determined to record the City's buildings for future generations. He started photographing Norwich in 1931, after acquiring a box camera, and in the years that followed built a comprehensive photographic survey of his home city.

For anyone interested in Norwich's heritage George's legacy is invaluable. His photographs illustrate the many changes made to the City's streets as a consequence of slum-clearance programmes, the Blitz and general redevelopment.

We have reproduced more than 100 of George's images. We are most grateful for his foresight and are also thankful that his son, Jonathan, has allowed us to print so much of his father's work, which can also be viewed at www.georgeplunkett.co.uk

# Index